TANA UMAGA
up close

the autobiography

TANA UMAGA

up close

WITH PAUL THOMAS

Hodder Moa

National Library of New Zealand Cataloguing-in-Publication Data
Umaga, Tana, 1973-
Tana Umaga up close / Tana Umaga with Paul Thomas.
ISBN 978-1-86971-119-1
1. Umaga, Tana, 1973- 2. All Blacks (Rugby team)
3. Rugby union football captains—New Zealand—Biography.
4. Rugby Union football players—New Zealand—Biography.
5. Rugby Union football. I. Thomas, Paul, 1951-
II. Title.
796.3330993—dc 22

A Hodder Moa Book
Published in 2007 by Hachette Livre NZ Ltd
4 Whetu Place, Mairangi Bay
Auckland, New Zealand

Designed and produced by Hachette Livre NZ Ltd
Printed by Printlink, New Zealand

Front and back jacket photography by Photosport.

To Rochelle and the kids
To Mum and Dad
To my sisters and brother
And to all those people who supported me throughout
my career and gave me a reason to write this book

Contents

Little Bro

Believe it or not, my first sporting love was soccer. My brother Mike was a big Liverpool fan and I was always in his room being the nuisance little brother. He used to buy *Shoot* magazine and we'd watch *Big League* with Brian Moore on Sunday afternoons. My favourite players were Trevor Brooking, Ian Rush, Kenny Dalgleish and Kevin Keegan.

No-one at our school played rugby. At lunchtime I played soccer and bullrush and after school I read soccer magazines. I wanted to play soccer for the school but so did everybody else: they had so many kids they had to pick names out of a hat and I missed out. I was gutted. I asked Dad if I could play club soccer and he took me down to the mall to enrol me in rugby. Seven years old and already an ex-soccer player. My first pair of boots were high tops with a silver fern on the side. I loved those boots and kept them immaculate. I played on the wing and, along with the inevitable cold mornings, my first rugby memories are of throwing the ball in underarm.

I was one of three boys at Wainuiomata Primary who made representative teams and a former All Black, Harold Pollock, came to our school to give us a talk and present the three of us with little silver fern badges. I loved that badge even more than my boots; I cherished it. I thought you got those badges for being an All Black which was right in a sense but not in the sense I had in mind. It wasn't until I became an All Black myself and was given bags of little silver fern badges to give away on school visits that I realised I'd been a bit naive. I also loved getting up at 3 in the morning to watch the All Blacks with the old man and for days afterwards went around writing 'I am an All Black' on light switches.

My parents had me when they were in their 40s; I was the youngest of five children, by seven years. My sisters had jobs and their own places and Mike left home when he was 20. My mother was a nurse and worked shifts — 7 am to 3 pm, 3 pm to 11 pm or 11 pm to 7 am — so often it was just me and Dad. We didn't talk much. He was a factory worker who worked hard and devoted much of his spare time to church activities. My parents had to work hard to put food on the table and we certainly never went without. With my siblings gone and both parents working, the school holidays were pretty slow around our place and I wasn't one to stay home and twiddle my thumbs.

I used to go around to the house of a friend from primary school, a Maori kid. It wasn't the most inviting place — there were clapped-out cars in the front yard — but there was always someone there. My friend had older brothers and sisters but no-one in the family had a job; they were either on benefits or still at school. I started dropping in after school, even if my friend wasn't there, because I just couldn't stay home. I'd just turn up: I'm sure I was annoying but they must have felt sorry for me.

There were a lot of people living in that three-bedroom house and it wasn't exactly genteel. The father was a sickness beneficiary. He had a TV in his room and rarely emerged, but he ran the household with an iron fist. I figured he was some sort of godfather figure. A lot of cousins came around, Black Power and Mongrel Mob guys who'd take their patches off before going inside to avoid trouble. Everyone else had to run errands for the father and jump to it when he wanted something but I just sat there watching them play cards. I learned to ride their home-made motorbike, got taken eeling and diving, and often ended up staying for dinner and hanging around till about 9 pm. They treated me as one of their own and I was grateful for it.

They weren't what you'd call a model family. The children didn't show their mother a lot of respect and my friend would steal from his sisters. I happily reaped the benefit of his ill-gotten gains but eventually his sisters figured out that I wasn't a very good liar: when they'd ask me if he'd pinched their money, I'd say nothing or mumble, 'I dunno.' Not surprisingly my mate got sick of my inability to lie through my teeth on his behalf and took to hanging out with other kids but I just kept on turning up on their doorstep because it was preferable to being home alone with nothing to do. The father was a disciplinarian, although not in the right way — at times it can't have been much fun living there — but he was the glue that held everything together. When he died they sold the house and the family drifted apart, but I still see some members of the family and their relatives.

I made more rep sides at intermediate school, playing alongside my future Wellington and Hurricanes team-mate Inoke Afeaki. I was playing in the midfield for my club but I wanted to see what it was like closer to the action so I went into the loose forwards. I didn't make the rep team as a loosie but they were short of a prop and called for volunteers. A bunch of us put our hands up so they had a race and chose the fastest runner, who happened to be me. I was quick and had a big sidestep: what more does a prop need? I also had stints at hooker, lock and number 8, which more than satisfied my curiosity about playing in the forwards. The last straw was ripping my ear when I yanked my head out of a scrum.

I looked up to Mike who was a well-known rugby player in Wainuiomata. I was a ball boy and used to watch him play for his first fifteen and later Wellington and was very proud to be his little brother. We lived just over the back of the local rugby club grounds and I'd go down there with him to field his kicks and boot the ball back to him. When I was just into my teens we did this drill: I'd stand on the 22, he'd stand on the goal-line near the posts, and I'd have to try to score in the corner. Then we swapped roles. He had a really long stride and once when I tried to tackle him my head got jammed between his legs, which was as painful as it was embarrassing. I was still crying when we got home and he copped it for hurting his little brother.

Parkway College's under-15 team took part in an annual tournament at Mount Albert Grammar and I got called in as a third former when they needed a couple of extra players. I was convinced the Napier Boys' High team had John Kirwan playing for them. The guy's name was actually Guy Curtis and I was to come up against him again later when he was playing for Otago and King Country. I couldn't get over how big our opponents were. I played fullback but didn't do a lot of tackling because I was too scared. The following year I was captain. We got a hiding from Auckland Grammar but managed to beat Shirley Boys' High to register our first-ever win in the tournament.

Our family had a Holden Torana automatic but Mum can't drive and Dad had gone to Samoa for three weeks so the car was just sitting in the garage. When Mum caught the bus to do her 3 to 11 pm shift, I decided to teach myself to drive. If I say so myself, I was a quick learner and cruised over to a mate's place to show off. I swung out really wide to turn into his driveway and a car whistled past on the inside, scaring the hell out of me. I drove straight home and put the car in the garage and the next night stuck to driving up and down Hair Street. A couple of days later I took the car to school to pick up some mates. As we went past the mall who should be standing at the bus stop but my mother, who'd had a doctor's appointment. I got a telling off but she got over it when I started driving her to work. The fact that I didn't have a driver's licence wasn't an issue, even when I was borrowing my mate Wesley Waiwai's car to get over to Porirua for Wellington touch team practice.

I was a bit of a rebel. Most Sunday afternoons after we'd been to church I'd go to my room, climb out the window, run around with my mates, slip back in the window, get into my pyjamas, and pretend I'd been there the whole time. I obviously wasn't much of an actor because I usually ended up getting a hiding.

I didn't like the fact that any elder, not just your parents, could hit you for things like talking in Sunday School or church — or sometimes for no apparent reason at all. I was no angel but I objected to getting hit all the time and it was just an added incentive to try to get out of it. Life seemed to revolve around church and Sunday School and when I turned 16, I'd had enough. Dad asked why I couldn't devote one day a week to church; the answer was because it was boring. Then I rubbed salt in the wound by deciding to play rugby league. It was a bit rough on my parents. Dad's still trying to get me to go to church.

I believe in God but don't necessarily believe that you find Him in church. Some rugby players are devout Christians but others are what they call Sunday Christians. I always wonder how Sunday Christians can go to church on Sunday as if they've been living that way during the week when they've actually been doing the opposite.

In 1998 I toured Samoa with New Zealand A. It was the first time I'd been there since I was four and I was looking forward to it, but it didn't quite live up to expectations. At the after-match function following the Manu Samoa game, one of the locals followed me into the toilet. He obviously had a few drinks under his belt. 'You're not Samoan,' he told me. 'You don't live here.' I got a bit of a shock and it stayed with me a long time. I was also annoyed because I'm proud of my Samoan heritage, although I have issues with some of the Samoan ways.

I visited my father's family whom I'd never met before. As is the custom, I'd saved up some money to give them. I spent the morning with them and gave them the money after church. They said thanks very much. When I got home, Dad told me his brother was very disappointed with the amount of money I'd given them because he'd wanted to get a new truck. I told my father to give his brother the message that if he wanted a new truck he and his kids should earn the money for it themselves rather than expecting me to do it for them. I also vowed that my uncle wouldn't get another cent from me and I've stayed true to that to this day. It left a sour taste in my mouth and I've never seen those relatives again. My father's view is that this is how we live, but he knows how I feel and has been very understanding. On the other hand, I've had a strong relationship with my relatives in Auckland and Wellington. I often stayed with my Auckland cousins during the school holidays and both they and my Wellington cousins gave me great support throughout my career.

A lot of Samoan families give money to the church even though they can't really afford it, and as a result the kids have to go without. Being the youngest, I didn't have it as tough as my sisters, who missed out on Christmas and birthday presents. And it's not just the church: there's also the extended family. You get the situation of a working couple with kids giving their hard-earned money to members of the wider family. If a family needs money they ring around to see how much they can raise and sometimes those who provide the hand-out don't even know the people it's going to.

My sisters Janice, Rachel and Sina looked after me when I was young; if I ever needed anything, I'd be on the phone to them. I'm very thankful that they've always been there for me to fall back on and very proud of what they've achieved in their lives, both in the sporting sense and career-wise. Janice and Sina have been through university as adults and Rachel has faced her illnesses and come through. They have always been there for me and had a big hand in who I am today.

Our son Cade was born at the end of 1993 when I was 20. It's hard for a Pacific Islander's partner to understand why you have to keep giving money to the extended family when there's a baby to look after. I said I couldn't do it. When I became a professional rugby player I told my parents they'd never have anything to worry about, but my kids weren't going to miss out because they'd decided to pass my money on to someone else. I still have battles with them. As an All Black I was often telling the young guys that even though they were now earning good money they had to learn to say 'no' because they couldn't keep shelling out for members of the church and the extended family.

But I wish I could speak Samoan. I spoke it as a child but at school I was the only one who could, so I figured if no-one else does, why should I? I regret it now though because I can't teach my kids.

When I was 15 I got caught wagging school. They got in touch with my mother who was in tears when I got home. She was very hard-working and wanted me to do well but I just didn't like school; all I wanted to do was hang out with my mates and play sport. I told her not to worry about it. The next day as I was waiting to catch the bus home from school, my sister Janice pulled up in her car. I thought, awesome, I'm getting a lift home. Then I noticed the plastic bags on the back seat. She said, 'Get in, you're coming to stay with me.' My parents couldn't really handle me. Wagging school was just the tip of the iceberg but I was past the stage of getting a hiding.

I stayed with Janice and her husband Gordon for two years until they moved out of Wainuiomata and I went back to Mum and Dad. Janice would run the rule over my friends; if she decided they were okay all I had to do was stay in touch; if I didn't ring, I'd be grounded. The difference between right and wrong had been instilled in me early on so there was no danger of me going too far but I can't say the academic side of things got much attention.

By that stage I'd become interested in rugby league. I used to devour *Big League* and *Rugby League Week*. My mates and I used to talk about it all the time and play it at lunchtime. We even had our own State of Origin based on which part of Wainuiomata you came from. My favourite players were Wally Lewis, Mal Meninga and Bradley Clyde.

In the fifth form, after a couple of years of avidly following league, a few of us decided to go along to training at Wainuiomata Rugby League Club. I was the only one who went back for more. I just got stuck in and enjoyed it; it was more brutal than rugby union but I liked the confrontation and knowing that you were going to get the ball, as opposed to rugby where the ball wasn't in play for as long and you couldn't rely on it getting out to you. It didn't seem like a new game because I'd followed it and watched it a lot on TV. I didn't know anyone there but it was a welcoming environment and I made a whole new set of friends.

But it was another black mark as far as my parents were concerned: they hated league and in fact my mother never watched me play a single game. When I made the seniors Dad sneaked along a couple of times, but my sisters and brother always came so I was never short of support.

Parkway College was a rugby school, although not a strong one. I was one of the few, even among the league players, who didn't turn out for a school team. In my fifth form year I was asked to play for the first fifteen. Lots of league players listened to music in the dressing room and I'd got into the habit so I listened to my Walkman before a pre-season game for the first fifteen. After we lost to Viard College — who were a good side — we were called into a meeting in the social studies auditorium. The coach questioned our attitude, saying some of us had been listening to music before the game and hadn't been ready to play. I assumed he was referring to me so when he went on to say that anyone who wanted to listen to music could leave now, it was an invitation I couldn't refuse and walked out. After that my appearances for the school were mainly restricted to filling in for my mates' teams. I once played four games on the same day: after two games of league in the morning, I played for the school in the afternoon, then got roped in to make up the numbers for the second fifteen. It was like that Weet-Bix ad: how many can you do? Four games in one day was my limit; I was shattered.

I was playing loose forward, number 13. I wanted to learn to tackle properly because I was always giving away penalties for going high, which I did because I wasn't a confident defender. I had a league-playing 'cousin' — that was what I called him, although we weren't related — called Pese who'd come down from Auckland to live with his sister. He taught me how to tackle, how to launch, how to time the hit, how to make driving tackles. I found some tackle pads in an op shop. They were ugly old things but once you've got some sort of protective gear your confidence grows. My 'cousin' played for us even though he was two years older. The coach couldn't say no, so if older guys wanted to play he'd let them. That was fine at the time but we ended up getting disqualified.

By now I was getting up to the usual mischief that's all part of growing up. The night before a rep trial there was a dance at which you paid a $20 cover charge and could drink as much as you wanted or as much as you could, which weren't necessarily the same thing. I scrounged the money from my sisters and drank all night. In the morning they couldn't wake me up. They made me have a bath, cooked up some pasta, and sent me off to play. I looked like crap and felt worse but managed to score a couple of tries. Not that it mattered: the coach of the team we played against happened to be the rep coach. Guess which team supplied lots of players to the reps. That was the way it worked back then.

I'd never won anything playing rugby but in my first season with league

I won Most Improved Player. I also had my first experience of being paid to play because the player of the match got $20; most of it went on shouting my mates lunch. I'd only planned to play for a year but after that I decided league was my game.

1991 was my last year at school. I knew I wanted to play professional rugby league so I really didn't pay much attention to what the teachers were saying. I have to admit I was far from an ideal student: I just sat there not taking anything in and throwing out the odd unhelpful comment. I really only went to school to keep my mother happy, but because my parents worked so hard they weren't there to monitor what I was or wasn't doing and homework fell into the second category. As far as I was concerned, schoolwork was something you did at school, not that I overdid it there, either.

I moved in with a mate, Rau Hura, and his sister and brother-in-law. They had a sleep-out where I crashed at weekends. I ended up moving my gear in and staying there in my sixth form year. I didn't pay rent but no-one seemed to mind as long as I helped with the chores. Just as my primary school mate's family had done, they took me in and made me feel part of the family. My parents would ask, 'When are you coming home?' The answer was always: 'Soon.'

The under-19 side had a couple of injuries so they asked if anyone wanted to play for them. I put my hand up, even though my mates in the team were a lot bigger than me and ended up playing for them for the rest of the season. In the final we played Upper Hutt who had Steve Kearney and Syd Eru, although Syd had been called up to Premiers which meant he couldn't play in the final. I'd heard a lot about Kearney — everyone said he was the best player in the grade — and went into the game determined to have a crack at him. That's the way I was throughout my career: when I came up against someone good, I lifted my game. If you're competitive, that's what you do. I wanted everyone to talk about Tana Umaga, not Steve Kearney. Well, I had a crack at him, alright — I got sent off for accidentally elbowing him in the face. Three other guys got sin-binned so we were down to nine men at one stage but they still couldn't score and we ended up winning. Luckily, Steve was a nice guy even then.

Under the coaching of Blue Delves we didn't lose a game that year or the next. Blue was the first coach who really made an impact on me. He was an autocrat and very direct: you were never left wondering what he meant. I had a few coaches like that in my career and quite enjoyed the hard-nosed approach because you knew exactly where you stood. Blue believed in me: he had me sussed as a lazy so-and-so but saw some potential and tried to get it out of me. He instilled the belief that I could achieve big things if I put my mind to it.

I keep in touch with mates from those days but I don't go visiting people. I don't even see my parents as much as I should. I've come full circle: these days I like staying home.

← **PLAYBACK**

JANICE AND RACHEL

*Tana's sisters **Janice** and **Rachel** live in Wainuiomata.*

Janice: Tana's the youngest; 12 years younger than me. What did Mum say? He was a mistake but we learn from our mistakes. Actually, I think she finally got it right. We had a big part in caring for him. After six months Mum went back to working nights. She was at home during the day, then we came home and Dad was home and so it was us and Dad who pretty much reared Tana. We had to change his damn nappies and all that kind of stuff. He was spoilt for a long time until he irritated us and we said, 'Mother, look after your child, he's getting out of hand. Give him a hiding or something.'

Rachel: But he could do no wrong in our mother's eyes . . .

Janice: No matter how much we tried to persuade her. Mind you, there was a good side to having a younger brother who couldn't talk back: you could blame him for everything. He was a good scapegoat. We used him quite a bit actually if we broke anything in the house — 'Oh, it was Tana.'

Rachel: But it wasn't that great when you'd go to buy something in the cake shop and he'd want something and the lady would say, 'You'd better ask your mother.' You're like, 'Hey, I'm only 13.'

Janice: In some ways he was a bit of an only child because there was such a gap. When we went off to work, we were 19 and 20 and he was eight. What the hell were we going to do with a child?

Rachel: Look, I've got eight-year-olds now and they don't want to hang around with me and I certainly don't want to hang around with them. We were teenagers, what did we care?

Janice: But we made sure that we went to just about every game he played in his league days.

Rachel: Someone had to.

Janice: Because he was a young kid and we were teenagers, we had to take him everywhere. We learnt to drive early and if he wanted to go somewhere, he'd just cry. I don't know how many times I told him, 'Wait until you're 15, you're going to get it. Me and you outside, you're going to get it.'

Rachel: Did you actually ever do that? Didn't he chicken out after he heard what you did to [brother] Michael?

Janice: Michael gave me this scar I'll have you know. Yeah, him and Mike — the boys were special. That's carried on actually: Tana has a special relationship with his mother.

Rachel: Because she nearly died having him.

Janice: She worked in maternity at Hutt Hospital and she felt a bit of a twinge. She said to the nurse that she felt like she wanted to push and the nurse said, 'No, no, you've got ages to go.' The nurse walked away but had to come running back because Mum had pushed the boy out. Mum goes, 'The baby's on the bed.' That was Mum. But she haemorrhaged quite heavily after that.

Rachel: He was born just before midnight so she would have finished her shift. But from there on he had four mothers until we'd had enough and we decided, 'I'm not a mother, I need a life.' But I always felt sorry for him after I'd left home. I found a letter my mother had written to me and he'd scrawled on the back, 'Hi sis, miss you, it's my birthday soon, send money.' Can we refer to him as Jonathan in the book? I call him that, but I'm the only one that does.

Janice: I'll tell you a story about Jonathan. My mother was looking for a name and Rachel had this sort of boyfriend.

Rachel: He wasn't a boyfriend, just a friend.

Janice: A really good friend. We were a hippy-style family of course. Anyway, her friend was Jonathan and Mum called her son Jonathan and all of us just about puked. Mum loved it because it's a good biblical name. We said, 'You can't call him Jonathan. What kind of name is Jonathan? When he grows up . . .' Anyway as soon as we heard that, we knew we needed to find a new name so we got the translation for Jonathan which is Ionatana and shortened it to Tana. And he's been called Tana ever since. I don't ever recall calling him Jonathan.

Rachel: I call him Jonathan; I even have him listed in my phone as Jonathan, because Jonathan's a lovely name.

Janice: Never, never, never, never. It's always been Tana.

Rachel: He had to change his name at primary school — there was him and Jonathan Higgs — so he took the name of Tana, I reckon because it was easier to spell.

Janice: Nah, we hated that name.

Rachel: Yeah, but you know what the alternative was? Dallas — from the TV show.

Janice: I think Dallas is a hell of a lot better than Jonathan. Dallas Umaga. Aren't you glad we gave him Tana? I mean, that's an iconic name now. We were brought up in Petone and came over here to Wainuiomata when [sister] Sina was at intermediate and I was at primary school. Tana was born and bred here; this is his stamping ground. It's now ours because we still live here. What we like about it, I suppose, is that you get a bit of the countryside but you're not too far away from the city. It's nice and relaxed.

Rachel: It's sleepy but that's the way it was designed. It was a dormitory town for people who worked in Wellington and the Hutt Valley.

Janice: There are beautiful hills and beautiful countryside; that's why a lot of people come to Wainuiomata — to walk. We walked a number of these hills during our childhood.

Rachel: You know, they've named a track after Tana and I don't think he's ever been on any of these bloody tracks.

Janice: He's not really into long distance walks; his training is very refined.

Rachel: I think I paid him once to just lift his feet so I could vacuum.

Janice: Tana lives just over the hill. He comes over here regularly. Part of it is he's got his big babysitting crew here, including his in-laws, and also a lot of his close childhood friends. He's always coming back and either helping out with the Wainuiomata Club or watching the league guys because that's where he started off in terms of his sporting public life. I've got a friend who wanted something signed for a lady who was leaving. Tana was this lady's favourite player so they'd sneaked this poster off her and wanted him to sign it. I was in the car with him so I told him to turn around and go sign something for my friend who we've known forever — we were all brought up together. And of course he just turned around. I knocked on the door. At first she thought it was just me and then it was, 'Oh my God, Tana Umaga,' and she was running up and down in her pyjamas and he's just standing there. She kept apologising and I said, 'Oh, for goodness sake, Karen, it's only Tana.' There are no airs and graces about that boy. He's a real home boy. I remember when he finally left for his first stint in Newcastle he felt so . . .

Rachel: What do you mean, Newcastle? When he was bloody five Mum had to go to Napier with him because he was going to be sick on the bus. He had to sit up the front.

Janice: Mum always went on his school trips, rugby trips especially. She kept them all in line. He's a pretty bad traveller. You don't want to take Tana on a trip with you if he's not driving.

Rachel: He was such a home boy. When he went to Greymouth — Greymouth for goodness sake — he was on the phone crying, 'I'm sick, I want to come home.' Then he went to Newcastle and before long he was on the phone saying, 'I want to come home.' Being the tough women we were, we were saying, 'For goodness sake, you're 18 years old, you're a man now,' and Mum was in the background going, 'Stop it, tell him to come home.' The next time he left, he took Rochelle with him. He said this time he had to stay because he knew if he came back we'd give him a hard time.

Janice: Over the years he's had a few offers and when people would say he's going to go here or go there, I'd say, 'No he's not.'

Rachel: No, he's not going very far, not for long anyway. Rugby was a big part of his life from the word go because Dad was a rugby nut. We were brought up on rugby. Dad's wish would've been to have had five boys. I can recall as a kid always being made to play rough. Dad was a wrestler, in the time of Steve Rickard, so we used to go watch him quite a bit.

Janice: He did it until he was about 42 to make some extra money. He travelled quite a bit during the weekends to wrestle with the likes of John Da Silva, Brutal Bob Miller, Gorgeous Teddy Williams and Robert The Bruce, so that left Mum at home with the kids.

Rachel: He wasn't flashy or anything. We went to see this bout at the Town Hall and we woke Michael up to find his father in a compromising position looking like he was going to die and Michael's like, 'Aaaahhh, my dad.'

Janice: Mum had to take the kids out but we were like, 'Come on, Dad, get him.' Tana actually didn't get to see his dad fight. He finished the year before Tana was born.

Rachel: Dad was very much into his sport and Mum was a foundation member of the PIC netball club. She's the athlete.

Janice: Tana will say that he got his sporting prowess from his mother. We say that too. My mum was still sprinting at 35 in what we called the Samoan Olympics — all the Samoan churches in Auckland. Sport was a big part of our lives as we used to travel around to watch Mum and Dad.

Rachel: Tana was raised on the sidelines of basketball and netball courts because we all played.

Janice: Lots of people remember Tana because of that. We all played sports and we all reached certain levels so he was always there on the sidelines with one of us. It's like Tana says, you either do sports or you go to church. But playing sport on Sunday is frowned upon in Samoa because Sunday is the day of rest and everything always happened on a Sunday.

Rachel: If you were at church you wouldn't get injured.

Janice: Tana was with Wainuiomata Juniors right from the word go. Mum and Dad were there every game. Mum on one side, Dad on the other because Mum would just yell. She was one of those walk-the-sideline mums. When she was seven or eight months pregnant with Tana, brother Michael was playing at The Strand and she couldn't be bothered walking along to where the steps were so she just slid down the bank. With Tana everything was about playing a game.

Janice: Mike had a big part in pushing him forward. From the get-go him and his brother . . .

Rachel: Were joined at the hip.

Janice: Well, they were and they clashed, right up until Tana reached that age where, 'Oh wow, Michael's doing all the things that I want to do,' and Michael became his idol.

Rachel: It was a sadness for me that Michael wasn't the first All Black because he had flair. Tana's got flair but it's a different sort of flair.

Janice: But also they're two different guys because Mike's a real extrovert, he just gets on with everybody and anybody, but he partied. Tana was always able to balance it a bit. And he's a bit of an introvert is our Tana.

Rachel: They'd spend hours together. I'd spend hours refereeing crappy games of rugby. But Tana played everything. Me and my husband coached him in basketball in his last couple of years at college. He could've played any sport, really. Actually, he could've played basketball. He still reckons he could.

Janice: Just after he received the Kel Tremain Award [the top honour for a New Zealand rugby player], he said he was thinking about retiring and was going to come back as a point guard for the Saints. He had a basketball hoop at home and was practising.

Rachel: When he first started out in sport we had a conversation about who was going to be the first international. You said Michael would be the first international and I said Tana would be the first All Black.

Janice: I thought we were talking about me. I've said to him that if it wasn't for the fact that I don't have a penis, I would've been the first All Black in the family.

Rachel: Nah, I would've been the first All Black, you're bloody useless. I said to him, 'You're so lucky you're a male because if I was a male I would've been the first All Black.' I reckon I would've done an effing good job of it. I sure as hell would've done a better job than you. But, of course, he's done a great job.

Janice: He's emulated what we would've done. Or what we would've been.

Rachel: He even looks like you now.

Janice: That's right. I actually said that I'd have dreads first and what does he go and do? He gets dreads. We've always been rugby mad. When Mike and Tana became good rugby players Dad was in heaven but of course there was that lapse when Tana played rugby league.

Rachel: Yeah, Dad's a staunch rugby man. He practically disowned Tana.

Janice: But he was sneaky, Dad: 'If you loved me, you'd give it up.' He wouldn't talk to Tana for a while because he played rugby league but every time Tana had a game you'd see Dad's car somewhere around and you'd know he'd be hidden behind a tree or something watching his son play.

Rachel: But Mum never went to a game because they were always on a Sunday.

Janice: And of course when Tana was playing NPC he was the bee's knees. Tana could do no wrong. We used to give him such a hard time: 'You are their only child, their only real child, we are nobody, we are just the plebs.' As much as he'd hate to admit it, he's very much like my father.

Rachel: No he's not.

Janice: He's a man of few words.

Rachel: A man of few words but the words he does say have weight and meaning.

Janice: He's a really intelligent kid. He did really well at primary school but once he got to college it just wasn't his thing. I remember him doing a quiz in some comic when he was 10 years old; one of the questions was, what would you like to be, and he wrote that he wanted to be an All Black. Once he got to college it was all about playing sport.

Rachel: He loves general knowledge things. He'll pick up anything: if you make a mistake, he'll throw it straight back at you. I suppose that's because on my mother's side they're all teachers. She did a lot in terms of bringing her family over here for education.

Janice: All the intelligence comes from Mum. The soft-heartedness comes from Dad. He's a real people person. Mum's tough and firm but she's fair. And funny.

Rachel: Good, quick wit — it runs in the family and we get that from our mother. Tana's got a wonderful, wicked sense of humour. Olo Brown's got to be one of the wittiest and most intelligent guys but here's something people don't know: Olo's family. It's something that Tana and Olo won't say, but his mother and our mother are sisters. That's how close the relationship is. We spend a lot of time with them. It was really good that Olo was still in the All Blacks when Tana got in. Of course, there was an age gap and also because Olo was 'in' with the likes of Fitzy, Tana put them up there a bit.

Janice: Leadership just seemed something that he was going to grow into because, not wanting to boast or anything, but we all displayed leadership qualities. It wasn't a surprise to us that he became All Black captain. It seemed like a natural thing, the obvious next step for him. What really got me was that Graham Henry saw that in him because Tana's not going to stand up and say, 'I'm this, I'm that.' Henry saw the kind of mana or influence that he had with other players. Before it was announced we were all thinking about it and following the papers but it's really hard to get anything out of Tana. I said, 'What's the point of having a brother that's a frickin All Black if he can't tell us anything?' He'd go only so far, then say, 'Oh, I can't sis,' so we'd try to get Rochelle to tell us. When Wellington was looking for a new captain after Norm Hewitt, Tana was being interviewed on the radio and they asked him if he'd stand up for the captaincy. I rang up and Tana goes, 'I think I know who this person is.' I asked him, 'What about you? You've got really good leadership qualities.' He said, 'Oh no,' then a couple of weeks later, bang, he's the captain. With the All Black captaincy he rang up and said, 'Can we get together at your house, sis? I've got something I want to say to the family.' But my place is too small and I'm too lazy so I rang up Rachel and said, 'Let's have it at your place.'

Rachel: My house is really small but I'm not lazy and I can cook.

Janice: So we ended up having it at Rachel's place. We were all sitting there and he goes, 'Right I've got something to tell you all.' There'd been a story in the papers that he was going to Leeds and Rochelle was pregnant but she hadn't told us that she was pregnant so we thought, Oh my God, what's he going to tell us? Maybe that she's having twins. He told us he was going to captain the All Blacks and I said, 'I'm not surprised, about bloody time.'

Rachel: He didn't say it straight away. First he said, 'Oh, I just want to tell you that Rochelle's pregnant,' and we went, 'Oh yay.' Then he went, 'Nah, nah, it's not that, we got you together because we're going to France,' and Mum gasped but tried to look happy, and then he went, 'Nah, it's not that either.' When he finally told us, we went, 'Yeah, right.'

Janice: It was like crying wolf.

Rachel: Mum and Dad were really proud. Mum's so into it. She said, 'I'm so happy, I prayed and prayed.' She's represented Tana at a number of awards and that's what she says to everybody: 'Parents, don't give your sons a hard time. You must pray for them.' That's what she did. Our parents are immigrants. Let's just say we struggled like every other family that came over and to see some of the fruits of their hard work was great. That's not to say that Tana's the only one, but it's such a big thing in this country and this society. Tana's attained the highest pinnacle. It's a great achievement for a couple from two small villages in Samoa who came here and bought their first house in Wainuiomata — a house that was freezing cold. For us, the achievement is more in terms of who Tana is. He's a well-rounded person and a great brother and uncle, all of those things. Everybody loves him.

Janice: Men play a big role in our culture because they're supposed to look after the women. When Tana became this big hit, all of a sudden he's it and everybody has to go to him. Every time something came up Dad would say, 'Oh Tana will have to see about that.' So he's been pushed into the sort of leadership role even within the family because of who he is.

Rachel: And sometimes we'll let him have that and other times we let him know who really is in charge — okay, that's enough, step back.

Janice: We like to think we had a part to play in it all by keeping his feet on the ground.

Rachel: We still know what his weaknesses are. We could bring him to tears just like that. I reckon that's why Tana didn't play yesterday [for Petone against Wainuiomata in Wellington club rugby] because we would've been barracking for the other side and we would've been right in his head: 'You can't catch number 13. You're too old.'

Janice: I wouldn't be surprised. He said he didn't want to play because he felt stink. I said, 'What, were you going to make a difference?'

Rachel: Not with us two on the sideline.

Janice: It was the worst-kept secret that he was retiring. He rang us from Scotland and said, 'I just thought I'd let you know this is my last game.' And I said, 'I think Rochelle told us that before you left.' He went ahead and made his little speech anyway and then you could almost tell that he cut us off because he just got tired of talking. We're big girls; as my cousin would say, we're more women than most, and him being the athlete he is, he used to give us a hard time about what we eat. So we knew he was starting to wind down because we saw the food change. I saw him in this café with pies and sausages rolls — he usually doesn't touch that sort of thing. Now he's in training to be a couch potato.

Rachel: I'm affected by bipolar disorder. During the last World Cup I appeared in a series of ads for the Like Minds Like Mine project. You know the catch phrase: 'Know me before you judge me.' They wanted me to get Tana involved and I felt pressured by the director to get him. Finally, I said to Tana, 'Look, it's totally up to you but they want that connection because it would be huge in terms of the wider population.' But he said to them, 'No, this is about my sister, it's her time.' I've always been really proud of him for that because we spent a lot of time being Tana Umaga's sisters, not Janice or Rachel.

Janice: What did we use to call ourselves? The Tussers. How does it feel to have a brother who's one of the most famous people in New Zealand? It irritates me sometimes. I took my married name at the beginning of this year after 20 years together because when I'm introduced people would say, 'Are you Tana Umaga's sister?' Not that I can't have an in-depth conversation about rugby. I travel quite a bit with my work and when I had my maiden name it was like, 'Oh, he's lovely.' What was funny about it was that they were all older women. The mothers and the grandmothers really loved him. Didn't matter which hotel I went to, I always got, 'Oh, he's so wonderful.' We get lots of people asking, 'Can you get Tana to sign this, can you get Tana to sign that?' It's sort of become our life for the last 10 years.

He's grown up now, finally. He's married with four kids, so he has to be. That's a huge responsibility. I mean, our conversations are like, 'Did you get the washing out?' 'Yeah, can't miss it, can't miss a day.' He's a good dad and he's a good carer and to us that's more important. It's great that he's achieved what he's achieved, but it means nothing unless you're able to look after your family and be the right kind of person because, as you've seen, it's gone, just like that, it's just a moment in time. Then you've got the rest of your life. He's part of a family who work with the same issues that a whole lot of other families do. He's dealing with just as many of the real issues in our society as anybody else. When he comes home, that's where he is. He's gone through his trials with stuff, and that's been well documented, and he's come through it really well. Sometimes you have to go through that. The other thing I like about Tana is his ability to reflect. Very few human beings are able to internalise the issues they go through in their life and then work through them and find a solution. A lot of human nature these days is really defensive but Tana takes it on the chin. He looks at it and reflects on it.

Rachel: Like after we told him he was fat that year. When you're running five paces back to run two paces forward there's something wrong.

Janice: That was 1998. He was the only one who was going to learn from that and he did. He went through things personally as well as professionally and it put him in good stead. He worked some things out in his personal life, too, and that's why he and Rochelle have been able to achieve what they've achieved and get to where they are today. Even with everything he's done and where they are today, we'd have to say that Rochelle has been a big part of that. She's the foundation, she's the rock.

Rachel: It's like they say: behind every great man there's a greater woman. And she's really happy about where she stands in the relationship. She's right there behind him but she doesn't overshadow him and she's never wanted to be in the limelight. She's his greatest supporter and his greatest critic.

Janice: He must feel henpecked sometimes because he's got so many women, including his daughters, coming at him from every angle.

Rachel: He just listens and says, 'Yes, Mother,' 'Yes, Rochelle,' 'Yes . . .'

Janice: And, of course, we're his harshest critics, we do give him a hard time. What the hell is happening with your team? Why is this going on? To be honest, we just run off at the mouth because we're so passionate, like every other New Zealander. But we were fortunate enough to have the All Black captain sitting right there so, yeah, I let him have it. Why is this guy playing? Why is he still there? And, of course, Tana, I don't how he does it, he just sits through it: 'Yes sis, you're right sis, please don't make fun of me, I'm telling you the truth here.' He's had quite a bit of that kind of constructive feedback. It just goes in one ear and out the other. It's like pulling teeth to actually get anything out of him. They're loyal, those bloody All Blacks. He's got a really kind soul. He'd rather do something for somebody than say no. He doesn't really like confrontation.

Rachel: We used to push him a lot — 'Come on, say no, I dare you.'

Janice: He's a cool brother; he cares. Mum and Dad have got a nice little place and he's able to support them. He's there to help us.

Rachel: You just have to ask.

Janice: For us, those things count for more. It's not hard for us to say that we've got a great brother.

Rachel: How many more superlatives could we use?

Janice: He's wonderful, lovely . . .

Rachel: Fabulicious.

Code Cracker

In 1990 I drove up to Auckland with some mates to watch Wainuiomata play Otahuhu in the final of the Lion Red Cup. Wainuiomata was becoming a real force to be reckoned with, on and off the field. Its animated supporters were renowned for massing behind the dead ball line at one end of the ground with their red and green flags and swapping ends at halftime by the most direct route: straight down the middle of the field. To rival fans and neutral observers we must have looked pretty rough and ready, if not downright menacing, but there was a family atmosphere at the club and they looked after their own. I was in the middle of this rabble, as we were sometimes called, and right into it: jumping up and down, abusing the other team when they lined up behind the goal-line then ducking behind big, fierce-looking blokes with tattoos, and marching the length of Carlaw Park as if we owned the place. Wainuiomata won, which was out of this world. As you do on those trips, we slept in the car and dossed in a mate's cousin's garage. The other thing you usually do is drink as much as you can, but guess who was the designated driver for the trip home. Being the youngest has its drawbacks, too.

At the end of the season the Under 19s played the Premier Reserves who were older and bigger. I played quite well and Ken Laban, the Premiers coach, asked me to train with them. I'd been playing loose forward, even though I was still quite skinny, so when the forwards set off to run laps around Wise

Park, I didn't wait to be told, I just went with them. When we finished, Ken asked me what the hell I was doing with the forwards — 'You're a back in this team' — and sent me off to do another set of laps with the backs. That was okay; fitness work wasn't hard graft for an enthusiastic young kid.

We started 1991 by winning a national nines tournament at Carlaw Park. It was a huge buzz playing with Johnny and David Lomax, who were as big as Mel Meninga in Wainuiomata, and their brothers Arnold and Tony; the Va'a brothers — Earl, Leonardo and Rio; and Heston and James Patea, and playing against Kiwis like Tea Ropati. We played a pre-season game against Manly. I was sent on with eight minutes to go and pulled off with two minutes left; I made two runs and one tackle but the adrenaline rush left me exhausted. The next day I was back at school and the centre of attention. That was when I decided I wanted to be a professional rugby league player and play in the NRL.

I stayed up in the Premiers for the whole season. One of my attributes is that I'm a good listener; I take things in. I learned that if a team-mate tackles someone low, you go over the top and put the ball-carrier away. Doing just that in the first game against Eastern Suburbs, I caught this guy in the face. He got up breathing fire; after the play-the-ball he chased me yelling that he was going to get me. I managed to stay out of his way but even when the game ended, I could see he was still seething. When I was talking to my sister after the game he came over, but instead of having a go at me, he gave her a kiss. He turned out to be a cousin of mine.

You win some and you lose some. In a game at Rugby League Park, I ran from dummy half and a guy called Phil Henry came over the top and raked my eye. He had a reputation as an enforcer, someone you didn't mess with. That was what guys like him did: they roughed up young blokes like me to try to unsettle them. I just said, 'Thank you,' and played the ball.

Our captain Alan Jackson and vice-captain Dwayne Gwiazdzinski kept me in line and taught me a lot. Whatever they told me to do, I just did it. If you did something wrong like drop the ball, they'd give it to you: 'Just catch the effing ball!' We had a tap penalty move where the wing would pass to the hooker, do a run-around, and take the ball and run straight into the defensive line. In one game I stepped and went straight through. The fullback got me but I saw our stand-off coming and off-loaded to him but he spilled it. Jacko gave me the 'Just hang on to the effing ball'. I thought, Christ, it wasn't that bad a pass. After the game Jacko gave it to me again but also told the stand-off he should have caught the effing pass. These days, some of the young guys take it personally if you give it to them: they sulk and fade into the background. They want their egos massaged.

I was a pretty slack trainer. Doing weights was too much like hard work; I went to the gym for a yarn and a catch-up — 'What did you get up to at the weekend?' I'd gone from Under 16s to Under 17s to Under 19s to Premiers without doing anything special or putting in any extra, but natural ability seemed to be working for me because I kept going up in the world.

It was a tough game in those days. The mindset was 'if you can run, you can play' or, to put it another way, 'if it's not broken, you're fine'. You got used to playing with injuries. I did my AC joint when I was 16 but only had a couple of weeks off because I didn't want to miss games. I fractured my wrist but cut the cast off rather than miss a big game. That wrist still gives me problems. My whole week revolved around playing football so I'd do just about anything not to miss out. I didn't like missing games for the Hurricanes or the All Blacks either but that was more because there was always that fear at the back of your mind that your replacement could have a blinder and you'd never get back in.

We didn't make the final of the Lion Red Cup but I had a pretty good year. Howie Tamati, the Junior Kiwis coach, came to watch me play. The Juniors had two games against Great Britain and it came as a real shock when I made the team. Usually they picked the team after a national tournament but Great Britain toured early in the season, so the announcement came out of the blue. I was at school and someone came running up to me waving a newspaper. It was a real buzz seeing my name in a national team but also hard to believe that I'd made the Junior Kiwis when I'd only been playing league for a couple of years.

We got together in Christchurch. I was rooming with the other centre, Paki Tuimavave. He was a 100 mph sort of guy, always wanting to do something, and if there was nothing else to do, he'd bounce a tennis ball against the wall. Steve Kearney was the captain and the other big-name players were Willie Poching and Brady Malam. After I scored a try in the first test in Greymouth, one of our wings, Solomon Kiri, said to me, 'No-one knew you before this but everyone will know you now.' He was a sort of elder statesman figure within the team, so that meant quite a lot. We won both tests and I made some good friends. I still see some of them now and again. The thing I remember about Howie is that he used to get us up to go for walks at 6.30 am which was a bit earlier than I was used to.

I made the Junior Kiwis again the following year, this time with Frank

Endacott as coach. Poching and Malam were there again, along with Ruben Wiki, Gene Ngamu and Joe Vagana. We played the Junior Kangaroos who included Steve Menzies, whom I marked, Nathan Barnes, who'd already played for Penrith, and Robbie Ross, who later played for Newcastle and the Melbourne Storm. In the first test in Rotorua we were ahead with a couple of minutes to go when I made the crucial mistake: I thought I could stop a move by coming in off my man but I took the wrong guy and they scored. We won the second test in Auckland, the first time the Junior Kiwis had ever beaten their Aussie counterparts. Frank was quite an innovative coach, even devising scrum moves which were virtually unheard of in league. He was harsh when he needed to be but when I apologised for the botched tackle that cost us the game, he just shrugged it off saying we had to move on.

Midway through 1991, my last year at school, Ken Laban had rung to say that Newcastle was interested in signing me. I really wanted a job but didn't have any qualifications — I didn't have School Certificate — and they assured me there'd be a job lined up for me when I got over there. I signed a two-year contract and thought I had it made.

It was hard leaving my family, especially my mother — I'm very much a mother's boy — but at the end of January I went over to Newcastle with Willie Poching and Brian Laumatia, who were on the same deal. I arrived with $100 in my pocket — a gift from my parents. We were picked up, dropped off at a motel, and pretty much left to our own devices. When some club officials turned up to take us out for dinner, I asked them when I'd be starting work. 'What do you mean?' was the reply. They told me I'd get a job eventually but they wanted me to settle in first. I felt let down. I got into a dark mood very quickly and made a lot of tearful phone calls home.

Food was a major issue because we had so little money. We used to go to Sizzler because we could have as much salad as we liked and get some protein from the mince in the Bolognese sauce. That was topped up by Tony Kemp and former All Black John Schuster who had us around for a barbecue.

The first time we went to training we were given a lift by Paul 'The Chief' Harragon because all the Newcastle teams trained at the same venue. We trained with the under-21 side which included Andrew Johns. He was a very relaxed dude; at first I took him for a country bumpkin because he wandered around with a piece of straw in his mouth. You trained all week with your team — Premiers, Reserve grade, Jersey Flegg — and at the end of the week played practice games against the other teams. The games weren't full on but they were pretty serious. We'd practise these plays all week with the nagging sense that we were being set up to be smashed, which proved to be the case. I'd never trained like that before.

We felt we weren't being looked after so we had a meeting with the club management to air our complaints. They moved us into a house owned by the club and had ladies come in to cook and clean and do laundry. Things were looking up. State of Origin wing Robbie O'Davis, who worked for the club, started taking an interest in us and their video analyst and scout likened me to Brad Mackay, the St George lock/centre who was one of my favourite players. I was thinking, this is what it's about, I could handle it here.

Willie and Brian felt otherwise; they reckoned the club should have looked after us properly from the start and were ready to go home. Brian said he knew I wanted to stay but he and Willie were out of there, which left me in a quandary. The Newcastle coach, David Waite, who later coached Great Britain, said that if I didn't want to be there, they wouldn't make me stay. I ummed and aaahed and eventually decided to go home.

I'd signed for two years and lasted two weeks.

I was soon back in Australia because Wainuiomata qualified for the international sevens tournament in Sydney by winning the national sevens. It felt like we were on the world stage because the tournament was being touted as a major international event. Against Penrith, their Kangaroo forward John Cartwright ran straight at me. Even though I weighed all of 80 kg I launched myself at him, but he just dropped his shoulder. If you watched the video carefully you could see that I managed to hang onto his sock so technically I didn't miss the tackle. Next up was Brisbane which meant I had to tackle Glen Lazarus. I didn't play that well because I was a bit star-struck and too busy getting autographs. When the tournament ended we found 15 dozen Powers Bitter in the manager's room. We had a good court session but I'm not surprised they don't make the stuff any more.

We beat Northcote in the final of the Lion Red Cup and Wainuiomata went off. The week before, having already secured a spot in the final, we went up to Ngongotaha and got beaten. Their centre tried to punch me and somehow his arm found its way into my mouth, so I bit him. He wanted to go on with it but the Lomax brothers stepped in and that was the end of that. It was great having those guys as your minders. On the luge the next day I stood up, like an idiot, and went over the handlebars, taking the skin off the palms of my hands. I couldn't train for three days because I couldn't handle the ball.

But after that I became disillusioned with league. The administrators seemed more interested in infighting than working out their differences for the good of the game. The players didn't want to play in representative sides and weren't striving to be the best they could be. When I took my son down to play league recently, I found many of the same people still there and still doing the same thing. No wonder we lose most of our good players to Australia.

I was living with Mike who was playing rugby for Petone and Wellington. At the end of the year I went along to a fund-raising function at Petone where Mike introduced me to his coach, Frank Walker. When I told him I wanted to play with my brother, he said, 'Come down and let's see how you go.' I thought it was just the beer talking.

I had to apply in writing to be reinstated as a rugby player. While my application was being processed, Wainuiomata had a game against the Canberra Raiders. My reinstatement hadn't come through so I figured why miss out on the opportunity to mark Mal Meninga in front of a full house at Fraser Park. When the Wellington Rugby Union found out that I'd played in that game, they were all set to slam the door on me so I had to write a begging letter. They accepted my plea with the warning that this was my last chance because they'd had enough of players flitting between the codes.

My first appearance for Petone was in a pre-season game against Avalon who had the cult figure Colin 'Pencil' O'Sullivan and Tony Ward, now manager of the Wellington Lions. I got a hostile reception from some spectators, both Avalon and Petone supporters; as far as they were concerned I wasn't welcome there and the sooner I buggered off back to league the better. Avalon worked this move with the fullback coming in running a straight line. I came in off my wing and smoked him which really got the crowd going — 'Get that dirty bastard out of here.' It was an eye-opener because I hadn't realised how unpopular leaguies were with the hard-core rugby folk.

I played at fullback a bit but preferred wing because I could do what I wanted. I made the Wellington Colts and when a couple of wings in the NPC squad went down injured Frank Walker thought I should have got the call, but it didn't happen, which was a pity because I might have got to play with Mike. Frank became a mentor. He's a person I can trust and who has always been there to talk to. As a coach he was a hard taskmaster who believed in hard work and 15-man rugby. Now and again he'd tell me that I looked uninterested and I'd tell him I was probably just tired.

As was very quickly drawn to my attention, Petone was a long-established,

Very little bro — Tana aged 3.

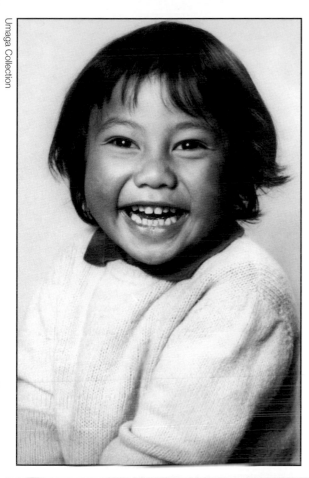

The Umaga siblings flanked by their proud parents. From left, standing: Paegauo Falefasa Ropati, Michael, Tana, Rachel and Tauese. Sitting: Sina (left) and Janice.

The Wainuiomata team celebrates after beating Northcote in the final of the 1992 Lion Red Cup at Carlaw Park. Tana is in the middle of the back row.

The 1992 Junior Kiwis. In the back row Tana (second from right) and Ruben Wiki (second from left) flank Joe Vagana. Willie Poching, the captain, is in the centre of the front row with future Kiwi Gene Ngamu to his right.

Now that's what you call Junior All Blacks. Twelve members of the 1994 New Zealand Under 21 team went all the way to the All Blacks. Back row (from left): Scott Lines, Chris Gibbes, Mark Atkinson, **Chresten Davis**, **Jonah Lomu**, Blair Foote. Third row: **Anton Oliver**, Alisdair McLean, Justin Collins, John Pothan, **Tana**, Adrian Cashmore. Second row: Jeff Marr (physio), **Daryl Gibson**, **Carlos Spencer**, **Kees Meeuws**, Boyd Gillespie, **Todd Miller**, Grant Allen (assistant coach). Front row: Shane Carter, Lin Colling (coach), **Justin Marshall**, **Taine Randell** (captain), Brendan Laney, Mike Banks (manager), **Andrew Mehrtens**.

Daddy Cool: Tana with Cade.

A sign of things to come: taking on the Springboks for Wellington in 1994. The Springboks in picture, from left, Hennie le Roux, James Small, and François Pienaar, were all members of South Africa's 1995 World Cup-winning team.

Tana tries to evade the clutches of Eroni Clarke in the 1995 Auckland-Wellington NPC game at Eden Park, won by the home side 13–10.

We're all professionals here: offloading in the tackle against the Queensland Reds in the first season of Super 12.

Storming past a Fijian defender on All Black debut at Albany in 1997.

Supported by Josh Kronfeld (left) and Justin Marshall, Tana heads for the try-line against Argentina at Athletic Park in 1997. A couple of hours earlier he'd been in hot water for being late to the pre game team meeting.

Rounding French prop Christian Califano on the way to a hat-trick of tries in what was the last test ever played at Athletic Park. A few months later at the 1999 World Cup it would be the French rooster's turn to crow.

Christian Cullen high-fives Tana after scoring a try against the Springboks in the Tri-Nations match at Carisbrook in 1999. The other Wellingtonian in the picture is Alama Ieremia.

If you can't beat 'em, bash 'em seemed to be Tonga's approach to their 1999 World Cup pool game against the All Blacks. Here Tana's a split second away from copping the high shot that left him wondering where his boots were.

traditional club. In league you turned up in whatever you wanted and wore jeans and a polo after the game but at Petone you were required to turn up in your number ones because you had to look like a team. The traditionalists didn't approve of me. I'd wear a shirt and tie with a cap and bomber jacket and get told I had to do something about my appearance. I'd say, 'Why can't it just be about the game?'

The old school guys always gathered in a particular corner and I could hear them abusing me. The other players told me not to worry about them. We had some good players — Jason O'Halloran, Tim and Simon Mannix, Martin Leslie — and won the Jubilee Cup in 1993, which was a big thing for me.

The standard of club rugby was much higher than it is today. The average age was mid- to late 20s whereas now a lot of the players are straight out of school. There were a lot of quality players, guys who were playing or had played first-class rugby, and the skill and intensity levels were higher. There was a natural pecking order in the team: you knew where you sat and what you had to do to get the respect of the older players.

I'd gone on the dole when I got back from Newcastle. I really believed my one chance of being a professional footballer had been and gone. Mike got me a job with the paving outfit he worked for, and then I did labouring work but that was really just a summer job because it was too cold in winter and work was scarce. In 1992 I got together with Rochelle, whom I'd known since school — we actually went out on a date before she moved out of Wainuiomata and we lost contact for a while — and the following year our son Cade was born. When she told me she was pregnant I freaked, as you do when you're 20. I was really living off her because she had a good job and we relied a lot on her family. My parents wanted me to marry her but we actually broke up although we still saw each other. She was at her parents' place with the baby, on the DPB. I wasn't welcome there, so I went over after everyone had gone to work and left before they got home. When Cade was five months old Rochelle went back to work and we moved in with her brother and his partner. I was building concrete dividers for the motorway, doing it tough on all fronts. My memories of what life was like during this period were still fresh when the next opportunity came along.

In 1994 Cade went to Te Kohanga Reo, I started playing for Wellington, and we got a two-bedroom flat in a block in Hutt Valley. It was nice to have our own space. We bought a sofa and armchairs from a second-hand shop, borrowed my sister's 16-inch TV, and got a table and chairs and a washing machine on hire purchase from Farmers. We didn't have a car. Mike was working for a bar called The Big Chill and had the use of a VW Beetle which was really an advertisement on wheels. When he went away they let me use it for a while. I was on the dole; I dropped our son off at Kohanga in the morning and picked him up in the afternoon; in between I killed time waiting for Rochelle to get home. I didn't think life was going to get much better so our focus was on making sure our son had what he needed.

In 1994 I made the New Zealand Colts along with Adrian Cashmore, Daryl Gibson, Jonah Lomu, Carlos Spencer, Andrew Mehrtens, Justin Marshall, Taine Randell, Chresten Davis, Kees Meeuws and Anton Oliver. I marked Jonah in the trial at the Porirua Police College; he was already an All Black by then so I figured if I went well against him I'd be in with a good chance. The first time he got the ball I went low but just got palmed off into the turf. I did a bit better after that, slowing him down until the cavalry arrived, and managed to score a couple of tries. I thought the star of the trial was a flanker from Canterbury called Daniel Charteris. He didn't make the team, yet a guy who didn't even take part in the trials did. Some of the other players told me the team had been picked beforehand.

We won our 'test' in Australia and I didn't play too badly. People were saying that I was one to keep an eye on but I was just cruising along. Rochelle and my sister Janice kept telling me I could be an All Black if I really put in the effort.

At the end of 1994, Mike was offered a stint in Italian club rugby but couldn't go, so they asked me. It seemed like a money-making opportunity, so I went for six months. Sometimes I got paid, sometimes I didn't; whatever money came my way got sent home to my wife. I was playing for Viadana, about an hour and a half from Milan. I enjoyed the food and the culture but the rugby was rubbish and even by those standards Viadana didn't set the world on fire; we didn't win a game in the first round. Rochelle came over for six weeks at Christmas, without Cade because we just couldn't afford it.

I went to the gym a lot in Italy because there wasn't much to do. What with the gym, the pasta and the bread, I started packing on weight. By 1996 I was over 100 kg and once I got serious about developing my explosiveness, speed and agility, the extra weight started turning into muscle.

After the 1995 World Cup, rugby went professional, seemingly overnight, which made me very happy. During the NPC the New Zealand Rugby Union put contracts in front of us but, after my experience with Newcastle, I was in no rush to sign. It was a three-year commitment and I wanted to make sure it would be what they said it would be. Not that I had a counter-offer from the rebel outfit, the World Rugby Corporation: Laurie Mains had drawn up a list of 100 New Zealand players worth signing but I didn't make the cut.

The NZRU told me that if I didn't sign, I'd miss out. I was one of the last to put pen to paper and I did so with the thought that one day they'd regret putting me under pressure.

I bought a car and we moved to another block of flats around the corner where we found ourselves living above the neighbour from hell. He used to bang on the ceiling with a broom handle whenever our son ran around. I tried to tell him that little kids had a tendency to do that but it made no difference. He went away for a few days but 'forgot' to de-programme his alarm clock which went off at two in the morning. The alarm was cranked up to maximum volume and rang for an hour so there was no way we could sleep through it. We rang Noise Control but by the time they got there it had stopped so there was nothing they could do. Our neighbour's power box was outside so when it happened the next night I went down with a torch and turned his power off. When he got back, he asked me if there'd been a power cut while he'd been away. I said, 'Dunno, mate.'

I was on $65,000 a year which worked out at $3,000 a month after tax. We saved as much as we could. The NZRU was supposed to pay us on the first of each month but if that fell on a weekend the money didn't go through until Monday night. The Christmas/New Year period was particularly bad. I'd ask why they couldn't pay us before Christmas; the simple, honest answer was that they couldn't be bothered. They were very hard to talk to; negotiating contracts was like pulling teeth and the players didn't feel looked after, which created an 'us and them' feeling. When I became an All Black in 1997 my income increased and by 1998 we'd saved $50,000 and were able to buy a house. As I'd vowed to do, I got my revenge: in 2000 I had a big year and was able to negotiate from a position of strength and secure a very good contract. I have a long memory for slights. At school one of the teachers told me that unless I bucked up, I'd never amount to anything. Our relationship went downhill after that and I even made her cry once. When I became an All Black she tracked me down to ask me to talk to her students. I did it and it was all sweetness and light but I was thinking, well, one of us still remembers what you said about me.

I never regretted walking out on Newcastle because I'm not a 'what if' kind of person; I don't look back, apart from filing away the names of people who've underestimated me or tried to put one over me. I don't dwell on things but I do learn from them. I learnt early on not to make the same mistake twice and to stand up for what you believe in. I saw rugby as a way to put food on the table and help my wife out by relieving some of the stress on her and contributing to the household. If rugby hadn't turned professional, we certainly wouldn't have what we've got today.

← PLAYBACK

KEN LABAN

Ken Laban played rugby for the Athletic and Wests clubs and represented Wellington. He then switched to league and played for and coached Wainuiomata Premiers. He remains actively involved in both codes through coaching and commentary work, notably for Sky Television, and is a community leader whose various roles include membership of the Hutt Valley District Health Board and managing the Tamaiti Whangai Project, a community programme in the Hutt Valley area working with disadvantaged children and families.

One of the unique things about Wainuiomata is that there are two sorts of immigrants: Maori and Pacific Islander. There are a big group of Ngati Porou who came down from the East coast in the 1950s and 60s and the great migration from the Pacific, particularly Samoa. A lot of people from both groups settled in Wainuiomata because of the cheap housing. They were seeking better opportunities for themselves work-wise and better opportunities for their children. A lot of the Pacific Islanders consciously made the decision to come to New Zealand and ensure that their children were born here so that they wouldn't have residency issues. My parents did that and I know that Tana's parents did, too. They were early settlers; they came with that first group in the 1950s. I live in the family home and we brought up our five kids here. There's a very close association between the Maori and Pacific Island communities here in Wainuiomata and it's typical that Tana, the son of an immigrant family from the islands, would marry Rochelle, the daughter of an immigrant family from the Ngati Porou.

Tana went to Parkway College and his parents still live in Parkway. His three sisters still live in Wainuiomata. The parents have a very strong association with the Congregational Christian Church of American Samoa and they and his sisters have a background of working in the community for the preservation of the Samoan language and culture. Rochelle's mother Flora is involved with Anglican Social Services and the Wainuiomata Marae and the family has a strong commitment to the maintenance and promotion of Maori culture and the Maori language.

Going back the best part of two decades now, most of the footballers in Wainuiomata have played more than one of the three footy codes: rugby union, rugby league and touch. A lot of blokes played all three; a few concentrated on just one. There's a whanau touch competition run under the auspices of the Wainuiomata Marae which is quite famous in this community for its simplicity and hilarity. Each team has to include two of the following: a kid under 12, a bloke over 40, or a woman. The effect of this rule was, and still is, that you could have three generations of a family playing together in the same team.

I guess an unintended outcome was that it forced kids at a very young age to take the field with adults, some of whom were very prominent athletes. There's that whole debate about when is a kid too young and when is the right time for an athlete, but in terms of the culture around the football scene in Wainuiomata, it's always been the case that if you're good enough, you're old enough. Tana was doing what a number of kids did when they were at school: he was playing rugby for the Parkway College first fifteen, he was playing for the Wainuiomata Rugby League Club, and he was playing touch with his family and friends in the summer, as well as his interest in basketball and a whole host of other things. So here was a very gifted athlete who was exposed to a pretty tough level of competition early in his life.

Piri Weepu is a typical Wainuiomata story: his dad is assistant manager of the Wainuiomata Rugby League Club and on the committee and his older brother Billy is the current captain. They sent Piri to boarding school at Te Aute College because that's where Billy went. Piri is a pipsqueak in comparison to Billy but when he got to Te Aute there was no rugby league so he was forced to play rugby. He was playing union for the college on Saturday, then driving home and playing league for Wainuiomata on Sunday. He ended up captain of the Te Aute first fifteen, captain of the Hawke's Bay Secondary Schools, and captain of the Hurricanes region schools team. Within a couple of years of leaving school he was in the Hurricanes and the Wellington Lions and the rest is history. It wasn't till Piri was in his second year as a professional rugby player that his parents went to their first game of rugby. To give you an idea of how humble it all is, Piri's dad Big Bill works on the oil ships that come in around Seaview. He's a kohanga baby, Piri, and his mum works at the local kohanga in Wood Street and is also part of the catering staff at Westpac Stadium, so you have the situation of Piri being out there playing for the Hurricanes or the All Blacks and his mother serving corporate guests up in the lounge. I've been in there commentating and ended up giving them a ride home because Piri's gone into town on the drink with the boys.

Tana played league in the days of the five-metre rule. It was a very different game to what it is today: the five-metre rule meant that once the ball was played, the defence line was in your face, so it was a very physically demanding game. They subsequently changed it to 10 metres and the game has become a lot more fluid and a lot less physical. Tana showed great promise early on. In 1991 he played for Wainuiomata Premiers against the first-grade side from Manly-Warringah in what was then the Winfield Cup competition. Graham Lowe was the coach and that Manly team had Martin Bella, Ian Roberts, Geoff Toovey, Cliff Lyons, Kevin Iro, Michael O'Connor and Matthew Ridge. They were all State of Origin players and Australian or New Zealand internationals; Tana was still at school. There would have been a crowd of 10 to 11,000 at Fraser Park in Lower Hutt. The Wainuiomata team had the Lomax brothers and some terrific footballers of that era but Tana didn't look out of place, not one bit.

In the week or so leading up to a big game it can get quite stressful and there was that whole dressing-room macho culture, and we're talking about a boy playing at that level for the first time. In the time he had on the park in the second half nobody would have picked that, but one thing we all did pick was that this was a kid who had great potential as an athlete. Even at 16 and 17 he was already hitting in defence with the same level of ferociousness as a Jerry Collins. He had a wonderful gift for timing in attack and defence which in a large part is unteachable. Those of us who are involved in coaching know that it's easy to teach structure, it's easy to teach drills and organise preparation programmes and all that sort of stuff. What you can't coach are things like speed, athleticism and natural talent.

He was exposed very early in his athletic life to a degree of competition and intensity well beyond his age; he was playing in significant competitions with serious athletes so there was no time for him to be immature. Well, he might have been but he had to keep it well hidden. At 16 or 17 years old he was taking the field with Johnny Lomax, a great player who was feared as one of the biggest hitters in the game. He played for Canberra and the Kiwis and fashioned a remarkable reputation for hardness and toughness. You can't be in an environment like that at 17 and not be influenced by it. Johnny was everything that Tana is: an absolute, no-nonsense, body-on-the-line player who'd try to score with every run and try to kill every person he tackled.

One of the things about the culture here in Wainuiomata, especially at the rugby league club, is that if you drop the ball at training they bite your head off. That's always been that culture in the place; there was no, 'Oh, that's okay.' That attitude's not prevalent among footballers over here. The environment is tough and as a result the kids that come out of it are tough. He was being exposed to that environment and level of competition at 16 when a lot of his peer group were behind the bike sheds sucking lollipops or whatever. You could imagine what Tana was going to be like at 23: mature beyond his years.

Jerry Collins was the same. Their upbringings just about mirror each other. I've seen a number of kids who haven't fulfilled their potential because they've been too protected. Having said that, I've also seen a lot of kids who've been rubbed out because we've elevated them too soon, so identifying those who are capable of doing it is a very subjective and selective process. Tana and Jerry just have that knack of knowing how to hit people. Because you're talking about a physical contact sport where physical dominance and intimidation and presence . . . well, that's the CV. If you haven't got that, you should go and buy a tennis racket.

Tana was in the Wainuiomata team that won both the Wellington championship and the national championship which was a very difficult thing to do given Auckland's dominance of New Zealand rugby league. They beat Northcote in the final; I think Bluey McLennan was their five-eighth. Tana played centre and finished up in the Junior Kiwis. He was destined for the Kiwis, there was no question about that. Before his 19th birthday he'd won a couple of Wellington championships, a national championship, represented the Junior Kiwis, and played for Wainuiomata against Manly, so he had achieved more in two years than a lot of my peers had achieved in a lifetime of trying to win championships and be successful. I suspect he probably thought, oh well I've done this, I've won every championship that I've been in, I've played for every representative team that I could play for . . . And at the same time his brother Michael, who was also a Wainuiomata boy, was playing rugby for Petone.

The Umagas were a rugby family anyway, as all immigrant Samoans are. This is a very big generalisation but it's also a fact that every Samoan who's part of the great migration to New Zealand grew up with rugby because there was no rugby league in Samoa in the 1950s, 60s and 70s. It's a recent thing. His dad, Falefasa, was a rugby player as well as being a wrestler, so it was always natural that Tana would go to rugby. But his initial reason for going was to play with Michael because Michael had indicated that he was going to go overseas and Tana wanted to play with his bro before he went. It was a similar story in that he went straight into the Wellington Colts and the Wellington team and the New Zealand Colts within a very short period of time. And the rest is history, really.

Let's be honest, rugby union isn't rocket science. Any idiot can play rugby union or league but the level you can play at consistently will dictate how successful you'll be. Tana already had the running power and the hitting power and the mental strength when he stepped into the professional environment. And even now, at the back end of his career and not really that motivated to play, he'd still be among the elite centres in world rugby. I just did the local radio commentary for the Petone-Avalon game: there was Tana, 34 years old and trying to look interested, and the first time his opposite number carried the ball, he knocked the bloke into next week. Tana was undefendable: three of the first four times he carried the ball, he offloaded in the tackle; he scored one try and set up three. And he's been like that for 17 seasons.

The thing that always appealed to people about Tana was the sheer physicality of his presence on attack and defence. That's why he was intimidating. People knew that if you didn't bash him and get him to the ground, he'd get the ball away in the tackle. And people knew that if you got him in a one-on-one situation, attacker against defender, he'd win it 95 per cent of the time. There are two things you can't coach: talent and toughness. He and Jerry Collins have got those in bucketloads and that's why they've been so successful.

Brian O'Driscoll was, and still is, one of the leading centre threequarters in world rugby. Given that they were the captains on the Lions tour, the contest between him and Tana over the course of the three-test series was always going to be a key factor in determining the result. So, if Brian O'Driscoll or anybody else thought that Tana wasn't going to go out and try and bash him — or that Brian wouldn't try to do the same to Tana — they were kidding themselves. If you scan a highlights tape, Tana was absolutely the crown prince of world rugby over the course of that series. And the fact that O'Driscoll got flipped and bounced and put out of the game, well, that's the reality of footy. It was his choice to leave the tennis racket at home. No-one will ever know whether Tana had a malicious intent but I'll say this: I'd be very disappointed if he didn't because it's a tough game. We can be romantic about it but people need to understand that rugby at the elite level is a tough, tough sport.

It was no surprise to me whatsoever that Graham Henry saw the maturity and leadership traits in him, or that as captain Tana conducted himself with humility and grace, or that he had the preparedness, the competence and the confidence to be a marvellous captain. What was a surprise to me was that he was appointed in the first place. Graham Henry probably doesn't realise it but he has made a most significant contribution to the Maori and Pacific Island communities. In 2005, after years and years of asking, he agreed to let the New Zealand Maori team have first choice of players ahead of the All Blacks, who were playing a warm-up game against Fiji. That allowed the New Zealand Maori to put their best-ever team on the park against the British and Irish Lions and record their most historic win. Then Graham took the decision to stand against the tide of what some of us suspect is still a significant anti-Pacific Island attitude among sections of the rugby community and the wider community and appoint Tana Umaga captain. I hope Graham Henry gets his due for what was, in my view, inspired leadership.

A strength and a weakness in Maori and Pacific Island communities is the ease with which we elevate young achievers. That's a very natural thing but we've promoted their achievements in areas where Maori and Pacific Islanders tend to excel, like sport and entertainment, beyond other things in their life that are also important. Tana was one of those who, because of his athleticism, was recognised as somebody special in our community very early in his life and we celebrated that, independent of anything else. Hindsight is a perfect science and I think we're better at doing that with the next generation of players than we were with Tana's generation. Tana would love to be better educated than he is but I don't think any of us in the community gave him much chance to do that because we were too busy celebrating his sporting achievements and he's certainly recognised that with the decision he's made, firstly to educate his own children and, secondly, in the very strong public commitment he's made through the television campaign to help parents educate their children.

Nothing Tana's done on the football field has surprised me one bit. But what I admire him for most is the fact that he's used his profile to encourage parents to get interested and involved in the education of their children. In the Maori and Pacific Island communities where young parenting and keeping families together has been a real struggle, a lot of people will take great heart from Tana's endorsement of the importance of numeracy and literacy and educating their children. That's a very mature thing for him to do. He's not well-educated in the formal sense himself but he's seen a lot of life, he's travelled the world many times, he's spent time in other cultures, he conducts himself with grace and class wherever he goes. In recent years he's also done a number of things in the community away from the cameras, a lot of unpaid work on junior sport and performing arts clinics and holiday programmes. I admire him more for that than his footy. His footy has been great but I'll leave that to everyone else.

Paint it Black

My brother Mike went to the 1995 World Cup with Manu Samoa. I'd thought of making myself available for Samoa too but he pointed out that I'd got my foot in the door by making the New Zealand Colts. At that stage I was still just playing for fun. Other guys were training hard but I was getting by on natural ability.

The Hurricanes 1996 pre-season fitness testing included a 3 km run around the pond in Porirua — not my cup of tea at all. I ran with Bill Cavubati who at 140-odd kg was built for comfort, not for speed. Everyone else had finished as we were starting our last lap. Frank Oliver, the coach, told me to hurry up so I took off and did the last lap in record time. My reward was to have to play all five 20-minute segments of the practice game.

With the All Blacks taking 36 players to South Africa I thought I might be in with a shout, but the four wings chosen were Jonah Lomu, Jeff Wilson, Glen Osborne and Eric Rush. Everyone was getting frustrated with me because I was cruising. The catalyst for change was my wife and sister Janice telling me I had to do extra training and get properly fit. I wanted to work on my speed in the off season so I consulted a specialist trainer, Glen Jenkins. He cost $45 an hour which seemed like a rip-off; I said I'd do it myself but Rochelle and Janice were on my case and knew me well enough to know that without someone to push me I wouldn't get out of first gear. At their insistence, I hired Glen and worked really hard over the summer. It was almost a wasted investment because apparently I came very close to not making the Hurricanes. If Frank Walker hadn't been one of the selectors I probably would have been cut.

In 1997 the Hurricanes made the Super 12 semi-finals playing an expansive brand of rugby that suited us to a T. We had a good side: Christian Cullen, Alama Ieremia, Jason O'Halloran, Steve Bachop and Jon Preston in the backline; an All Black front row of Bull Allen, Norm Hewitt and Phil Coffin; Mark Cooksley and Dion Waller at lock; Filo Tiatia, Chresten Davis and Martin Leslie in the loose forwards; and some good depth in the form of guys like Jarrod Cunningham and Marty Berry. We had a simple game plan: ruck and run; just get the ball back and run the opposition off their feet. The pack laid the platform and I scored a lot of tries running off Cully.

The All Black selectors were looking for a big wing and I was the next biggest after Jonah, who was sick, and Joeli Vidiri, who was ineligible. I got a call from John Hart telling me I was in the Barbarians — the shadow All Black team — for the trial in Rotorua. He wanted me to come up to Auckland for the announcement and press conference at North Harbour stadium. Because we'd made the semi-finals, I had to go up and back on the same day but on the way out to the airport for the return flight we got caught in gridlock before we'd even reached the harbour bridge. I was with All Black selector and assistant coach Gordon Hunter, a former cop. He made a phone call and we pulled off the main road into a park in Northcote where a helicopter landed. Gordon had organised a chopper to get me to the airport on time. I thought, so this is what it's like being an All Black.

When the team assembled in Rotorua I kept my head down and stuck close to the guys I knew. I was rooming with Jeff Wilson but when I woke up in the morning there was no sign of him. When he eventually turned up I asked him where he'd been. It was one of those times when you wish you'd never asked: he said I'd snored so loudly he'd relocated to the physio's room to try to get some sleep. I told him I'd been really tired.

Because my room-mate had disappeared, I'd gone down to breakfast by myself. The old guard — Sean Fitzpatrick, Zinzan Brooke, Olo Brown, Ian Jones — were sitting at a big table. I didn't really want to sit with them — I thought that would be presumptuous — but I didn't want to be rude either so I parked myself on the end of the table. As he was reading the business pages Zinny had a bright idea: seeing the stock market was going so well, why didn't everyone in the team put $500 into a share-trading fund. I thought, oh no, I can't afford that sort of money. When they looked at me, I kept my eyes down. Some of the younger guys filed in and sat at another table. I got up for some more cereal and went and sat with them.

The snoring quickly became an issue. There was a bed, recently occupied by J. Wilson, in the physio's room, so I confided in the physio Dave Abercrombie, asking if he'd mind if I slept there. It had the benefit that at around 10.30 or 11 pm Zinny and Co would come in for treatment so I could lie there listening to their stories about the old days. The downside was that I couldn't get off to sleep until they left because if I dozed off they'd wake me up to tell me to shut up. The other option was to take a fold-up bed or mattress into the baggage room. It was the best solution all round because otherwise I would have been keeping my room-mate awake or keeping myself awake by worrying about keeping my room-mate awake.

In 1999 I always roomed with Cully because he could sleep through anything, whereas the almost imperceptible hum of the refrigerator was enough to keep some other guys awake. It got to the point where guys were saying they wouldn't room with me but in the end it worked in my favour because in 2000 I started getting my own room. It's one of my lesser known achievements: I was the youngest All Black to do that without being captain. Usually only the captain and senior players had their own rooms. The light sleepers weren't too happy about it but I figured it was their own fault for making such a fuss. Actually, I know what it's like to share with a snorer: when Wellington played King Country in Te Kuiti in 1994 I shared a motel room with my brother Mike and ended up chucking things at him. Now he had a real problem.

After a tough trial — the Barbarians won 29–22 — we went up to Albany for the test against Fiji. I was nervous because I was very conscious of coming into a team whose nucleus had been together for a long time with Auckland and the All Blacks. Every Pacific Islander looked up to Michael Jones — I remembered watching him score the first try in the 1987 World Cup final — and now here I was standing next to him during the national anthems. He was talking to me, promising that they'd look after me out there. As it turned out, it was the only test he played that year because he did his knee for the second time. You don't swap your first All Black jersey but Fitzy swapped his and gave me his Fijian jersey which was a great gesture.

Anton Oliver, Taine Randell, Charles Riechelmann and Ofisa Tonu'u had also made their debuts. Under the benign eye of the Godfather, Frank Bunce, we had a big night celebrating becoming All Blacks, getting back to the hotel as the sun was coming up. There was a team meeting at 8.30 am so we went straight into it, still in our number ones, which caused a lot of amusement. Well, three of us did: Anton had crashed out in his room. His roomie Charlie copped some flak for not waking Anton up. Frank, meanwhile, had had a shower and got changed and looked for all the world as if he'd gone to bed early with a good book and a cup of cocoa. Ofisa had some trouble staying awake while Harty was talking, which did nothing to lighten the coach's dim view of the debutants. Afterwards Frank told us that you never, ever went to a meeting in your number ones.

The next test — against Argentina in Wellington — was a big game for me, my first test at home in front of family and friends. It got off to an inauspicious start. We had a daily sheet telling us what time meetings were, what time we had to be on the bus, and so on. About 10 minutes before the pre-game team meeting was due to start I took my gear down to put it on the bus. I had my headphones on so I was in a bit of a world of my own. I was going to stop off on the team room floor and leave my gear there but decided to put it on the bus and get it over and done with. I got down to the lobby and went out to the bus. Ofisa, who was a dirty dirty [a player who isn't starting or who isn't on the bench], was there. He stared at me. 'What's wrong?' he said. 'Why aren't you in the meeting?' I realised to my horror that I'd misread the daily sheet and got the times mixed up.

I ran back inside, sprinted up the stairs to the team room, and tried to slip in to the meeting without drawing attention to myself. The chairs were arranged in a crescent so I sat on the end. Harty was in mid-sentence; he stared at me but I didn't look up once while he was speaking. When he'd finished, I went and apologised; he told me to get on the bus. I thought, it's only my second test and I've already blown it twice. No-one spoke to me. I was telling myself you'd better have a bloody good game today or it could be your last. During the game I made a break from inside our 22; I was tackled just short of the line but offloaded to Josh Kronfeld who scored. Zinny, who hadn't spoken to me since I'd baulked at his plan to storm the share market, came over: 'If you'd been on time for the meeting, Tana,' he said, 'you'd have scored the try yourself.' I just smiled thinking, Jeez, he does know my name after all.

I did have a good game that day but unfortunately I didn't really finish out the season: I got an injury and it just kind of petered out. I was left out for the last Tri-Nations game against the Aussies at Carisbrook. That was disappointing but I had to refocus quickly because I really wanted to make the end-of-year tour which meant having a good national championship season. It was Frank Walker's last season as coach and I wanted to do well for him but that didn't work out because our campaign never really took off.

The touring team was being announced the day after our last game which was against Auckland. We were doing well but late in the game I damaged the metatarsal bone in my foot. It was so painful I couldn't walk. I had to remain in Auckland to see a surgeon and was staying with Ofisa when he got the phone call telling him he hadn't made the team. Then he had to pass the phone over to me: I'd made it subject to fitness. Ofisa had been looking after me, helping me with a contraption that poured icy water over my foot, and talking about what a great tour it was going to be. All in all it was a tough weekend.

The diagnosis was that I had a dislocated bone which wasn't worth operating on. I had two weeks to get myself right, which meant plenty of physio and rest. The fitness test involved sprinting on a concrete surface in the cricket nets at the University of Auckland sports complex. Martin Toomey, the fitness adviser, told me to run up and down the concrete wicket six times. I was pretty sure it was going to hurt and I was right. I'm sure he saw me limping but I was trying not to show any pain. I told him, 'Sweet as.' I don't think he entirely believed me but he went along with it. The foot ached throughout the whole tour but I wasn't going to tell anyone and I haven't had a problem with it since.

Jonah came back for that tour, relegating me to the mid-week team captained by Todd Blackadder, whom I hadn't met before. He was a good man, someone you could talk to, and I enjoyed playing under him. We had some good sessions after games, so much so that the management felt we were drinking too much, which we were, and told us not to go out anymore. That didn't stop us partying and the partying didn't stop us winning all our games. We were having fun, trying to help the test team and not be too much of a nuisance, but whatever we did, we looked after each other and backed up the next day. I had so much respect for the way Toddy led us that at our last court session I got up and told him he could be my captain anytime. I even encouraged him to come to Wellington and be my captain, which didn't go down too well with incumbent Hurricanes captain Bull Allen.

The last game of the tour, against England at Twickenham, ended in a draw, depriving us of a perfect winning record for the year. The English players did a lap of honour. We were thinking, what are these guys on? They seemed to think they were God's gift to rugby and it was that arrogance that made them the side I loved to beat. Some of their players weren't bad blokes when you got to know them but the whole English rugby scene was hard to take.

We had meeting after meeting. John Hart talked and talked and eventually people stopped listening and focused on what Fitzy and Zinny had to say. I tended to listen to Frank Bunce. Hart was a good motivator because there was a lot of passion behind his words, but sometimes you were hearing stuff you'd heard before.

That tour was really the end of an era. Zinny bowed out at the end of it and Fitzy struggled with the injury that led him to pull the pin on his career early in 1998. Then Frank Bunce, who on top of everything else was the defensive co-ordinator in the backline, decided to look to France and the selectors called time on him. It was a massive loss because they were the key figures: they told everyone what to do and how we were going to play the game. They were Hart's men, the guys he talked to and relied on.

They were born competitors who did their utmost to make sure no-one ever got anything over them. It wasn't about emotion: their professional standards and pride wouldn't let them have bad games. Zinny hated losing, so he expected you to do your best. He certainly didn't mince his words (I wouldn't play any of his off-field games because I was scared he'd yell at me) which was something I'd got used to in league. I enjoyed every moment of the tour. There wasn't much pressure on me and it was such a successful side that the possibility of defeat never entered your mind. The mere presence of those three guys created such confidence that you were never conscious of the weight of expectation.

The tour reduced the off-season training window and when I resumed playing I noticed I wasn't as sharp. I felt that I wasn't playing to the standard of the previous year but wasn't too worried: Frank Oliver and Graham Taylor still picked me, so I thought 'she'll be right'. The Hurricanes started with a hiss and a roar, winning both games in South Africa and beating the Chiefs when we got back. The media started talking us up as finalists, the team started believing what they were reading and hearing, and individuals started thinking they were better than they really were. We had the talent but complacency crept in and things just didn't come together. I was one of those resting on the previous year's laurels.

After a disappointing Super 12 I had a mixed game in the All Black trial at

Albany: Glen Osborne got around me twice but I scored a couple of tries so while I wasn't that happy with my performance, I thought I'd done enough. The next morning, before the team was named, I was called into the coaches' room for an audience with Hart and his co-selectors Gordon Hunter and Peter Sloane. Wayne Smith, who'd come in as backs coach but wasn't a selector, was also there. They told me I'd missed out because of my defence, which was a bit of a shock because I regarded that as one of the stronger parts of my game.

I could certainly tackle but they were introducing a new defensive system that Smithy had devised and I was having trouble adjusting to it, much to the amusement of Andrew Mehrtens and Justin Marshall. Previously we'd used either drift or man on man defence, but under this system you numbered off from the outside which meant the winger had to stay on the last man, whereas I had a penchant for coming off my wing. At the meeting at which he introduced the new system, Smithy asked me who I'd take if Alama Ieremia came in off his line. The right answer was that I'd stay on the last man but I said I'd come in and take the next guy, which gave Marshall and Mehrts a good laugh. It was alright for them: they'd had five months to get their heads around it because Smithy had used the system with the Crusaders.

Maybe I should have seen the writing on the wall given that Joeli Vidiri was now available for New Zealand and Jonah was back and Jeff Wilson had to be fitted into the mix, but I took it hard. I had to pack my bags and get on a bus with the other players who hadn't made it to link up with the New Zealand A team. Luckily I had a few mates in the As. I was rooming with Eroni Clarke, which was good because he knew what it was like to be an All Black and then suddenly not be one. We joked about reinventing ourselves as Polynesian versions of Josh Kronfeld but realised it wouldn't work because we couldn't run all day like Josh and didn't have his extra-long arms. We played England in Hamilton on an atrocious night. Jonah played the first half because the coaches wanted him to get game time and I played the second. When England tried to run the ball out of their 22, I came off my wing and snotted a guy. Kevin Nepia was quick to point out that Smithy wouldn't be happy but it stopped the movement in its tracks.

New Zealand A then toured Samoa under Graham Henry and Frank Oliver. Ofisa had told me a lot about Graham, mostly on the theme of him being an ultra-hardworking coach who spent hour upon hour watching videos. There wasn't much evidence of that: it was a very relaxed environment and Graham seemed more focused on fishing than training. It didn't come as a big surprise to me when not long afterwards he announced he was off to coach Wales.

I roomed with Glen Osborne, which is always an experience. You mightn't suspect it from his public image but he's obsessively tidy. I'm not a slob but I don't always fold my clothes or arrange my shoes in a neat row. He'd brought his fan mail with him, explaining that he replied to every letter he received. He encouraged me to do the same but I pointed out that with my handwriting it was hardly worth it.

The rugby was rough and tough, especially the game against the President's XV who seemed to target the Samoans in our side. The kicks and punches were raining in and Filo Tiatia was getting beaten up in every ruck. I found myself on the bottom of a ruck staring up at the sky through a little gap in the pile of bodies. Next thing the sky was blocked out by an evil eye and a fist came whistling through the gap and smacked me in the face. It got to the stage where their captain, who'd played in New Zealand, had to rein them in. I guess they were down on us because we were representing another country and maybe there was some jealousy because we'd made a bit of a name for ourselves. The Manu Samoa game was fine because their team contained a lot of guys we'd played with in New Zealand.

1998 will always be remembered as the year the All Blacks dropped five tests in a row. People told me it was a good year to miss out on the All Blacks but there's no such thing and I was very determined to get back in for the 1999 World Cup. I played sevens for the first time and started popping up everywhere during the Super 12 after Frank Walker told me to up my work rate and get more involved.

Apart from the World Cup itself, my most vivid memory from 1999 is the SAS camp. I suspect most of the guys who did it would say the same. It's the hardest thing I've ever done. We spent the first night in a hangar sleeping on camping mattresses. There were complaints about my snoring, so I assume I got some sleep. We were woken up at 4.30 am and split into groups of five, each with an SAS man. The others in my group were Craig Dowd, Alama Ieremia, Norm Hewitt and Charles Riechelmann. Everyone had a turn at leading the group. We were all carrying injuries so if the other groups had to climb a mountain, we had to go around it. We had to do things like put on overalls and boots and swim 10 lengths of a pool. (I have to admit I didn't actually do that because of the injury and the fact that I hate swimming.) We had to pull a trailer loaded with jerry cans filled with water and carry ammunition boxes full of sand across 100 metres of swamp and then rearrange them so that the pictures on the boxes fitted together. We had to drag ammo boxes over dunes back to where we'd started from.

Our meagre rations had to last four meals from breakfast through to breakfast the next morning but some teams had wolfed their food by lunch-time. We drank lots of tea with plenty of sugar and I remember licking the dregs out of marmite jars and jam packets. The coaches stood around watching and trying to motivate us to keep going but all you could think was, whose crazy idea was this?

Our SAS guy never said a word. I called him Master Chief and kept cracking jokes, which was just my way of dealing with it. There were some strong wills in our team which led to arguments over how we should go about building a bridge from three pieces of wood and a rope. I don't need to be top dog so I'd just say, 'Whatever, no need to get angry.' When it got dark the SAS guy took us out of the swamp and told us to find a place to sleep. Our overalls and boots were wet but I was so tired I didn't care. We had a blanket each but the SAS guy had a little tent with a mosquito net; he probably had extra rations too. The others 'slept' on the top of a rise but I spent the night in a hollow with part of the blanket over my head listening to the angry whine of mosquitos wanting a piece of me. The wind got up during the night and in the morning I found Alama huddled next to me.

After breakfast — tea and biscuits — we had to carry logs up a hill, dig holes, erect the poles, and get a team member up the pole. Then we walked to the road where the trucks were waiting to pick us up. We came across Josh, Filo and Cully who had the sourest faces I'd ever seen, although Cully was never at his chirpiest when he was being made to do something. The fact that Josh was so snaky says it all because he actually enjoyed that sort of stuff; in fact, he was the only one of us the SAS would have taken. They wouldn't have touched me with a bargepole: when our SAS guy delivered his assessments of us, all he said to me was that I talked too much. We were starved, sleep deprived, utterly buggered, and secure in the knowledge that we'd never do anything as hard again, certainly not on a rugby field.

Before the World Cup we had a camp in Palmerston North. The coaches told us we were going to Taupo for some R and R but the bus turned off the Desert Road. Guys were looking around, wondering if it was a short cut, but then the bus stopped next to some poles and jerry cans and the penny dropped. Along with our faces. We had to carry the poles and jerry cans along a road to a big dam where army guys were waiting for us with rubber dinghies with three oars.

It was blowing a gale and we had to paddle out to a little island and back. The others in my team were Jonah, Andrew Blowers, Pita Alatini, Alama and Reuben Thorne. While we were arguing about where the guys with the oars should sit, Kronfeld's team came past and swiped one of our oars. Pita and I were laughing and singing 'Row, row, row your boat gently down the stream.' Not surprisingly, we came last.

We also did some abseiling which I found quite exhilarating. Glen Osborne, one of the funniest men you'll ever meet, is normally into everyone, making fun of them to their face, but now the boot was on the other foot because he was scared out of his wits. We were yelling at him to jump and he was screaming at us to shut up. He was so slow I told him he looked like Michael Jackson doing the moonwalk. Eventually he got the hang of it and enjoyed it so much he did it again.

Going into the World Cup it was obvious that we didn't have the calibre of leadership we'd had in 1997. I'm not sure Taine Randell and his second in command Jeff Wilson had the team's respect. The heavy loss to Australia in the last Tri-Nations game was a stark illustration of the problem: in tough times you need talk and focus but no-one was saying anything. In those situations Fitzpatrick and Brooke would have had plenty to say, telling us how we were going to get back into the game. It was a lesson I absorbed and drew on when I became captain: everyone talks when you're winning but when things aren't going so well it goes quiet and everyone looks for someone else to step up and do the talking. The pressure that had built up during the run of losses in 1998 was starting to get to Hart and Randell. We knew that if we came home with the World Cup, 1998 would be forgotten so there was a big push for us to do well.

Our first pool match was against Tonga. I was hit high and knocked out in the first few minutes and didn't remember a thing about the first half. For some reason I kept asking Cully, 'Where are my boots?' The Tongans put in one cheap shot after another. One of our players just didn't want to know and I got quite angry. We just needed to muscle up and show them that we were there to play.

I've never watched that 1999 semi-final. We were all over France in the first half and if there was any complacency going into the game, it grew when we built up a good lead; we thought it was enough to get us home. Then we made mistakes, the French came back, and the confidence slowly seeped out of us. It was a nightmare: there was a sense of powerlessness in that you could see it slipping away but couldn't do anything to stop it. You always have to look at yourself first, and I made errors I hadn't made in the whole tournament. I'd caught every high kick that came my way but in the semi-final I went up for one and dropped it.

I'd started every test that year bar the romp against Italy but in the third place play-off game against the Springboks in Cardiff I was pulled off at halftime, which I saw as a sign that I'd lost the coaches' confidence. John Mayhew, the team doctor, wanted to cut me around the eye so, technically, it would be a blood bin. I wanted to know what was wrong with the old blood on the towel trick but he said the officials would need to see a cut.

We had to stick around for the final so a lot of us had a couple of big nights as a way of numbing the hurt. We'd get up at lunch-time and meet at the pub. Sensing that I was really down, Wayne Smith pulled me aside. 'You're a superstar,' he said. 'Remember that. You'll rise from this.' I thought, you're just pissed, man; you've said that to everyone.

When we heard what was going on at home everyone wanted to stay in England. A lot of guys did. My wife had come over but our son was at home, so we came back. Harty and Taine took the brunt of it. I felt for them: the way people went after them, you'd have thought there was no one else in the team. We were all to blame for what happened that day. If we'd been poor all tournament, you could have blamed the coach but we'd played pretty well, especially against England. It wasn't as if he came in at halftime and said, 'It's in the bag, you can relax now.'

← PLAYBACK

FRANK WALKER

*A long-serving Petone, Wellington, and New Zealand Maori hooker renowned for his hard-nosed approach, **Frank Walker** coached both Petone and Wellington.*

The first year I had him, 1993, he was just one of those raw, talented kids with the whole world on his shoulders. He turned up for his first game in a pair of black jeans and a black top and earphones. I'm not sure if I sent him home straightaway but he certainly got the message: 'If you're going to play for Petone, you don't come dressed like that.' I told him to buy a white shirt and tie and some proper trou. He was certainly a kid who had a lot of talent. Every time he got the ball he'd make a line break.

He wasn't much smaller than he is now but he was a bit thin up top. He didn't do much weights in those days. He didn't even do any bloody running. In fact, he struggled with work. We got him a job with some paving contractors but he preferred to spend all day sitting in the truck listening to music rather than working. His attitude to training was pretty similar and on the paddock he didn't go looking for work. He was one of those lazy buggers who sat on the wing and waited for the ball to come to him and only wanted to run with the ball, although he could tackle. It took a while to nurse him out of that — I was quite surprised when he actually played for the All Blacks that he was one of their high work-rate players. Of all the players I've been involved with, he and Allan Hewson would probably be the most talented. Those guys just had exceptional talent.

It was all natural ability. He had no problems in playing rugby. He certainly knew what lines to run and everything. He did have a problem with his hands sometimes, a bit like his brother, but he got better and better. I was quite keen to play him at fullback. I thought he'd be the sort of kid who could really adapt to fullback. Centre was the other position that I thought he could make a pretty good fist of, which he did in the end, of course. When I was coaching Wellington I actually played him at centre against Counties and he went pretty well. His only problem with fullback was that he didn't like kicking very much, or he couldn't kick, so if he was in trouble he'd rather run it out than kick it, but my team philosophy in those days was that your first option was to pass, your second option was to pass, your third option was to pass, and maybe your fourth or fifth was the kick. We had a pretty good club team and we didn't kick the ball much, we just liked to run it all over the place. Halfway through the 1994 season [Wellington coach] David Kirk said to me, 'What do you think about Tana? Is he worth selecting?' and I said, 'Hell, yeah.'

When I first came across him he already had mental toughness; he was so determined when things weren't going right for him that he'd tough it out. But he just had that sort of lazy ambience about him, head down, shoulders forward, not saying much, just shrugging his shoulders. The moment he got the ball, though, he was different altogether. It just released some sort of inner power and he was away. It was getting him to go look for that ball. I used to quote him the example of a guy like Grant Batty: the way Bats used to go and look for work — he was over on the other wing, he was in the middle, he was in rucks and mauls, he was everywhere. I was always saying to Tana, 'Get a tape of Grant Batty and see the way he played. That's how I want to see you play.'

It's almost as though a couple of years later something clicked in him and he was just a complete footballer. He was a good work-horse too; he never ever got injured, he was available to play all the time. It wasn't until he hurt his knee at the World Cup in Australia in 2003 that he had a major injury.

In 1996 he and Filo Tiatia didn't make the All Black trial and I had a crack about it. John Hart rang me up and blasted me: who did I think I was trying to promote two players who he didn't think had the ability to become All Blacks? I wasn't quite so impressed by Filo but I was certainly pushing Tana. So that was a real cold blast from John Hart. He said as far as he was concerned they would never become All Blacks. So it was funny when after the last Super 12 match in 1997 Hart came into the changing rooms and gave Tana the good news.

I was a Hurricanes selector that year and [Hurricanes coach] Frank Oliver originally wasn't going to pick Tana. Frank said that if he got Manasa Bari, the Fijian winger who played for Otago, he wasn't going to pick Tana. Bari and Alex Telea were going to be his wingers. I couldn't believe it. He just said Tana's work rate wasn't up to scratch. I didn't tell Tana at the time but he overheard a conversation I was having with someone and said, 'Why didn't you tell me?' It spurred him on, I think, getting a bit of a fright because his work rate went from zero to the top level. He got fitter too and made the All Blacks that year.

When he didn't get that All Black trial in 1996, he rang me up to say he had a contract to go and play for the North Queensland Cowboys, what should he do? I said give it one more season and if he didn't make the All Blacks or at least an All Black trial, go. He also talked to his brother Mike about it; he and Mike were pretty close and he relied a lot on Mike in all his decisions he made. So he stayed and he made the All Blacks and gave me his second All Black jersey, which was fantastic of him.

At Petone we used to take turns to clean up and afterwards we'd have a few drinking games as a shout from the club for cleaning up. We'd set these rugby questions and if he reckoned he was right, he'd always stand up and say so, even if everyone else was saying he was wrong. He was the only kid who actually did that. He wasn't shy to stand up for himself and I thought that was something for a young kid in his first year with a team. So he had something special even then. It never made any difference — in fact, he'd end up having to double-drink — but he always stuck up for himself which I suppose sort of paved the way to him becoming an All Black captain. I didn't think in my wildest dreams he'd be an All Black captain but he obviously grew into it.

Even when he was a young fella he actually talked a lot within the team about where everyone should be standing or about defence and things like that. He always had something to say, which I thought was quite forward for a guy of his age. It wasn't until he became a captain with Wellington and the Hurricanes that it sort of dawned on me that he was a hell of a lot brighter than he looked and had been right from the start. When he became All Black captain with that huge responsibility he did a fantastic job. It was probably the rise and fall of him because I think he got quite down at times with all the pressure that was put on him as All Black captain and it got to the stage where he really wasn't enjoying it. I think if he hadn't been captain, he might still be playing at that level.

I'm talking about the public pressure and the media pressure. He used to come and see me here at work a fair bit and there'd be kids trailing behind him and he'd spend 20 minutes signing autographs. You'd have fathers and mothers coming up and saying, 'Would you sign this for my son or my daughter?' After a while it just got too tiresome for him to come in and have a talk because we couldn't actually have a talk. He didn't mind it but he didn't have a life of his own. And, of course, if he misbehaved at any stage, they'd put the public spotlight on him.

In 1999 Petone went to the Singapore Sevens, which we won, but when we came back we were kicked off the plane. One of our young guys, Toddy Williams, was a hyperactive sort of kid, mad as a hatter, and he'd had a couple of beers. As we got on the plane Toddy was all over the place, jumping up and down and being a silly bugger just as he normally did, and this security guard went and told the captain. We sat down on the plane and the security guards came on board. I said to Tana, 'What do you reckon?' He said, 'If Toddy goes, we all go.' I said, 'Oh? Do you think that's wise?' and he said, 'Yup'. So the call came that they were going to take Toddy off the plane and Tana stood up and said, 'If he goes, we all go.' And the guard said, 'Well, he's going,' and Tana said, 'Well, we're all going.' So the guard said, 'Okay, you lot, off the plane.' In hindsight, it wasn't the best thing to do as far as publicity went but that was Tana. He was saying, 'We're a team. If he goes, we all go.' The players slept in the airport that night. I went and found a motel.

When we arrived back in Wellington the media was there and all they kept asking was why had we been thrown off the plane? We said, 'We just won the Singapore Sevens, why don't you ask us about that?' but they weren't interested in that. A lot of it went towards Tana because he was an All Black. He was an amazing sevens player; I don't know why Gordon Tietjens didn't pick him earlier. He was big enough and strong enough to be a forward and fast enough to be the fastest back on the field.

He's had a few scrapes. I remember we were down in the Deep South and they weren't going to let him on the plane in the morning. I said I'd look after him and make sure he didn't get into trouble. He was never a problem at night but the morning was another matter. He didn't run out of steam, he gained steam.

In terms of his influence on Wellington and the Hurricanes, the first thing you'd say is that he's been a big draw card. He's one of these players you like to go and watch — he was always doing something exciting and being a game breaker. You don't get many game breakers and with Tana and Jonah and Cully you had a bagful of them in the team. Those three were a huge attraction and put a lot of money in Wellington rugby's coffers. After 1997, Tana became a sort of Wellington icon, especially with kids. And the greatest thing about it is that he's been very, very loyal to Wellington. I'm sure Auckland were putting pressure on him to go there at once stage. There's been pressure for him to shift, but he always said to me, 'Wellington's my home and I'm not going anywhere. If I leave Wellington it won't be to any other side in New Zealand, it would be to go overseas.'

If you talk to Rodney So'oialo and Jerry Collins and those guys about who has been an influence for them, the first guy they talk about is Tana. They've all looked up to him, especially the Island boys, and he's been a kind of godfather to them through all these years. It doesn't matter that he's a back, they've always looked up to Tana.

How will he go as a coach? The main thing for a coach is that he's got to be a good selector. A lot of coaches have been good selectors rather than good technical coaches, the Brian Lochores and the Ian Upstons. It's just a matter of him getting the selections right because he'll be fine at man management and talking to the players and those aspects of the game. [Former Petone and Wellington coach] Ian Upston was a great guy: he'd drink with us, we'd play cricket with him in the weekends and have a few beers with him. But as he used to tell the guys, when it came to picking a team he had no friends. That was his outstanding ability: to go that step above everyone when it came to picking teams. I think that's one of the key strengths of any successful coach and selector. A coach also needs to have the respect of his senior players. Tana has some pretty high profile players in his team at Toulon; he'll need their respect and I'm sure he'll have it. That's a big thing and a good starting point.

Smith's Dream

The World Cup semi-final loss taught me some harsh lessons: you can't afford to drop your standards or take things for granted, you can't give up, you've got to keep trying for the full 80 minutes. After Michael Jones suffered his season-ending knee injury in 1997, he wrote a letter to the All Blacks wishing us well and warning us never to take our place in the team or the jersey for granted. He reminded us that all those people in black jerseys and black face paint we saw from the bus on the way to a game were going along to watch the jersey as much as they were going to watch us. Those words came back to me as I struggled to come to terms with the disappointment of the World Cup. I resolved to make sure I didn't repeat my mistakes and to really get out there and give it a crack in 2000.

Wayne Smith and Tony Gilbert were the new All Black coaches. I had a lot of respect for Smithy: technically he's brilliant and you won't find anyone who works harder or has a greater passion for rugby and the All Blacks. I didn't really know Tony Gilbert. Anton Oliver and the other Otago players reckoned he was a good motivator and a good team man and that was how I found him. Their double act was an NZRU call; Smithy didn't have any choice in the matter. It seemed a little strange that he couldn't choose his assistant. Peter Thorburn, the third selector, was another good man.

Andrew Martin came on board as manager. While he might not have been a breath of fresh air, I didn't actually mind him. As you'd expect from someone with his military background, he was very regimented which rubbed some of the senior players up the wrong way. Sometimes, though, that needs to happen; sometimes one or two guys might be getting away with too much or wanting to do too much and need to be brought back to the pack, just to impose a bit of discipline and deliver the message that there are no cliques or special treatment for anyone in this team. Apart from me getting my own room, of course.

The All Black tradition was that you started at the front of the bus and worked your way towards the back. You bided your time and moved back when you felt the time was right. With a number of senior players having left, the new captain, Toddy Blackadder, suggested that it was time for me to leave the front of the bus. I was a bit hesitant because I still saw myself as the new guy but in fact I was becoming one of the more experienced players. I went and sat next to Christian Cullen who'd moved towards the back but he didn't like having anyone next to him so he told me to beat it. He'd played more tests than me so I sat in front of him.

I was happy with Toddy as captain; my respect for him was unwavering. He knew his limitations but he just kept going anyway, throwing his body into everything. As far as I'm concerned you earn respect on the field. I don't really care what you do off the field, but if you're in amongst it doing the best you can when you're out there, you'll gain respect. And vice versa: if you don't front up out there, you'll lose respect. With Toddy you always knew he'd give you everything he had and because he earned respect on the field, you took more notice of him off the field.

Toddy was able to connect with the players and you could feel the culture changing. When I came into the All Blacks in 1997, you had a group of older, experienced players from the same era and mainly from Auckland who sat at the back of the bus and pretty much dictated things. They did all the talking. The younger guys sat up the front, didn't look back, and only spoke when we were spoken to.

Alama Ieremia had told me, as Norm Hewitt had told him, that when you come in you just keep your head down and work away; if you're given a duty, make sure you do it and do it well. In my first year, I was on the laundry committee. I used to take everyone's gear down to the laundry but the real work started when it came back. The gear was all numbered or named, so I'd take it into the team room and arrange it in neat piles by number or name.

I took great pride in knowing that whenever anyone came in looking for their gear, they didn't have to hunt through a great pile of stuff. My predecessor, Andrew Mehrtens, had done it that way and passed on the tip. I just got on and did it as a way of keeping people off my back.

Toddy and the new coaches tried to create a more inclusive culture. The dynamics had changed anyway because the back seat now consisted of Mehrts, Taine Randell and Justin Marshall. It wasn't that they didn't command respect but they certainly weren't as intimidating as Zinzan and Robin Brooke, Ian Jones, Michael Jones and Frank Bunce. I'd been in the Colts with these guys, after all. Besides, whenever you looked at them, they were fooling around. The back seat was now occupied by three of the biggest jokers in the team.

I had my first encounter that year with Gilbert Enoka, a sports psychologist who's now the All Blacks mental skills coach and who became a close friend. He's taught me a lot and helped me to grow up. I used to sit in his room and talk to him and, without even realising it, I was being helped. The term sports psychology conjures up a picture of a prima donna sports star lying on a sofa having a whinge to a nerd in a bow tie whose first question is always: 'Did your mother make you play with dolls when you were a kid?' We had one at the Hurricanes but I didn't find him as effective as Gilbert whose style is never to push or intrude: when you're ready to talk, he'll talk and he offers suggestions rather than trying to impose a solution: 'Why don't we try this?' or 'Well, if you want to, we can.' Whenever he's in his room, his door's open; you can walk in and he'll drop what he's doing and just sit and chat. I learnt a lot from him about keeping in the now, helping with leadership, and coping with leadership.

I suppose most people's recollections of Tri-Nations 2000 centre on the Wallaby test in Sydney, widely regarded as one of the best games of all time. To be honest, it wasn't a game that stood out for me. We started well: things just went right for us and we scored three tries before they'd settled down. Then they came back and it see-sawed right to the end when Taine did well to offload to the big guy — Jonah. The game that sticks in the memory for all the wrong reasons was the one we lost to the Aussies in Wellington. We thought we had it won, so it was pretty heartbreaking. The coaches took it really hard. Then we lost to South Africa away in a game that was all over the place. I thought I'd played well and still had the mindset of feeling good if I'd had a good game, regardless of the result.

On the way back we stopped off in Sydney for a review and some soul-searching. The coaches were wondering why some players weren't able to get up for the last game, given that we could have won the Tri-Nations. They asked me how Cully and I were able to get ourselves up whereas some others struggled. I said something really silly — I think I was a bit hung over — but in a sense it wasn't that silly because it illustrated how Christian and I fed off each other. I told them that when we felt something needed to be done, we'd ask each other, 'Who are you going to be?' The answer would be something like, 'I'll be Batman and you be Superman,' meaning that we were going to try to do something special. I was getting funny looks so I tried again, explaining that we were just competitive and loved to play. Cully and I enjoyed what we did and had a laugh at the back there; we'd developed an ability to run off each other and feed off each other. I knew he could create things but I also knew he was a good support player so I could rely on him to be there if I got my hands free. They just looked at me and said, 'Oh, okay. Thanks a lot.'

Smithy, TG and Peter Thorburn were very thorough in looking for ways to motivate and improve players. Looking back, you can see that they were starting to build up data on players to establish who they could count on — similar to what's been done in the last few years.

Earlier we'd beaten the South Africans in Christchurch but I didn't think I'd played well. I used to concentrate almost exclusively on myself: if I had a good game I'd be happy; on the other hand, if we won but I believed I'd had a bad game, I'd be down. I'd become my own harshest critic, partly because I always wanted to do well and partly in response to being left out in 1998 and feeling that I'd let myself and the team down by dropping my standards in 1999. If I felt that I'd had a bad game, I'd get into a very black mood and that was when I'd hit the grog with a vengeance.

That night we started late. I had a few with the team, then went out with some friends and drank some more. I was drinking to forget. I'd done it before and it worked for me: I'd drink, get drunk, wake up in the morning, feel bad, and then start the week. It was like washing away the whole episode so I could start again on Monday having wiped the slate clean.

But this night some guy filmed me staggering around the centre of Christchurch. It wasn't a particularly pretty sight but I wasn't causing anyone any harm. When I got back to Wellington on Sunday, there was a reception committee of film crews and journalists at the airport. They were firing questions at me but I didn't know what they were talking about. The NZRU media person who was there to meet me said there was a video of me walking through Christchurch drunk. I was like, 'So?' Then television crews staked out my house. I was telling my wife not to open the door and wondering what the hell was going on. I hid in the toilet while Rochelle told them to go away or she'd call the police. 'We just want to talk,' they said. It just came out of nowhere. No-one had anticipated it snowballing like that.

The footage aired on TV3. It was what it was and people knew what it was but it affected my family, which shook me up. My mother cried because she'd seen me on TV drunk. People were talking about me, saying I was a role model and had to behave in a certain way. I was thinking, yeah, I suppose I am but I still want to live my life my way. I also wondered what I'd done that was so wrong and why it was being presented as if I was the only rugby player who got drunk. My stubborn side came to the fore: 'I'll do what I want, when I want, so don't try to tell me what to do.' I got some support from the coaches who could see it wasn't a major issue, as could everyone close to me. I didn't talk to TV3 after that, which was absolutely no skin off my nose because I didn't like talking to the media anyway. And in an ironic twist it turned out that the guy who filmed me was wanted by the police.

You had to wonder where we'd got to. We soon found out because, from then on, All Blacks' social misdemeanours were big news stories and there was no stigma attached to snitching to the media if you saw an All Black overdoing it socially. But life went on, I carried on playing footy, and it went away.

People say elite sportsmen don't drink. Back then I only drank at weekends; later I stopped drinking during the season except when we had a bye or at the end of a tournament. That's probably worse in the sense that you save it up and go on a binge. It's a release: the pressure's off, for the time being at least, so you can relax and let your hair down.

Football players aren't unique in associating a good time with drinking. I get angry sometimes when I hear people talking about rugby's booze culture as if we're the only people in society who ever get on the grog. I once spoke to a group of young accountants; afterwards I asked one of them what the rest of the night held. 'It's Friday night,' he said. 'We'll go to the pub, get drunk, go home. That's what we always do.' For the same reason rugby players do it — to unwind. It's not a rugby culture or a sporting culture; for better or worse, it's the New Zealand culture.

I'm not making excuses or saying society is to blame. I did what I did and I had to live with the consequences. Sometimes I have to take a look at myself and ask why I do this but I do it because I enjoy it. I've had to realise that there will be repercussions if things go wrong and I behave badly; that's what I have to live with and deal with. Other people have to live with the fact that now and again I'm going to let my hair down.

That year I won the Kelvin Tremain Memorial Trophy for rugby personality of the year. The Steinlager Awards dinner fell in the short gap between the NPC final and the All Blacks going to Europe. Before I went on a tour we'd always have a family dinner, a get-together at which we'd have a talk and my parents would say prayers for me. All Blacks were supposed to go to the awards night in Auckland but I didn't want to. Andrew Martin rang to ask me to go but I told him that I wanted to spend the time before we went away with my family and playing with my baby girl. He said I was going to win the main award so it would be really good if I was there. When that didn't change my mind, he put it on me that I had to go, making pointed reference to the terms of my contract. No doubt he was being put under pressure by the sponsors but I got angry and said I didn't play for awards, I played for the jersey. He backed off and came back later to tell me not to worry about it.

I copped a bit over that as well. There was no disrespect intended to the memory of Kel Tremain or the organisers; I just did what I thought was right which was to stay with my family. I have to say I don't like going to awards dinners, I feel uncomfortable. They seem to get bigger and bigger and less focused on the players. I don't have a problem with that — the game isn't just about the players — as long as I don't have to go.

I made the move to centre on that end-of-year tour. Debate over who should be the All Black centre had raged since 1998 when they'd tried a number of guys, the likes of Caleb Ralph, Scott McLeod and Eroni Clarke. At the outset Frank Bunce had come out and said I was the right guy and you'd have to say he knows a thing or two about the position.

My move to 13 didn't put an end to the debate; if anything it stirred it up because there was a strong — or at least vocal — body of opinion that I was better on the wing. It didn't affect me. I'd become good at not listening to the radio or reading the papers. I never listened to talkback anyway — I learnt early on not to listen to people who I didn't respect or whose opinions I didn't respect — but I had friends and family who did; they'd get a bit wound up and give me a ring to let me know what was being said.

The critics reckoned that I was wasted there but I wanted to get more involved in the game on defence as well as attack. On the wing you don't make many tackles or decisions. I wanted to try to influence the game more

We are not amused: referee Steve Walsh declines to high-five after Tana's try against the base of the goal-post in the 2000 NPC semi-final against Auckland at Eden Park. Wellington went on to beat Canterbury in the final.

Watched by his Canterbury opponents and All Black team-mates, from left, Richie McCaw, Brad Thorn, and Greg Somerville, Tana kicks ahead in the 2001 Ranfurly Shield challenge which Wellington lost 29–31. This game was his first encounter with McCaw and the closest he got to winning the shield.

Do what I say, not what I do: giving Richie McCaw a quiet word of advice and encouragement before his debut against Ireland at Lansdowne Road, Dublin, in 2001. McCaw was man of the match while Tana had an extremely forgettable afternoon.

Tana and assistant coach Robbie Deans manage to keep a lid on their emotions after the All Blacks' narrow win over Argentina in Buenos Aires on the 2001 end-of-year tour.

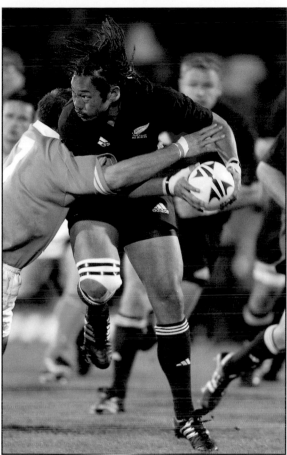

Honorary Canterblack: Tana looks to get a pass away against Ireland at Carisbrook in 2002, a game in which the coaches felt he was off the pace, despite running down Brian O'Driscoll.

Doug Howlett supports Tana as he makes the most of rare possession in the All Blacks' draw with France at Stade de France in 2002.

Enjoying a ringside seat view of Jerry Collins' monster hit on Welshman Colin Charvis at Hamilton in 2003. Delight quickly turned to concern. Realising that Charvis has been knocked out, Tana ensures that he doesn't swallow his tongue.

Despite Phil Waugh's efforts, Tana scores in his 50th test, the 50–21 romp at Telstra Stadium in 2003.

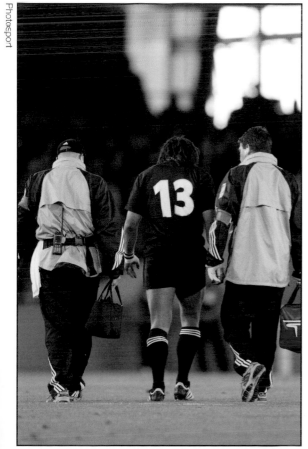

Escorted by physio Steve Muir (left) and team doctor John Mayhew, Tana limps out of the 2003 World Cup after injuring his knee in the opening pool game against Italy.

Under new management: in May 2004 recently appointed coach Graham Henry announced that Tana would become the first Pacific Islander to captain the All Blacks.

Followed by Justin Marshall, Tana leads the All Blacks out for the first time — against England at Carisbrook in 2004. The World Cup holders were thrashed 36–3.

Singing in the rain: Tana hoists the Bledisloe Cup after beating the Wallabies 16–7 in the opening game of the 2004 Tri-Nations at Wellington.

It's not tiddlywinks: all business during the 2004 Tri-Nations clash with the Springboks in Christchurch.

Holding aloft another cherished trophy, the Dave Gallaher Cup, after the All Blacks' stunning 45–6 demolition of France in Paris in 2004.

Garlanded with sweets — a Samoan tradition — and holding the mere presented by the New Zealand Rugby Union, Tana addresses the crowd after playing his 100th Super 12 game in which the Hurricanes beat the Blues for the first time.

and to do that you have to get closer in. In fact, it was just a matter of time before I moved in because to be a wing first and foremost you have to be fast and it just seemed to me that there were players around who were faster than me and who could do most of the things I did. In other words, it just seemed like a smart career move. When the opportunity came up, I took it and enjoyed it, and the people who mattered were happy with how I performed in the role.

Do I wish I'd done it earlier? Yes and no. Yes, because I'd always liked playing centre anyway; no, because the opportunity to become an All Black centre didn't present itself, apart from at the 1999 World Cup. The selectors knew I could play centre because I'd done it at club level for a few years but they didn't believe I could do it at international level. I'm not sure why they thought Christian could, given that he hadn't played there since he was at school. In retrospect you could say that we had the right personnel but didn't have them in the right positions.

We beat the French in Paris and then went down to Marseille for the second test. Marseille was a very different kettle of fish: the comforts of Paris were just a memory. We stayed in a run-down concrete block of a hotel; something was always breaking down and something else was always getting fixed. As for the game itself, they came at us with such intensity; they looked like men possessed — and that was just the spectators. We played at a soccer ground with a moat between the crowd and the field but it still felt like they were right on top of us. It was intimidating but I actually quite enjoy those environments. The crowd really hyped the French players up and they got stuck into us. We couldn't handle the heat from the crowd or the French team's intensity. It dawned on me that day that some of our players were a little bit scared; they went missing in action. I was playing centre and there were forwards coming out and standing by me; I ended up going in to try to do their job. As a player you remember these things; you remember the guys who waved the white flag in tough times and pressure situations.

I didn't pass that information on to the coaches. I didn't see that as my job. I assumed they'd seen it for themselves and didn't believe I had the experience or a position of responsibility that entitled me to do that. Once I became the All Black captain, I definitely put in my two cents' worth and asked for players who would serve in the trenches.

It was an enjoyable tour, partly because I had some good friends in the team: Filo Tiatia, Jason O'Halloran and Pita Alatini. Toddy's credo was that everyone's got a voice, there's no us and them, we're all one. Wayne and Tony pushed the same message. At the end of the tour a young player on his first tour thanked me for helping him and talking to him and not making him feel like the new boy at the front of the bus. That meant a lot to me because I knew what it was like. I didn't agree with some of the so-called traditions that were really just about making the younger guys do things for the sake of it. I didn't like it when it was done to me, so I wasn't going to let it happen to others. I learned from Toddy's example that even though you're the captain you've still got to be able to talk to everyone and everyone's got to feel that they can talk to you.

I wasn't really surprised when Toddy was dropped in 2001. He was a grafter and a competitor and an inspirational leader but as a player he wasn't what we needed at the time. A captain has to be a player first and foremost. You've got to be able to command your place in the team and from what I'd seen and heard that wasn't the case with Toddy. You don't want to be picked just because you're the captain. I know I wouldn't and, being the person he is, nor would Toddy.

Anton succeeded him and I became vice-captain. Hatchie and I had got to know each other on the 1994 New Zealand Colts tour. I'd hung out with him quite a bit and we'd become good friends. I learnt a lot from him about honesty as a captain and standing up for what you think is right. That year I underwent a major change in outlook: whereas previously I was happy as long as I'd played well, the result and the team effort came to mean a lot more to me. Anton had seen that I was inclined to be a little bit individualistic and, at times, a bit selfish. He told me he thought I was one of those players who were too involved in themselves and their own games to be a leader. I'd learnt from the example set by Toddy and Smithy and I'd developed from being in a team environment where everybody had a voice. It was a big change for me, and not always a pleasant one when it involved hurting for the team even when I'd played well, but I'd come to understand that in the bigger picture individual performances don't matter.

In the 2001 Tri-Nations the Wallabies beat us easily in Dunedin which was a bitter pill for the coaches and players to swallow. But that was just the appetiser. In the return game in Sydney we thought we were there but yet again they weaselled their way back, as good sides do. I was particularly gutted because I was one of the tacklers hanging on to Toutai Kefu when he went in beside the posts. Something snapped inside Smithy that night. He's a passionate person who loves the black jersey and would do anything for it and for the team but after the game he looked like a beaten man. He wore a blank stare and you could tell that he was questioning himself and wondering what more he could do?

Gilbert Enoka told me to stick close to Smithy, which I did. I told him, 'These things happen; we've just got to learn from it.' 'That's what we said last year, Tana,' he said. 'We were meant to learn from it then but we haven't.' I was telling him that we couldn't let it get us down, but the horse had bolted. I'd never seen a coach take defeat so hard. I had to tell him not to question himself because he was doing a good job; we were the ones who were out there doing it and it was up to us to implement the plan and not make mistakes. As I said about Harty and the 1999 World Cup, in the end it's not about the coach; the players have to go out there and play. If individual errors are costing you games, there's a limit to what the coach can do about it. Either the players improve or he stops picking them.

Then it all went south. I couldn't believe what happened. Smithy told the NZRU board that he wanted to test his record and credentials against anyone else who thought they could do the job in order to ensure that he was still the right man to coach the All Blacks. It was a selfless gesture but it gave the board an easy out and they made the mistake of taking it. I believed — and still believe — that Smithy was on the right track. He was doing what the current panel have done over the past couple of years, methodically weeding out players who looked the goods at Super 12 level but couldn't be counted on to deliver at test level. I thought we were positioning ourselves well heading towards the 2003 World Cup so it came as a real shock when he and Tony Gilbert got the axe and Gilbert Enoka went not long after. I felt for Smithy because I'd become close to him and he'd helped my game a lot but, as they say, life moves on. I still had my goals; I still wanted to be an All Black and was looking forward to the World Cup.

When I spoke to Smithy afterwards, he said he had options and was in a good space. Getting out of New Zealand was probably the best thing he could have done. I just don't think he coped with the scrutiny and pressures of being a head coach. He was the sort of person who took everything on his own shoulders because he didn't want to worry anyone else but it weighed him down. He obviously learnt from that experience because he was a changed man when he came back to the All Blacks in 2004. He was a lot more relaxed and had learnt to focus on what he could control and not worry about things that were outside his control. It's a good skill to have.

John Mitchell and Robbie Deans came in for the end-of-year tour of Ireland, Scotland and Argentina. I hadn't worked with Robbie before and hadn't seen Mitch for years, and when we got together in Auckland it was clear that they had different ideas about a whole host of things. They brought in new blood like Richie McCaw and Aaron Mauger but that always has to be at someone's expense. Pita Alatini had been our player of the Tri-Nations but before we left Auckland Mitchell told me they were going to try something different for the Irish test and Aaron would be in the midfield with me. That was their prerogative but I felt for Pita who was a good mate. It was a setback from which he never recovered. Aaron's a class player, as he showed on that tour, so who's to say it wasn't a fair decision, but after that Ala just never got a chance. That was his last tour and he was subsequently dropped from the Hurricanes. He wouldn't be the last player whose career effectively ended under those coaches.

We had a couple of mid-week games but instead of having a mid-week team and a test team there was a Zig team and a Zag team. I found it quite funny. You're either in the test team or you're not; it doesn't matter what they're called, and making up silly names doesn't change the fact that everybody wants to be in the test team. It was one of those little mind games coaches play which rarely come off and are usually ridiculed by the players. There were quite a lot of them on that tour and if nothing else they caused amusement, which I suppose was a good thing.

Before the start of the Irish test I was standing next to Richie McCaw, who was making his debut. I remembered standing next to Michael Jones before my first test and thought I'd have a quiet word in his ear during the anthem. 'Just do what you've been doing, mate,' I told him. 'Play the game that you've been playing all year.' Which he did, so successfully that he was Man of the Match. I, on the other hand, had an absolute shocker.

At training Mitchell introduced pairs of white gloves for the forward and back who'd missed the most tackles in the previous game. Presumably the idea was to punish the bad boys by embarrassing them. I knew I'd missed a few tackles so I wasn't surprised to get first use of these brand new white gloves. The weather and ground conditions were typically Scottish so I just ploughed into the nearest puddle and groped around in the mud. After that, the gloves were so brown you couldn't really notice them and they were unwearable for a couple of days. Anton got rid of them, so that was the only time I wore them.

We wanted to be treated as grown-up individuals but they were treating us like children. We responded by laughing at their little mind games. Anton and I talked a lot about how things had changed. He was really struggling with it and, being the straight-shooter he is, he confronted them and told them their approach was annoying people. It was good for the team because some things got changed. Whether it was good for Anton in the longer term is another matter.

In his autobiography Anton wrote about the disrespect the coaches showed Andrew Martin, but it wasn't just them. There was a group of senior players who didn't like him because he laid down rules and regulations. Some of them were a bit outdated, like having to shave, but you either start with a softly-softly approach trying to be everyone's friend and work your way up or you come in looking to stamp your authority, which, given his background, was always going to be 'the Colonel's' way. But he loosened up as he came to understand the environment. I got along with him. What you saw was what you got: when you talked to him you knew he'd be honest and upfront and you'd go away knowing exactly where you stood, which was all you wanted.

Perhaps the new coaches just couldn't accept that under the management structure the Colonel was the boss but they seemed quick to form a negative opinion of him and proceeded to disrespect him, which I thought was wrong. They were supposedly all working together within the management team but when Mitchell and Deans saw some players making fun of the Colonel, they went along with it instead of trying to support him. There was a court session in Scotland at which things just got out of hand and they went out of their way to belittle him.

As coaches they had worthwhile ideas and were good technically. It seemed to me, though, that Mitchell was a bit young and insecure. There was one meeting at which he talked to us quite passionately. When he'd finished he came over and said to Deans, who was standing behind me, 'How do you think that went?' It sounded like he was seeking positive reinforcement, and Deans gave it to him. That was when I started to feel that Mitchell wasn't completely confident in his role and that in some ways Deans was the power behind the throne, supplying Mitch with the messages he wanted put across. Of the two, I had more of a problem with Robbie, whose man-management style left a lot to be desired.

The last game of the tour was in Argentina. This was just after 9/11 so everyone was a bit wary of flying in and out of the USA, but when we were airborne I just wanted to get home. We had a nightmare transit through Miami, spending two hours standing in queues. Marty Holah put his bag down because he was sick of carrying it around and got barked at by a cop.

There are three venues where I felt intimidated the first time I played there: Marseille, Ellis Park and Buenos Aires. We played at the Boca Juniors soccer ground and it felt like there were four floors of people looking straight down on us. The stands were old and rickety and the noise reverberated around, bouncing from one side to the other and making the crowd seem bigger than it really was. We sneaked a win in a tough game and ended up in a good nightclub where the roof opened when it got too hot. I hadn't seen that before.

Buenos Aires is different, and I enjoyed it, but wherever I travel I come away appreciating New Zealand even more. In Argentina, as in South Africa, you're very aware of the beggars and the shanty towns. Kiwis can moan about their taxes and the money that goes into social welfare and I suppose there are always those who try to rip off the system, but I'd much prefer that we look after the people at the bottom, than have them begging in the street. I hope our country never gets to the point where there are so many people living in cardboard boxes that they call it a town.

← **PLAYBACK**

WAYNE SMITH

Even when I first came across Tana in 1998 he was his own man — very independent and strong-minded, almost just for the sake of it sometimes. You'd have to put it down to his upbringing and family background because two high-achieving young men have emerged from it. Mike Umaga was probably a few years too early for professional rugby but he's done very well. Tana's parents obviously brought him up to be true to himself.

I wouldn't say he was self-destructive but he had some behavioural issues linked to going out on the grog. Tana had to change because of the way he was going and my most abiding memory of that 2000–01 period is of the change in him. In the end that sort of change can only come from within. From my point of view Tony Gilbert was a really good man to work alongside and I think he had quite an influence on Tana. Wherever it came from, becoming the man he is today involved a big shift.

In terms of his transition to centre, I would've loved to have thought of it in 1999 and put it to John Hart — maybe it would have changed history. Having said that, the guy we had there was a pretty good footballer. I wasn't a selector then but my gut feeling at the time was that Harty made a pretty logical decision putting Christian Cullen at centre, given what he wanted to do elsewhere. Christian actually played pretty well there and it's very easy to look back and find reasons for why you won or lost. But the fact that Tana was wasted on the wing didn't become apparent to me till 2000: he had this incredible skill level, the ability of offload, and presence on defence.

I made him vice-captain on a hunch. I had candidates like Justin Marshall and Andrew Mehrtens but I felt Tana was the right choice. He was who he was and handled things a certain way but he was an independent thinker, a person who cared deeply about the team, and had a lot of mana. We were introducing peer reviews and honesty, an environment where people could say what they were thinking or feeling, so it became an easier decision. He was a success in the role.

After we lost to the Wallabies in Dunedin in 2001 Tana said to me that he wasn't sure if he liked being vice-captain because he couldn't get on the piss and forget about the loss. He had to think about it and about how to fix it and that was a hurtful process. Prior to that he'd drowned his sorrows after a loss but that was a sign of his emerging maturity. That loss hurt him a lot and he focused on getting things back on track, which we did with a good win against the Springboks the next weekend.

There really wasn't a discussion about the captaincy in 2004. One of the first things Graham Henry said when we got together as a coaching/selection team was that Tana appeared to be the outstanding leader in the country. I agreed with that and so did Steve Hansen so it wasn't a big issue. We were excited at the thought of being associated with the first Polynesian captain and because we knew what Tana would bring to the role.

We didn't coach very well in 2004, mainly because the three of us had been working with a certain type of person in the UK and prior to that we'd been successful working with a certain type of person in New Zealand. We didn't appreciate that there'd been a generational change. Tana was the captain and out front but the rest of them became social loafers, letting him do all the work. There wasn't a hell of a positive team environment because one man was having to do so much stuff.

At the end of the Tri-Nations we reviewed the season and there was a sort of epiphany when we understood where we had a problem. We'd been saying, 'They can't do this, they won't do that, we can't get a spark out of them,' and then at a certain point we realised that *we* were the problem. That was great because if *we* were the problem, *we* could be the solution. One of the big parts of the solution was to grow leaders around Tana because we knew we couldn't leave him out there carrying the burden by himself. From that point on he became a great leader. He could delegate and he could confront people because we created a brutal facts regime throughout the whole team, an environment in which you could be brutally honest.

We did some good work on the 2004 end-of-year tour: the team developed, we started to play good rugby and we grew people who were prepared to stand up. By 2005, that process was well and truly in place. When Tana held a press conference at the height of the O'Driscoll affair, he was flanked by the senior players. That was a real statement that they were right behind the captain. I don't know that it would have happened previously. Because the team had grown to love Tana and we'd developed a leadership group around him, the mood in the team turned against the Lions and it created a huge feeling and desire to get behind Tana and produce a really positive performance for him.

I think he changed as a person during his two years in the captaincy. He became a better person and a better rugby player and came to be seen as a great leader within the community, in fact in the country as a whole.

I think he gave up too soon athletically but I can't answer for him personally. He had things he wanted to do as a father and a husband which didn't fit in with being captain of the All Blacks. But athletically he certainly had more to give. It will be interesting to see how he goes as a coach. He's certainly got the characteristics: he thinks deeply about the game and he's open to learning. I think his challenge is going to be coaching his old mates Gregan, Oliver and Mehrtens, but they're all competitive and professional guys so it might work bloody well. I certainly wouldn't bet against him.

The Battle of Wounded Knee

The only non-Crusaders in the 2002 All Blacks squad were me, Jonah Lomu, Doug Howlett and Marty Holah, which didn't sit well with everyone. The Crusaders players were used to winning, having romped through the Super 12 without losing a game and were always going to be well-represented, but for one franchise to dominate the squad to that extent felt a little strange. Anton Oliver had done his Achilles tendon, opening the way for Reuben Thorne to become captain, while Aaron Mauger took over from me as vice-captain.

I injured my knee towards the end of the Super 12 and missed the opening test against Italy. Next up was a two-test series against Ireland. John Mitchell and Robbie Deans and the selectors, Kieran Crowley and Mark Shaw, were concerned about my speed coming off the knee injury and were wary about putting me up against Brian O'Driscoll, but I got the nod for the first test in Dunedin. It was a freezing day and a scrappy game which we won unconvincingly. At one point O'Driscoll snapped up a loose ball and took off; I had to turn and chase but I ran him down, no mean feat. Afterwards, a member of the management team told me I didn't look too slow for someone whose speed times supposedly weren't up to test rugby, which made me wonder if I was on the way out. I didn't have to wonder for long; I didn't even make the bench for the second test in Auckland. Jonah, in fact, was the only non-Crusader in the starting fifteen.

Mark Robinson, who'd played well for the Crusaders, took the centre spot and kept it for the first Tri-Nations game against the Wallabies in Christchurch. After coming through another fitness test, I was on the bench for the Springboks game in Wellington. Mark got injured, I got onto the field, I played well, and kept the spot for the rest of the tournament. It was the old story of one person's misfortune being someone else's opportunity and I grabbed it with both hands.

It was a tough time, though, because I didn't know where I stood or what the coaches were thinking. Despite being a senior player, I got no feedback at all — just, 'No, you're not in this week.' That was pretty typical of the Mitchell/Deans man-management style, which wasn't what I was used to. With the squad system, players like to know where they stand. Where are they in the pecking order? What do they need to do to get picked? What aspects of their game do they need to work on? But I got no feedback from those two and it was hard not to think that being a non-Crusader I was behind the eight-ball anyway. But I never let it get me down; on the contrary, it just made me more determined to prove to them that I still had what it takes to play at that level.

There were one or two suggestions in the media that there might have been an element of racism behind the team's vanilla complexion. I suppose that if you'd dwelt on skin colour and the type of player they were picking, you could have jumped to that conclusion but I don't think there was anything racist about it. It was just the way it was. Mitchell and Deans had a core group of players whom they valued and listened to, and it didn't include me. That was fine with me; I just thought I had to prove myself to them. I didn't want to rock the boat but if I had something to contribute, I'd still speak up. I had a good relationship with Reuben. His promotion wasn't a big step in the sense that he'd already become a senior figure in the team because of his leadership qualities and the work he'd put into his game. He was a good captain who was liked and respected by the players because he was a deep thinker whose actions backed up his words on and off the field.

We lost to the Wallabies in Sydney in the last minute — again. It was becoming a rugby version of Groundhog Day. The game in Durban will always be remembered for the spectator from hell Pieter van Zyl's attack on referee David McHugh. I was wondering what the hell's going on here when I saw him trundle onto the field. Next thing, Richie McCaw and A. J. Venter were trying to haul him off the referee and getting in a few shots themselves. It was surreal. Up till that point the level of crowd noise and animosity were par for the course and I didn't think McHugh had made any particularly bad calls, although I'd have to say I wouldn't rate him as one of the better referees. The Springbok players were as shocked as we were.

During the NPC the coaches indicated that some first-rank All Blacks would skip the end-of-year tour to freshen up for the World Cup. Not having had an off-season since 1998 I figured I was in line to be rested, which I didn't really mind. The coaches asked Taine Randell, whom they'd previously ignored, to captain what was going to be a development side. Taine knew the score but wanted to go out with a bang and prove them wrong. He rang me to ask if I was keen to come along and give him a hand. We'd played quite a bit together but it wasn't as if we rang each other every weekend, so it took some guts for him to ask. I thought, well, why not? What had happened at the start of the international season was still fresh in my mind. Would I have got back in if Mark Robinson hadn't been injured? Could I be certain that I'd be picked in 2003? I talked it over with my wife who told me to go, so I said, okay. The coaches asked me if I was sure.

We had a good group: some guys who were on their first tour and others who were coming back. Christian Cullen was in the second category but it wasn't much of a comeback for him as he only played one game. Before the side to play England was announced, Deans pulled Cully out of a team meeting; when he returned it was obvious from his expression that he wouldn't be playing. It should have been done earlier; it was no way to treat someone who'd played so many tests and had such standing in the game. It certainly didn't impress the players, although there was no disrespect to Ben Blair who was a good player in his own right. The non-Crusaders got together and agreed that we just had to watch our backs and try to hang in there.

People were saying that Cully's knee wasn't 100 per cent and he'd lost a yard of pace, but he still had the nous to be in the right place at the right time. He didn't take it well — not many people would have but he takes it worse than most — and I didn't see him for a couple of days. Cully hadn't had a great year but he was a special player who still had plenty to offer the team. You could speculate all day about why they would take someone of his stature and experience on that tour and not use him.

We had an opportunity to beat England but didn't take it and drew the French game 20–20 despite getting monstered in the scrums and losing nearly every lineout. At one stage I suggested to Taine that we should try something else. He said, 'We've tried everything but they just keep picking off our ball.' That's the problem with a young side: at the top level it's all about knowing what you need to do to hang in there and close out games. We also got into trouble against Wales but Doug Howlett and Daniel Braid had blinders and we came back in the second half playing some good rugby. Taine went off — he'd had problems with his calf for years — so I took over the captaincy, which was a proud moment. I'd captained Wellington in 2002 so I had a bit of experience but I didn't say much apart from that if we hung in there, we'd get on top of them. Which we did: we scored a couple of late tries to blow the scoreline out and end the tour on a positive note.

Looking at who was left at home, it wasn't a huge stretch to assume that if you were on that tour, you were on the outer. But I just like to play and my philosophy was always that when you get an opportunity to play for the All Blacks, you take it. You never know what's around the corner and there were a few boxes to be ticked before anyone could pack their bags for the World Cup: you'd have to play Super 12, produce some form, avoid injury, and get picked. It's interesting to look at who went on that tour: Tony Woodcock, Keven Mealamu, Keith Robinson, Ali Williams and Rodney So'oialo all made their debuts and it was the only time Mitchell and Deans ever picked Carl Hayman, who's been the cornerstone of the All Black scrum for the last few years.

We started 2003 by losing another game to England that we should have won. We had enough opportunities but didn't take them, and England showed their experience. When they were a man down, Martin Johnson stood up and gave the 'on me' call: he took the ball from lineouts and they drove it and shut us out. It was Rodney's first test at home and Ma'a Nonu's debut so the dismissive media reaction would have been particularly hard on them. The pundits were saying we weren't up to it but we were a young side and that England team was a tough outfit at the best of times, let alone first up.

The test against Wales in Hamilton was notable for Jerry Collins' tackle on Colin Charvis. Charvis was actually running towards my channel; I was lining him up when I saw Jerry coming from outside me and I knew it was going to be big. It was a big, big hit, one of the bigger ones I'd seen, and my immediate reaction was, Yeah! I was right behind them as Jerry drove him back; I saw Charvis go limp and his eyes roll back. My excitement gave way to dread. I was aware of the danger of him swallowing his mouth guard and choking so I just did what I'd been taught: rolled him over, took out his mouth guard, and kept his tongue out of his throat. I thought I'd done the right thing but when I came off the All Black team doctor John Mayhew told me I shouldn't have moved him because he might have had a damaged neck. I asked what was I meant to do: let him choke or take the gamble that he hadn't hurt his neck? I was right there and I've been knocked out on the footy field and that was what it looked like to me. But it makes you think: what do you do next time?

Anton Oliver had a couple of lapses in his defensive decision-making in the test against France in Christchurch and that was the end of him. I'd seen what he had to offer and what he did in a game and if they'd been willing to work with him, it wouldn't have been a problem. Virtually overnight he went from being the first-choice hooker to the fifth or sixth-ranked, which just didn't seem right for such a highly experienced All Black and former captain.

We went into the Tri-Nations with a more balanced side than we'd had in previous years and really fired, playing a good brand of rugby. Everything clicked and we put 50 points on South Africa in Pretoria and Australia in Sydney, scoring a lot of tries. I didn't sense those performances coming because we'd made so many changes throughout the first three games and hadn't really settled on a starting line-up. My own form was average. I felt really tired. I'd had an arduous Super 12 captaining the Hurricanes and working my arse off to keep us competitive in some games. We made the semis which meant one week off, then back into camp. I think it caught up with me during the Tri-Nations and I didn't feel I made a major contribution to those performances. I did what I was meant to do and no more, which wasn't my game. I aimed to do my job plus contribute around the field and help out. In the South African game, for instance, I must have only touched the ball a couple of times. The Australian game was my 50th test so I had motivation and the honour of handing out the jerseys but again I thought I'd just done enough to get through. I suppose if there's ever a good time to turn in an average performance it's when everyone else is on fire. The home games were a lot tighter. We didn't play as well as we had on the road but the other two teams played a lot better. To be part of the team that won the Bledisloe Cup after having tried and failed for so long was a great feeling and enormously satisfying.

We had a series of camps leading into the World Cup. I was in the remedial training group, the same old predominantly brown faces, who did a lot of extra running and fitness work after training sessions. I'd been in it every year since 1997. I arrived in Nelson for the third camp feeling tired and went down crook. It absolutely flattened me: I couldn't get out of bed; I couldn't eat. For the first two days I just slept; on the third day I had some soup. Doc Mayhew didn't think there was anything more to it than being worn down; I guess it was just a case of the body needing to recharge. I stayed in bed for the whole five days and my weight went from 102 kg to 96 kg. By the time the camp wound up I was well again and my body fat count was unbelievable. It certainly made a change to have the nutritionist tell me that my body fat was unhealthily low.

I was really looking forward to the World Cup. I'd been building up for it since 1999; all my training had been focused on it. Everything was looking good in the lead-up: I was enjoying Melbourne — my sister-in-law lives there, so Rochelle and I had been there before; we were training well; and we had had good digs. In the first game against Italy I was feeling good; I got the ball in a half gap and if I'd dummied and gone I probably would have scored but I passed to Brad Thorn who got the try. Around the 20-minute mark we had a move off a scrum; I was meant to cut with Carlos Spencer but the Italians pushed up hard and he got the ball going backwards so I held back to try and help him out. Carlos got barrelled just as he gave me the ball and fell on my leg, hyper-extending the left knee. I got up and tried to walk it off, telling the medical team that I was okay. I should have asked for a second opinion. I stayed on for a couple of minutes but I couldn't run. The knee felt sloppy and unstable so I limped to the sideline. I'd had my heart and mind set on the World Cup for four years and had lasted all of 21 minutes.

They put my bed up on phone books so that it was tilted backwards to stop the swelling going to my knee and I woke up every two hours to ice it. The surgeon thought I'd ruptured my posterior cruciate ligament. You're better off going the whole hog because partial ruptures might require an operation that can sideline you for a year. If it's completely ruptured then it's useless and there's no point having an operation; all you can do is build up the muscles around it. It looked like it was gone, which gave me some hope: league players usually come back from this injury within three weeks because you can train other muscles to function as the knee's stopping mechanism. They didn't even strap it and within a few days I was cycling with the seat down low so that the knee was always flexing. I was going through some pain but at least it was movement and I started to think that I might be a goer. I did plenty of cycling and pool work and icing and spent a lot of time in my room with guys popping in to say hello.

I took control of the DDs, the dirty dirties. They were mostly young guys who were getting disgruntled with going to training to hold tackle pads. I told them that whatever they did, they musn't go to their mates who were in the team and moan about not playing and the way things were going; if they felt that way they could come and see me and we could console each other because we were all going through the same thing. We had to support the guys who were playing and one way of doing that was to carry the load for them in terms of all the promotional obligations. As well as that I was training twice a day, getting lots of physio, and trying to learn some songs on the guitar, but there was also down time when I sat around wondering if it was worth it and whether there was a realistic chance of getting onto the field.

About 10 days after the injury I tried to run. It was an ugly sight but at least I was out there jogging and getting a lot of support from the boys watching me run around the field. I did a lot of work on my quads and hamstrings and calves to build up the muscles around the knee and coming up to the quarter-final it was actually feeling good; I was running quite freely. The acid test was lateral movement. I thought I'd just go as hard as I could and if it buckled, it buckled. The first two steps were fine but as I went to take the next step the knee buckled and the pain was horrendous. Then I moved my leg and the pain was gone. I had no idea what had happened but it felt like the knee had locked up and then released. The medical team said it was nothing to worry about, the knee was probably still cutting in and out. I kept up with the gym work and had another run after the quarter-final and the same thing happened: it locked up as I side-stepped, only this time it stayed locked up for a while. It was so painful that I could hardly walk.

Deansy was there watching so I pretended I was okay and tried to walk as normally as possible. We were training just across the road from the hotel so the walk back was only about 400 metres but it seemed to take an eternity and every step hurt. When I got into my room I just closed the door and lay down on the bed. I knew something wasn't right and I was pretty sure Deans knew that, too. The next time I tried the knee out both the coaches were there. The same thing happened: they were asking if I was alright and I was saying yeah, it was just a bit achy. This time, though, I sat down. The next day they told me I wasn't in the team for the semi.

It was pretty gut-wrenching because I'd worked hard to get back and no-one could explain what was wrong; as far as the medics were concerned, I'd recovered from the initial injury. But I have no issues with not being picked:

as the coaches said, I wasn't 100 per cent. I tried to get back, I think I did everything I could have done, but it wasn't enough. What I did have an issue with was the fact that they had another specialist centre in Ma'a Nonu but didn't play him. I thought they should have stuck with him and really given him an opportunity. I don't know if it would have made a difference to the final outcome but it would have made a difference to Ma'a.

The DDs were sent to Sydney a day early to do promotions. Some of Steve Devine's mates turned up and a few of the boys took the opportunity to enjoy Sydney nightlife. I wouldn't know what time those guys got to bed. I didn't get into it, partly because I still thought I was in with a chance of playing if we got through to the final but mainly because I just wasn't in the mood. At least I had my wife and kids and parents there. They'd come over to watch the last three games and the only good thing about not playing was that I was able to spend quite a bit of time with them.

The semi-final was another slow-motion train wreck. The Wallabies played well: they'd done their homework, as Australian teams always do, and they came to play. Their crowd lifted them and they played their guts out. We tried to play the expansive game which had worked for us all year but they were able to shut us down. It was *déjà vu*, complete with the same terrible sick feeling but with an added sense of uselessness because there was nothing I could do about it. I felt for the boys and it was a credit to them that they got up to beat France in the play-off game for third and fourth a few days later, so that we at least finished a place higher than in 1999.

Back home I just moped around. I was pretty useless, really. After the 1999 World Cup I'd set myself one big goal and it had come to nothing. I'd signed a four-year contract rather than the usual two or three with the idea of getting to the World Cup, winning it, and having one more year. That was the plan but it wasn't to be. I'd turned down an invitation to Adrian Cashmore's stag party in Las Vegas — I'd just spent a couple of months in Australia and didn't want to go away again — but my wife got sick of me mooching around and told me to go.

So I went. I met up with Carlos Spencer and Craig Innes in Los Angeles and we flew to Las Vegas together. You fly in over the white desert and suddenly there's the city. It's tempting to call it an oasis but the only green bits are the football field and the golf courses. The rest of the crew were Filo Tiatia and Charles Riechelmann, who were playing rugby with Adrian in Japan, and Cashie's dad. We were staying at the MGM Grand, all six of us in two rooms.

We got there first, so we got the beds. The programme was pretty simple: get drunk and gamble or vice versa. Seeing I don't gamble I didn't do anything I couldn't have done without leaving home. I've never gambled in my life and don't understand why people do it, which I suppose is a good thing. After one day of it, I was done; the other guys kept going but I spent most of the second day in bed. At one stage I tried to go for a walk. I was hung over to start with and the bells and lights in the casino made my headache worse. It was such a big casino that it took me ages to find an exit and when I finally did, a security guard wouldn't let me use it so I had to keep looking. That was really it for me: I'd had enough; I just wanted to go home. The other boys were still going strong and keen to go again the next night but I went to bed early because I had a flight in the morning. It was good to get away and do something different with mates and when I got back, it was time to move on. I'd gotten over my World Cup disappointment and was ready to focus on what I was going to do next.

When I resumed training in January, though, the knee was still locking up. Further scans didn't reveal anything so I got in touch with Stu Walsh, the surgeon. He thought he knew what it was and wanted me to go up to Auckland for arthroscopic surgery. Clearly, all that rehab I'd done at the World Cup hadn't fixed it so my wife and I went up a couple of weeks before the first pre-season game. Stu got into the knee and found that a piece of meniscus was flapping around inside the joint. What was happening was that as it flapped around it was sometimes getting stuck in the joint, hence the locking up and the pain. He cut the piece of meniscus out — I've still got it in a jar — and two weeks later I played 15 or so minutes against the Brumbies in the first pre-season game.

To be honest, I can't say I was too upset or surprised when John Mitchell got the sack. As everyone knows, he dug himself a hole by distancing himself from people. As Michael Jones said in that letter, you can't take the fans for granted and under Mitch we took a lot of things for granted. I knew it wasn't right, us trying to seal ourselves off from everyone else. I understand the way it works: you do what you have to do for sponsors because without sponsors we don't get paid. And it's not just the All Blacks; it's the game all the way down to the grass roots. All Blacks have a responsibility to the country and to the game as a whole; they're the front men for every aspiring rugby player in New Zealand and that's something you need to learn. I learnt it early and made sure that I didn't forget it. But Mitchell and Robbie Deans had the view that they didn't need to focus on anything except the on-field performance because if they got the end result, the rest would take care of itself. It was a high-risk strategy because it meant there weren't going to be too many people rallying around them if the end result wasn't forthcoming. It was a tough couple of years with them in charge. I didn't feel sorry for them because I remembered the contemptuous way they cast aside experienced and valuable players. I'm a big believer in karma and that was certainly a case of what goes around, comes around.

← PLAYBACK

ANTON OLIVER

Tana and I go back to the Colts in 1994. I don't generally spend a lot of time with backs as they don't have anything interesting to offer but he always had a sense of himself, he was always his own man. Back then he had a confidence based around his ability to play sport. His evolution saw that slowly morph into a confidence based on himself as a person and his ability to deal with people.

We made our All Black test debuts together and went out on the piss together. That was the expectation. We came up in an era when alcohol was a big part of things, not only in celebrating success but also as a test of manhood as in how much could you handle. It was binge drinking — none or a hundred — and I drank just as much if not more than him. The difference was that I didn't get feisty. There were consequences in some of the trouble that followed him around but it's all relative: down in Dunedin we got away with murder because it was seen as student culture and accepted whereas in Auckland or Wellington you couldn't do that. The Xavier Rush incident would be an example of that. Dunedin was a place where you could express yourself — all kinds of shenanigans that Marc Ellis has talked about endlessly. We were all students and even when we became rugby players we still saw ourselves as students.

Being a young forward, particularly a young tight forward which was rare, I was given a rough time when I came into the All Blacks. It was different for the backs because the senior back, Frank Bunce, was very inclusive and warm; he's a nice guy and they didn't need to be obsequious or fawning around him. As a young forward, and especially not being part of the Auckland club, you had to know your place in the pecking order. I struggle to understand how we won games because I didn't understand the inner circle and how they worked. They were very hard-nosed and professional and hard on each other — if you didn't live up to what was expected, it would be made known through public admonishment. They won games because they had high standards. Graham Henry calls them ruthless. We never really played as a team; we relied on giving the ball to talented individuals like Tana and Jonah. I didn't understand how that group worked but they'd spent a lot of time in the trenches together and were very tight, but I wasn't part of it.

Wayne Smith started trying to turn it around. It was a tough assignment — heading in a new direction, changing cultures — but I felt we were making some real progress. In the end, after another year without the Bledisloe Cup, Smithy's and Tony's heads were on the block. Poor Smithy, he's such a good bugger; he was so honest he slit his own throat, but I believe he has found his right niche now.

I'd been captain under Wayne and Tony Gilbert. During the transition period to Mitchell and Deans I was getting information from people in the management set-up that I was close to. The new coaches were picking a team based on form after each round of the NPC and the selections fluctuated wildly: one week Andrew Mehrtens was captain, next week it was Scott Robertson. I wasn't featuring at all so it was bizarre to get a phone call summoning me to Christchurch to inform me I was captain for the end-of-year tour. Tana and Justin Marshall were the two people I sort of trusted so when injury took Marshy out of the tour I felt quite exposed.

There was a lot of change in the area of support staff and you felt that the coaches were on a slow but inexorable march towards removing anything and everything that Wayne and Tony had put in place, for no other reason than that it was their legacy. That tour was about stamping their mark on the team — the new bosses were going to eradicate all trace of the previous regime and have all the players channelling through the two of them which meant the end for the likes of Andrew Martin and Lipi Sinnott. They didn't want people who could think for themselves. They really bawled out Nathan Mauger; it was completely unacceptable and I had guys coming up to me asking what was going on. I asked Tana and Reuben Thorne to go with me to confront them over it. To their credit they stopped.

I was massively surprised to get back in 2003 after the Achilles injury in 2002. I came out of the trouble at the Highlanders all over the place and down on confidence and had no idea how I made it. One of the problems in that loss to England was that we had Marshy who was the game player for the Crusaders, Carlos who was the game player for the Blues, and Tana who did it for the Hurricanes and there was real conflict over what was going to happen when the shit hit the fan. Marshy would run a few yards looking for an opportunity, then give it to Carlos who'd do the same, then give to Tana who'd get smashed. They were three very strong individuals: I think Tana's attitude was to keep his mouth shut and see where it went. Marshy was definitely Deans' chap so he was pushing it uphill there.

I didn't play that well against England — there was hesitancy and self-doubt. Against the French in Christchurch, though, I thought I played well, although the lineouts weren't great — the French managed again to be very disruptive. But I got dumped. The rationale wasn't solid, that was my gripe. Christian Cullen got the same treatment but he took it personally.

People think I have a grudge against Mitchell and Deans, but I don't. It's just my assessment of what happened. I didn't have any issues with Deans because I rarely talked to him. I think he was a bit of a Machiavellian figure — an intelligent orchestrator who managed to get his way in most things relatively unseen. John Mitchell just got the job too early. They had some fantastic success and their egos got away from them. They wanted to be judged on their results and they were. They were pretty off-hand with the media and sponsors and it always comes around.

After the 2003 World Cup at which Tana was injured, I gave him a ring. There was talk that he was right to play but they wouldn't pick him, and I said to him, 'They got you as well; they got all the "dissenting" characters. It took them a bit longer in your case but they got you in the end, too.'

The role reversal when Tana became captain was good for me because I was out of the limelight. There's something attractive and enticing about being in the limelight — you say stuff and people listen, which can be used for tremendous good — but for me it was good not wanting to be top dog. I never got comfortable with it and I was glad to not have that role again. It was good for me to use my experience and be a henchman, a right hand man. On the 2004 tour Norm Maxwell and I were outside the leadership group and really didn't do a lot, which made it a magnificent tour. We were in the back seat and the leadership group, then in nascent form and trying to take over, had not figured out where the back seat fitted in with them.

In 2005, I was injured for the Lions tour but was happy to help out wherever I could for Tana, as I've done for Richie McCaw. I know the pressure they're under so I did whatever I could do to relieve the load. When the pressure came on Tana, he really withdrew. He's had his own room for a long time because of his snoring — he's like a Husqvarna chainsaw, you can hear him through a five foot concrete wall — and because of that he's always been able to shrink away and make it difficult to get to him. Like in Ireland in 2005 when he was copping a lot, he'd be on the phone to Rochelle, she'd ring Gilbert Enoka, he'd get hold of me, and I'd knock on his door and say, 'Right we're going for a beer.'

Not many New Zealanders have experienced what he went though during that

Lions tour, particularly the media hysteria that followed the O'Driscoll tackle and the week of intense character assassination that followed (Alistair Campbell, of Tony Blair spin doctor fame, had to earn his way somehow). After that second test, Tana had his jersey over his head and was crying because he'd been booed on his home ground because the place was half-full of Lions supporters. It really affected him and what he'd been through all week just came pouring out. I gave him a hug and told him, 'Get it out, fella.' I don't know why people say to stop crying.

He really stamped his mark in that Lions series. We lost two in a row in 2004 and he had some self-doubt and thought about retiring, as did [All Black manager] Darren Shand after some shenanigans on the part of a couple of senior players. Tana was going down the same path as Todd and myself, being a one-year wonder, not actually achieving anything. Gilbert Enoka needs to be recognised because he challenged Tana's natural reluctance to be a talker off the field. He really pushed Tana's leadership role, deferring to him as the captain and giving him the last word. Slowly but surely Tana started to function as a leader. He'd always had the ability — when things got to melting point, he'd flare — but you have to lead and front issues all the time. Gilbert did a really smart job in cultivating his leadership; he always had it in him but Gilbert brought it out.

He insisted Tana lead the haka and the public attached a huge amount of significance to Tana's role there; they translocated those qualities onto Tana in much the same way as happened with Buck Shelford and which never happened with Taine Randell. It was a huge thing for the New Zealand public and kind of legitimised his spot as leader. All captains have doubts — will they back me? — but doing that lessened the doubt and increased his mana.

Tana's influence on Wellington hasn't been replicated elsewhere, say by Todd Blackadder in Canterbury or Carlos or Sean Fitzpatrick in Auckland. Because of the culture and the hierarchical nature of the Samoan community, he's almost revered. I think it became a negative for him and the Wellington rugby community. I don't think it is healthy for so many to be deferential to one person — albeit for respectful reasons: it restricts other players' growth and leadership potential and places a lot of pressure on the individual (Tana) who is held in such high regard. So, in my opinion, it is both the right time for Tana, and for Hurricanes and Wellington rugby, that he has made the decision to end his career in Wellington. It should not be met with any sadness or melancholy, rather an acceptance that it is the natural order of things and the boat will keep sailing regardless of who is on her decks.

Captana

For the 2004 Hurricanes the Super 12 had ended two weeks earlier than we'd hoped. The upside was no training, which meant I could sleep in. So when the phone rang, I just rolled over thinking it can't be for me because no-one who knows me would be ringing this early. My wife answered and handed me the phone. The conversation went like this:

'Hi Tana, it's Graham Henry here.'

'Whatever. Who is it?'

'No, no, it's Graham Henry.'

'Oh, okay. What can I do for you?'

He said if I wasn't doing anything — and seeing the Hurricanes weren't in the semi-finals I obviously wasn't doing much — he was going to be in Wellington and would like to meet. My wife reckoned he was going to ask me to captain the All Blacks. Ever the pessimist and mindful of Michael Jones' warning about taking things for granted, I thought it was more likely that the new coach wanted to make some changes and my services would no longer be required. Talk about glass half-full or glass half-empty: my wife was convinced I was going to be offered the captaincy while I was thinking it was good of Graham to break it to me face to face rather than letting me read it in the paper. As they say: think the worst and you'll never be disappointed.

We met at the City Life Apartments. It was the first time I'd seen him since the fishing trip otherwise known as the 1998 New Zealand A tour of Samoa. After some small talk he laid it on me: would I like to captain the All Blacks? I was stunned. When I snapped out of it my first thought was geez, that's amazing; my second thought was geez, that's a big job and a big-time commitment for a bloke with a young family. I asked Graham if I could think about it overnight and get back to him, which I think surprised him a bit. I guess most people would have jumped at it but it wasn't just about me: it concerned others so I had to make sure that it was alright with them. My wife said, 'Yeah, go for it.' She also said, not for the first time, 'I told you so.' The next day I rang Graham to accept.

There was a lot of media interest, with an emphasis on me being the first Pacific Islander to captain the All Blacks. Just before the announcement, NZRU deputy chief executive Steve Tew asked me if I'd sorted things out with TV3; he got a bit of a shock when I replied that it hadn't been talked about. TV3 was the NZRU's free-to-air partner so in the normal course of events they'd expect to have access to the All Black captain. When Graham Henry walked in, Steve took it up with him. Graham asked me, 'Have we sorted it out?' I said, 'Not really. We haven't even talked about it.' He smiled and said, 'Well, you just need to change your mind, I suppose.' 'I suppose I do,' I said, 'if I want to keep the job.' And that was pretty much it. It went with the territory: being captain meant I just had to roll with it and do what I had to do. I hadn't forgotten my grievance — I never do — but the thought of having to talk to them again didn't bother me that much.

Graham Henry, Steve Hansen and Wayne Smith had all returned to New Zealand after stints coaching in the UK and our training took on a very European flavour. We were training twice a day with a lot of contact. We started with two tests against England, the newly crowned world champions who'd beaten us the last two times we'd played them, so the enthusiasm levels were high. We also had a few old All Blacks coming back — Carl Hayman, Keith Robinson, Xavier Rush — and new blood in the form of Jono Gibbes, Mose Tuiali'i and Sam Tuitupou. But after that initial phase we seemed to be doing the same thing all the time; a clear structure isn't a bad thing, but the long training sessions meant that players coming straight off a demanding Super 12 programme were being hammered. The new All Black coaches didn't think we'd trained enough during the Super 12; when they'd put that view to Hurricanes coach Colin Cooper, he'd wondered when he was meant to fit in these extra training sessions. Besides, he was more concerned with ensuring that his players were fresh for the weekend. It was very tough adjusting to the new regime's style and expectations, especially as their thinking and methods were largely based on what they'd picked up from a different rugby culture.

I quickly found out that there was a huge difference between being a player, even a vice-captain, and being captain. The role involved doing many things that I hadn't previously got caught up in, such as the captain's press conference the day before a game. I felt that I had to do a lot of the talking and that burden really weighed on me. Looking back, I believe that instead of focusing on playing, I focused on being the captain and performing the various duties that were part and parcel of that role. Earlier in my career I'd been self-focused to a fault; now I just wanted to make sure that everything was going right within the team.

The team flew to South Africa on the Sunday after we'd played Australia in Sydney but I was granted leave to be present for the birth of Lily-Kate, our second daughter. It really hurt me to miss my son's birth and I was very anxious to be there. The doctor had told us that because our daughter was quite big, it was safe for her to be induced a week or two early, which my wife was happy about. Things worked out well. I flew back from Sydney on the Sunday morning, the baby arrived around 8 pm, I stayed the night at the hospital with my wife and daughter, and flew out to Sydney at 6 the next morning to catch a connecting flight to South Africa. Happily, I've been there for the births of all three of my daughters.

By this stage the players were tired and stale and we weren't performing. The training hadn't let up; it was full on the whole time. From what I could pick up, the boys had just had enough. They were sick and tired of beating each other up during the week, then having to play a game at the weekend. We were lethargic in Sydney and worse in Johannesburg where the Springboks ran rampant with Marius Joubert scoring three tries, the first after I'd missed him. All three teams won their home games and lost their away games but we ended up last on bonus points.

After the coaches had done their review, they called a meeting in Wellington involving the three of them and Darren Shand the manager, Gilbert Enoka the mental skills coach, Richie McCaw the vice-captain, and me. I decided it was time for a few home truths and advised Richie beforehand to leave it to me. I spelt it out: we were training too hard; we had nothing left for the games; they had to realise that we'd already played a competition before they got hold of us and we weren't going to get any fitter during the international window. What we needed was quality rather than quantity; that would keep us fresh for the games and enable us to produce the intensity we all wanted. Poor Richie was sitting there with an 'oh my gosh' expression on his face: it was his first meeting of this sort with the coaches and I'd just gone in there and let them have it. I really stressed the point that we were training for too long — it must have been mentioned three or four times — and finally Graham said, 'Okay, I get it, it's sunk in, we can get off that now.'

I didn't know how they'd react. We'd been through that getting to know you period when you get a feel for each other and see where things are going but this was the first really frank and open discussion I'd had with them. My view was that I had nothing to lose and these things needed to be said for the greater good. I'd had a good run in the All Black jersey so if it cost me my job, so be it. It must have been a bit nerve-wracking for Richie, though, because he was in the opposite situation. To their credit, the coaches took it on board and I kept my job.

The leadership group emerged from this meeting. The coaches told me I couldn't do it all and had to step back a bit and delegate, which was fine with me; I knew that things hadn't gone as well as they should have. We talked about the make-up of the leadership group. Apart from me and Richie, the names under discussion were Chris Jack, Aaron Mauger, Greg Somerville, Keven Mealamu, Byron Kelleher, Mils Muliaina and Doug Howlett.

The player I really wanted in there was Jerry Collins but they were very reluctant. In their eyes he was a one-dimensional player and they didn't know if they'd be selecting him in future. I argued that, based on my experience of playing with and without him, the one dimension he certainly possessed was the one dimension every team needs: intimidation. You need someone who has the opposition looking over their shoulders to see if he's coming and he was the one guy who had that. It was something we hadn't had for a long time. Our successful teams have had the likes of Sean Fitzpatrick, Zinzan Brooke and Buck Shelford, relentless players who created a little bit of uncertainty and fear. Without Jerry we didn't have that. I also knew that if I asked Jerry to do something, he'd do it, no questions asked. He was a rock for me, someone in the pack who I could go to if I needed something done; if he couldn't do it himself, he'd make sure that the guys who could realised what was needed.

The previous coach had just wanted him to run hard and straight and tackle hard so that's what he did. But he's always been a skilful player and when the new panel asked him to expand his repertoire, it wasn't very hard for him because he's got all the skills and we've now seen a complete game from him. As he always says, he's a soldier: tell him how you want him to play and he'll play that way. A few weeks later they told me Jerry was in.

The creation of the leadership group was a big call by the coaches because they were more or less saying these players will be in our All Black team. That was a good thing for the players concerned because it's great to have that certainty but it came with the pressure that we had to be seen to deserve that status. Within the group we were very clear that being there didn't mean we were assured of our spot; we put pressure on ourselves to be the best players in our positions so that the other players would listen to us and respect us as a leadership group.

During the NPC we'd play on Saturday and have a leadership meeting on Sunday so that was your weekend. I found these Sundays quite beneficial. The aim was to develop leadership across the board: we had discussions about how we were going to live and work and function as a team, what we expected of each other, what was best for the team. The management spelt out what they wanted to do and invited our feedback. We talked about how we wanted to be remembered, about leaving a legacy of our own to add to the existing All Black legacy. There was a big push for us to strive to be remembered as having enhanced the All Black mystique. We talked a lot about the pressures of becoming an All Black and the importance of not being overawed by it: you had to embrace being an All Black and the challenge of enhancing the jersey; you had to try to make it your own and add your own individual history to it.

The time commitment that went with being All Black captain was growing because in addition to the leadership meetings, there were other discussions that the coaches wanted me to sit in on. But it was time well spent as the improvement in our performances from that time on demonstrated.

I had a break after the Tri-Nations and did some individual training with the Wellington trainer Andrew Beardmore, a top operator whom I'd used a few times. We had to fit around his role with the Wellington Lions but for a few weeks I just worked on my fitness, speed, strength and agility. It was refreshing. In rugby environments you're always being told where to go and when. You've got to be here at this time, you have an hour's break, then you've got to be there at that time, and throughout it you're hanging around with the same guys. It's always good to get out of that structured regime and be able to do what you want. I enjoyed the break and played some good rugby in the NPC.

The leadership group had talked about the structure of the end-of-year tour and targeted the French test as the game in which we wanted to make our mark. Our planning for the World Cup started then. We'd also tried to develop our understanding of the haka and had brought in Derek Lardelli to assist in that process. Throughout my All Black career we'd had various people talk to us about the haka but Derek managed to make everything clearer. He explained what the haka is and what it means to New Zealanders and how we're linked to each other: we've all got people who have meant a lot to us buried in New Zealand and they're intertwined within the earth. The earth is what grounds us and is where we gain our strength from. That explanation really resonated with the players.

On that tour we started doing the haka at the captain's run at the match venue the day before the game. We'd get together in the middle and talk about what was in front of us and then do the haka just for ourselves or to the other boys. The first time we did it was before the game in Rome and afterwards everyone was abuzz. The DDs who were watching said it was spine tingling. That started it: it was really an impromptu thing but after that we did it all the time. I felt I played well against Italy. I could feel the difference in myself compared to that last Tri-Nations game: I felt a lot lighter in mind and body and rather than feeling lethargic, I wanted to get involved.

At an airport stopover en route to Cardiff, Graham told me I wouldn't be playing against Wales. I knew it was coming because earlier he'd mentioned that they were planning to have Richie captain the team at some point but when it actually happens to you, your heart drops, your throat tightens up, and you feel like you're going to start crying. I'd been expecting it but it's something you never want to hear. I signalled Jerry over. He said, 'So what was that about? What are you up to in Wales?' 'Not much,' I said. 'I'm not playing.' 'Well,' he said, 'neither am I.' I was pretty gutted but I knew what it was for. I also knew it meant that I had a bloody good chance of playing against France which was the big game, the main event.

The Millennium Stadium and the surroundings are brilliant but the playing surface is poor. Every time we've been there the turf has been churned up or there's been no grass which makes it really stodgy. The Welsh crowd was in fine voice; it was a close game so they got right into it and it was quite something to experience. Richie and Chris Jack had brilliant games, showing their leadership. You could see the leadership group starting to work because those guys understood that when things had to be done, they had to stand up and take responsibility. There was relief that we came away with a one-point win, but also a lot of satisfaction at the way we got there. It was Piri

Weepu's first test. He comes from Wainuiomata and I know his family very well. I knew how they'd be feeling and I felt a lot of pride myself watching this young guy whom I'd known since he was a little kid come through. And I was very happy the next day when they announced the team to play France.

I didn't do much in Paris. I'd seen all the sights before so I just stayed in my room and read books. It was very anti-social but I just couldn't be bothered going anywhere. Besides, winter was setting in and I'm not too partial to the cold. At a leadership group meeting the question of who would lead the haka came up because Rico Gear wasn't in the 22. Aaron Mauger suggested that I should do it. Piri was on the bench so I put his name forward but it was only his second test and the others felt it was too big an honour for someone just starting his All Black career. Carl Hayman's name came up but he didn't want to do it. They did a good sales job — the haka is best led by the leader of the team, someone who has respect — and in the end I agreed.

In the build-up to the game I was more nervous about the haka than the match itself, which was probably a good thing. Rico's advice was to be calm and make sure they could hear the words. I spoke with Lipi Sinnott, a good friend of mine, who stressed the importance of being very deliberate and not rushing it. I practised in my room until I was sure I had the words right. We had a rehearsal on Stade de France the day before the game which seemed to go alright judging by the 'yeahs' and slaps on the back from the boys.

On match day, I just slipped into game mode and did what I usually do. The French crowd is one of the best because they really respect the haka. It was quiet; I wanted to give it everything but also had to remember not to rush it. I got through it but was taken aback by what happened afterwards: I got heaps of letters and emails, a lot of them from Maori people, saying how pleased they were to see someone lead the haka with pride. My wife is Maori and her family is very much rooted in Maori tradition and culture so it was nice to know that they and other Maori were proud of the way I did it. Personally I was just happy that I didn't stuff it up.

We took control of the game early on. Having played the French in Paris in 2002 when they'd taken our forward pack apart and forced us to live off scraps, it was great to go back there and do it to them. I may be a back but I know how the game is played; it's no good having a Rolls-Royce backline if you've got a Morris Minor pack. Our forward play came of age that day, reflecting the work that Graham Henry and especially Steve Hansen had done. They'd set out to give our set piece work a makeover and that game was the coming out party.

It was also satisfying to see my mate Anton Oliver make such an emphatic comeback. He's written about how he wept when he was presented with his All Black jersey before the game against Italy. I was taken aback; I think we all were. It goes by numbers so the first guy to get his jersey is number one, the loosehead prop, followed by the hooker. Anton started crying straightaway. The jerseys were being handed out but everyone was looking at him thinking what the hell? I'd been through a bit with him so I had some idea of what was happening and where he was coming from; I knew how much it meant to him. For a while we'd had a running joke about which of us would reach 50 test caps first but then he got injured in 2002 and dropped in 2003 and he got stuck in the 40s. Whatever anyone might have thought of a grown man crying, they were in no doubt about what it meant to some people to wear the All Black jersey. I think everyone's abiding memory of that test is Anton's cynical little smirk when the French had to go to golden oldies scrums. The wheel had come full circle because on previous occasions the French prop Pieter de Villiers had crushed our scrum.

Dan Carter really announced himself as an international first-five that day. He reads and conducts the game so well and is always willing to take on information. The defence when they laid siege to our line in the second half was another huge tick for the leadership group because they were the guys who stood up and were talking the whole time. Previously when we'd been under the hammer I'd had to do most of the talking, but in the space of a few months we had a bunch of leaders out there urging their team-mates not to give an inch. It just shows that if you give some people a bit of leadership and responsibility and a role within the team — a job they can call their own — they can use it as a foundation and build on it. The growth of the leadership group and the individuals within it was evident that day.

I felt vindicated by Jerry's performance; he really got into them. The one thing Jerry always wants to do is play rugby. If you take that away from him, you'll just make him angry. He'll seethe away and when he gets back out on the field, look out. The selectors have done that with him a couple of times and it certainly worked that day. It pays to do it on tour so he can't sneak home and have a game on the sly for his club Norths, which he's been known to do.

Sylvain Marconnet was one of their front row casualties but he didn't get hurt in a scrum: he tried to take the ball up and got smashed by Jerry. That's what he brings to the game. In Australia they call him 'Cement' because that's what he feels like when you run into him. Players understand that when you're playing against Jerry Collins, you've always got to know where he is because you don't want to look up and find yourself carting the ball straight into his channel. Teams are good at making up plays that keep their ball carriers away from him but he goes chasing them. It's something he takes pride in.

We were playing for the Dave Gallaher Cup that day. We first played for it on the 2000 tour when we won in Paris on Armistice Day and lost in Marseille and I've learnt a lot about him since then. Around that 2004 French game there was a big focus on Dave Gallaher and the New Zealand soldiers who gave their lives in Europe. Anton Oliver's a good historian who's done a lot of research on Dave Gallaher and he gave us a talk and showed clips on the big screen. The message, particularly to the younger guys, was that he's part of their history because he's part of the history of the jersey.

I've taken a keen interest in Dave Gallaher because he was the first All Black captain. I've been to his gravesite in a Belgian war cemetery, and to Passchendaele, scene of the horrific battle in 1917 in which he lost his life. On the 2005 Grand Slam tour a group of us went to his birthplace in Ramelton, County Donegal, Ireland. At that time Ireland wasn't my destination of choice but I really wanted to do it and it was an amazing journey. I loved playing for his trophy; for me, it's one of the most important trophies the All Blacks play for, one of those that you hold close to your heart.

He was 44 years old when he was killed. He went off to the war because he wanted to be with his brothers and look after them, which I can relate to. I'd like to think I'd do the same. I personally didn't lose anyone in the wars but a great many of us did; my wife lost an uncle. As a country we lost Dave Gallaher, the father of the All Blacks. Like many New Zealanders I pay my respects to them all on Anzac Day.

PLAYBACK ←

GRAHAM HENRY

You think of a few things when you apply for the All Black coaching job and one of those was who would captain this team. I saw Tana as that person. Why? Because he was a world-class player so he had the ability to lead by example, he related well to everybody in the group regardless of whether they were Pacific Islander, Maori or European, and he was his own person.

I think his appointment gave the Polynesian rugby player more self-respect, not that they needed it but they probably thought that they did, if you understand my logic. The Polynesian rugby player is a very important part of the All Black machine. I'm amazed by the number of times I get asked by reporters, sometimes New Zealand reporters, about importing all these players from the Pacific Islands. They don't understand that there are more Polynesian people living in this country than anywhere else in the world, and they are a very important and integral part of our New Zealand culture. A lot of people fail to see that; probably some New Zealanders fail to see that, particularly those who live in the South Island.

I was lucky that in my development as a rugby coach I had a lot of contact with Polynesian people. Auckland is the largest Polynesian city in the world; I coached at various levels — Auckland Under 21s, Auckland B and Auckland A — and was headmaster of a school which had a high ratio of Polynesian students. I was also lucky enough to mix with some outstanding Polynesian players like Michael Jones, Eroni Clarke, Olo Brown, Junior Tonu'u and Mata'afa Keenan whom I coached at University.

When I first coached Auckland I used to drop the odd 'Jesus' or 'Christ' at training — it was just part of the vocabulary. As we walked off the training field one day Michael and Eroni put their arms round me and said, 'Coach, would you mind not using those words?' I said, 'Guys, look, I'm terribly sorry, I'll do my best not to do that again.' That was a hell of a good learning curve, to be able to mix with those sorts of people over a long period of time. It was very helpful in understanding what was important to them: whanau, their respect for elders, and so on. I came to understand that they were very respectful people and often that respectfulness stopped them saying things that perhaps they should say.

Tana, however, was quite black and white on many things and made his opinion very clear. He didn't pussyfoot around, he was pretty bold in his leadership, and he made statements which were all about standards. I guess over the years he'd had an interesting development as a rugby player: he was always his own person and that probably didn't always fall positively with the establishment. But he learnt from those things and he developed into an all-round sportsman, an outstanding athlete who was totally committed to doing the job. He was hugely competitive, which I think was a major asset, but he also understood where players were in their development because he'd been through it himself. But the biggest thing about Tana was that if he believed in something he stood up and made a statement and was very clear. There was no ambiguity. He had firm ideas about standards, both on and off the field, and he didn't want to compromise those standards. If he felt people's standards were falling backwards, he would certainly make it very clear that we needed to do something about it or the group needed to do something about it, whereas a lot of Polynesian guys wouldn't have said anything or would have pussyfooted around.

We were having a coffee one morning on tour and he said to me, 'Ted, what's the story with these bloody team talks? Are they for you or for us?' I was pretty serious about these team talks; I thought they were very important. I'd been doing them since 1977 so they'd become ingrained, part of the ritual. And I thought, oh okay, I've been fooling myself for 30 years. So I've made them a lot shorter. I still talk but they're a lot shorter and I never get uptight about them anymore.

We learned a lot in the 2004 Tri-Nations. We got beaten in both away games and finished last in the competition. When we analysed it, we came up with a number of reasons why we hadn't done the business — one was that the other sides were quite good, which was a bit of a pity. Another was our collective ability to be self-reliant so we went through quite an extensive leadership development campaign and that made a huge difference. Gilbert Enoka was the facilitator of that and he's done an outstanding job. We all benefited greatly from that. Tana obviously benefited greatly because the other leaders in the team came forward and led, and he was able to play. An example of that was the game in Paris in 2004 when it all came together. From that point on, the side has played pretty good rugby.

I think captaincy is really about leading by example and using the other guys around you. If you try to captain a side in isolation, that's a recipe for disaster, but if you lead by example and lead in your particular area and use the other guys in the team to lead, that's the ideal, and that's where Tana got to. That leadership group developed into a pretty potent force which allowed Tana to concentrate on playing his game.

Zinzan Brooke was an outstanding captain. There was a good balance because Fitzy was captain of the All Blacks and Zinzan was captain of the Blues and Auckland and they helped each other and were very supportive of each other. Zinzan had a lot of Tana's qualities; he had the ability to motivate and relate to all the guys in the team, no matter what their backgrounds were. Martin Johnson was outstanding as captain of the Lions. He was a world-class player and had huge respect from his players — when he spoke, they listened. He didn't say a lot but when he opened his trap, everybody shut up and listened. Not only was he a fabulous lock forward, probably the best in the world in his time, he also had tremendous respect and knew the game. And he was a big man so he had some physical presence. Pat Lam captained the Auckland Colts for a couple of years and he was an outstanding leader as well, a very astute captain who understood the game, as he proved at international level with Manu Samoa. So I've had a bit of luck in this area; I've been blessed with top captains.

I knew six months or thereabouts beforehand that Tana was going to finish at the end of 2005. I respected his reasons and that was where it started and finished basically. I would have been delighted if he'd stayed on but his reasons were so strong and *he*'d made the decision. I didn't try to twist his arm or change his mind because I could see that it was important to him and that was what he wanted to do. I just respected the decision and wished him well and got on with it.

I think far too many outstanding rugby players get fast-tracked into coaching rather than doing the apprenticeship and very few of them have been successful. Tana's going to be coaching at second-division level in France which won't be highly competitive; he's also going to have some good, experienced players whose knowledge he can call on. So if he's got ambitions to coach, he's going to buy some time and have that experience before he gets into a highly competitive environment.

He's a guy who obviously had some rough edges initially but learned a lot from the game and developed into a world class player and leader of men who was totally respected by the guys he played with and the guys he played against. I have a huge amount of time for him. I think he can do anything he likes really. If it's not rugby coaching, he could be the prime minister.

But you can tell him that I didn't go fishing when we were in Samoa.

Lion King

The leadership group continued to meet during the 2005 Super 12 although the make-up had been tweaked with Doug Howlett and Mose Tuiali'i making way for Rodney So'oialo and Carl Hayman. I'm a big Doug Howlett fan — I don't think you'll find a more professional athlete. He's got the latest training techniques and is always working on his body so it might look to some as if he's overly focused on himself, but he was a proven performer and I couldn't believe they'd cut him from the group. The coaches indicated that they wanted him to concentrate on playing football but it was hard for me to take.

The British and Irish Lions tour had created tremendous interest and anticipation which the All Blacks shared. I'd met Brian O'Driscoll, Jonny Wilkinson and some of their other players doing advertisements for adidas and we'd got on quite well. When the Lions arrived we had a media launch with them and it was all very friendly. That was then.

My recollections of the warm-up game against Fiji at Albany are of trying not to get hurt and scoring a try from a move we'd practised a lot. It's very satisfying when the execution in a game mirrors what you've been doing at training. We got through the game unscathed, scoring a lot of tries, and took some confidence from the fact that things we'd been working on were starting to come to fruition.

I was very enthusiastic going into the first test in Christchurch. I'd been looking forward to it for two years and couldn't wait to give it everything I had. Not even some of the worst weather Christchurch could throw at us could change that. Everyone knows — or thinks they know — what happened in the first 90 seconds. I went into a ruck and cleaned out Brian O'Driscoll. I was standing over the ball trying to protect it when he bounced back to have another crack at disrupting our possession. We were tussling as he tried to get through and I grabbed his leg to try to unbalance him, a technique I'd used before and still use to this day. What I didn't realise was that Keven Mealamu was doing the same thing on the other side of the ruck. As I got one of O'Driscoll's legs up, Keven hoisted his other leg and drove him back. He ended up with both feet off the ground, not in control of himself or the situation, a position rugby players often find themselves in. When we let him go he came down and what happened, happened. I didn't think anything of it, I just took off.

When the whistle blew and he was being attended to by his medical staff, I was completely focused on the job in hand. The game I'd been preparing for since the 2003 World Cup had just started, the pressure was on, and I was concentrating on what we were going to do next. It didn't really occur to me to go and check on what was happening in their camp. There was no conscious decision not to go over: I didn't do it then because I didn't do it, period; I'd never done it for anybody else. I was a competitive animal out there. The flipside of that was my bedside manner when my players got injured: if I saw someone in my team on the ground, I'd say, 'What's wrong with you? Just get up.' I was always telling cousin Jerry that. When they carted O'Driscoll off I thought Jesus, major, then I put it out of my mind and got on with the game.

I didn't go and see him after the game but I ran into a group of their players who weren't going to the after-match function and asked Richard Hill how Brian was. He said he'd gone to hospital. Again, I didn't think anything of it. When we got back to the hotel after the dinner, Keven and I were told that we'd been cited so we had a meeting with NZRU lawyer Steve Cottrell to run through what had happened. While we were doing that, news came through that the Citing Commissioner had ruled there was no case to answer. We were relieved but not surprised; from the outset our view was that since there'd been no malice or intent, the matter shouldn't go any further.

The Lions leadership and their high-powered spin doctor Alistair Campbell wouldn't take 'no case to answer' for an answer and found a way to take the matter much further. The sustained personal attack they launched against me was hard to believe and even harder to stomach. You don't want to take it personally but it's almost impossible not to when another player, a guy you had some respect for, attacks your character in the most direct and damning terms. My first thought was geez, don't be a sook; there's no use crying about it, man, it's over. On the other hand I could understand how bitterly disappointed O'Driscoll was. He would have been just like me: buzzing with anticipation, really up for it, and desperate to make a point on the field.

There was a lot of talk about the Lions' response to the haka. Someone had supposedly advised O'Driscoll to kneel down and pick a blade of grass, which he'd done, and we'd supposedly regarded that as disrespectful. The truth was we didn't care what they did. I noticed him doing it but just thought, oh, that's different. Opposition teams had tried a variety of responses and our attitude was always the same: whatever. We didn't understand what he was doing so they were one up on us there, but it's rubbish to suggest that it had anything to do with what happened at that ruck. The media tends to provide interpretations of what they think has happened, as opposed to what actually did happen, and it's often all that speculation which creates the angst and inflames the situation.

At first, the kerfuffle didn't really bother me. It was a case of, oh well that's the way it is. But it just snowballed and O'Driscoll kept going on about the fact that I hadn't rung him to say sorry. I'd actually tried to get hold of him on the Monday via the Lions' media liaison person but I never heard back. By this stage we were in Wellington and it just kept cranking up and I was getting a bit angry. I finally obtained his number and got hold of him but it wasn't a warm exchange. He was still angry that I hadn't gone over to see how he was and once he'd got that off his chest, he accused me of being involved in a lot of off-the-ball incidents. The Lions hadn't been impressed with the way I'd played, he said, and I had to watch it. I said, 'Don't talk to me about off-the-ball incidents, talk to your own players.' (With all the fuss the Lions had made over the O'Driscoll incident, it had almost been overlooked that their lock Danny Grewcock, a player with a history of foul play, had been cited, found guilty, and banned for biting Keven Mealamu.) 'Look at Grewcock,' I said. 'He's a meathead.' 'Yeah, he is a meathead,' he said. "You can't change that but we're better than that. We shouldn't play like those guys. We thought you were a gentleman.'

While he went on along those lines, I was thinking to myself, hang on, this is a game I take seriously. And I did: I aimed to let an opponent know I was out there and get into his mind so that next time he'd have a look to see if I was coming. I'd body-check him on the way through or if I came up quickly and the pass didn't go to him, I'd still give him a little reminder that I was around so he knew that if he didn't have his wits about him, he could get hit, and hit hard. I had no qualms about it; that was how I played. That's the gamesmanship of rugby. Players sledge. I sledged a bit and did so in that game. I was always trying to get an edge and in that respect I was no different to a lot of players. But when he started talking about off-the-ball stuff and me not being a gentleman I thought, oh, you're reaching now. I never went out to commit foul play: I didn't punch guys on the ground or stomp on them. So I said, 'Oh well, mate, we'll just have to agree to disagree. I'm sorry for what happened to you but there was no intent in it; it was one of those unfortunate things that happen in rugby.' He said, 'Yeah, but you could've helped it.' 'Okay, mate,' I said, 'all the best.' And that was where we left it.

Instead of trying to get on the front foot straight away, our PR strategy was to let the storm blow itself out. But it didn't blow itself out and when I eventually held a press conference a few days later it felt like a hollow exercise. By that stage I was all for just taking it on the chin and getting on with it, but our media people wanted to respond to what had become a pretty relentless and inflammatory — as in 'I could have died' — campaign. I'd been getting a lot of support from the team all week and at the press conference I was backed up by the leadership group which was great, even though the exercise itself felt like it was all a bit late. Whether it could have been nipped in the bud is a moot point given the intensity of their media blitz but for a couple of days they had the floor to themselves and they made the most of it. Even when I was being bombarded with questions I couldn't help seeing the funny side of it: poor little me surrounded by all those big, burly forwards as if I couldn't protect myself. It was good to have my say but I wanted to do my talking on the field. Clive Woodward had talked his team up, saying they were the best prepared Lions ever and wouldn't repeat the mistakes of the 2001 Lions tour of Australia, which was a crack at Graham Henry who'd coached that team. That kind of thing — attacking our people, talking themselves up — just steeled us. We wanted to show them that they weren't as good as they thought they were and Woodward wasn't as good as he thought he was.

They started the second test very well, scoring under the posts virtually from the kick-off. I wasn't worried because we hadn't had the ball or played any rugby. My message was let's get the ball, get down there, and give it a crack. They launched another attack but this time they dropped the ball. I picked it up and gave it to Daniel Carter because I knew he'd do something with it and I was able to run off him and score. It was a team try, pure and simple. I didn't see it as some sort of personal statement — 'straight back at you' — because I never felt like it was me against them.

At times, though, they seemed to think it was them against me. As a ruck broke up, Paul O'Connell loomed over me ranting and raving. As I got up, their props Julian White and Gethin Jenkins started pushing and shoving. I knew it was going to happen at some stage so I just said, 'Come on, any time, just bring it.' I backed away slowly looking at them and saying, 'Are you going to start playing soon or what?' Later, when O'Connell went down, I went over to him as he was rolling around the ground and said, 'Mate, don't give up now, we're just getting started.' He jumped straight up. When Stephen Jones came on for Jonny Wilkinson he took the ball up yelling, 'For our captain!' like something out of *Braveheart*. I said, 'Are you serious?' You could see how they were trying to motivate themselves but it became quite laughable. I got into some of their forwards about being a bit chubby and after the game Jenkins said to Steve Hansen, who'd coached him when he'd been with Wales, 'Can you tell Tana it's nothing personal, it's just the game.' That was a bit rich coming from them. I told Steve I didn't see any of it in personal terms. During the game I hadn't thought about the stuff they'd been saying about me all week until their players started having a crack at me. I didn't go out that night but the guys who did ran into a bunch of Lions and reckoned some of them were good guys.

We'd won the series but there was another test to be played and the coaches were onto us, telling us that a clean sweep would make a real statement about where we were as a team. I was all for that. My attitude was let's give it to them; let's send them home with nothing. We prepared well in Auckland but started the game lethargically. It felt like the edge wasn't there because we'd won the series and weren't expecting much from the Lions who didn't have much to play for and were already being ridiculed by their media. I was getting steamed up with the way we were playing even before I got yellow-carded, without any warning, for lying on the wrong side and slowing their ball down. I was furious with the team and yelled, 'Get in there!' We scored two tries while I was in the bin. I don't know whether my sin-binning sparked them up or they were just better off without me yelling at them. I scored a couple of tries, which was satisfying, but the encouraging thing about that game was that we came away with a good win despite being without Dan Carter and Richie McCaw who were seen as our key players. That series was like my World Cup, so to play some of the best rugby of my career and lead the team to a clean sweep made me a very proud man.

The Lions supporters were some of the best I've ever come across. They were here to have fun and didn't let the results get in the way of a good time. Westpac Stadium was an amazing sight with those huge swathes of red. It was as if the Lions had more support than we did. They were a brilliant crowd: they made a lot of noise and supported their team wholeheartedly and, unlike their soccer counterparts, didn't turn sour when the results didn't go their way. After the Christchurch test there were Lions supporters everywhere, but the only trouble came from locals.

It was a mentally draining series — especially for me with the O'Driscoll carry-on — so getting up for the Tri-Nations wasn't easy. On the other hand, the emphatic nature of our victories had given us a lot of confidence. Realising where we were mentally, the coaches gave us some time off to get away and freshen up before the first game against South Africa in Cape Town. It didn't work because we lost, mainly due to rustiness. In that game Victor Matfield took out Byron Kelleher and got away scot-free. Even though Byron was knocked out, Matfield didn't even get cited, but that's what happens in rugby and you've just got to live with it. On a positive note, Piri Weepu came on and showed that he could handle playing at that level. Our forwards didn't lay a platform, our game didn't come together, and the team seemed out of sync. Afterwards Richie was saying that he just hadn't felt right and that's what having a couple of weeks off and not being together as a team can do. The coaches were far from happy and we had to work hard for the rest of the tournament.

Since the All Blacks had assembled after the Super 12 we'd been practising a new haka, 'Kapa O Pango', with the aim of unleashing it on the Lions. I really wanted to do it in that series but it dawned on me that the players hadn't learnt it properly and weren't performing it well enough. The last thing I wanted to do was jump the gun with an innovation that would challenge people's thinking and generate debate.

There was a divide between the leadership group, who'd done a lot of work with Derek Lardelli gaining an understanding of what the haka meant and what would be achieved in terms of the team's legacy by introducing a new version, and the rest of the team who hadn't spent as much time on it or had it explained in the same depth. When the leaders spoke to the team about it, the message didn't get through because we didn't have Derek's passion, understanding and knowledge. The younger All Blacks weren't really buying into what we were saying. They were asking us who were we to change something that had been a part of All Black history for so long.

It seemed that the younger players weren't comfortable with it and didn't really want to do it so when we were in South Africa, the leadership group asked Gilbert Enoka to run a meeting with the rest of the team to establish exactly where they were on it. Gilbert confirmed our impressions: the others were questioning why we needed a new haka and what qualified us to drive the change. The leadership group knew we were adding to the haka, not diminishing it, but we also understood that it was a big step and we couldn't push it. We decided to wait until we got back to New Zealand and have Derek talk to the rest of the team.

In Sydney we were on the back foot very quickly. The Wallabies worked a blindside move and Dan Carter missed Drew Mitchell, which wasn't normal. For me, the key when you get behind or things aren't happening is to stay task-focused because there's no use dwelling on why you're in the situation you're in; you don't have time for that. You've got to concentrate on what you can do about it, starting now. I talked a lot about the importance of getting our hands on the ball because if you've got the ball and can retain it, things will happen for you. That's what we talked about when we found ourselves behind the posts, down 13–0 in as many minutes: let's get the ball, run some plays, and get ourselves into the game. When things are going wrong the captain needs to stay calm. Panic is contagious and even those who don't catch it are likely to be saying, 'Look at this idiot,' whereas if the team can see that the leader's calm and confident they'll take reassurance from that. On the other hand, you can't say nothing; you've just got to make sure that what you say is direct, to the point, and covers what needs to be done.

Sometimes when things weren't going well I was inclined to get a bit angry and take over. In one test I called a lineout from midfield. Richie came across and said, 'Hey, you can't call that because we've called something else and we'll just get mixed up.' That was the right thing for him to do and I backed off. Most games ebb and flow and sometimes you can get onto one of those spirals when mistake follows mistake and you just can't gain any control and the heads start to drop. That's when the captain has got to step up and make demands of the players he believes will make a difference. I'd go to Paul Tito: 'I need this lineout, "Fish".' Or to Jerry: 'I need a big hit.' Or to Chris Masoe: 'Get me the ball back.' It gives them a focus. Against the Springboks at Jade Stadium in 2004 we were behind and struggling; I put it on Keven Mealamu who said, 'No worries, boss, we'll get it.' I like that. That's the response you want when you demand something special from a player. It showed Keven's leadership and willingness to take responsibility: he said the boys would step up and they did.

We were aiming to introduce 'Kapa O Pango' when we played the Springboks in Dunedin. Derek Lardelli talked to the young guys in a very enlightening way and they got it: they realised that we weren't trying to be different just for the sake of it. We were acutely aware that if we did the new haka, we had to win the game because there'd be a real backlash if we changed the haka and lost. There was pressure to ensure that this player-driven initiative was seen as a positive development. We didn't want it to come totally out of the blue so Darren Shand and Scott Compton, our media man, briefed the Sky TV commentators, enabling them to explain to the viewers what was happening. I had the honour — and anxiety — of leading it. Doing it really fired us up: the look on the Springboks' faces and the reaction of the crowd when we all went down on one knee was fantastic. It was a tough, seesaw game but I never thought we'd lose because our will was so strong. To their credit, the South Africans responded in the right spirit with John Smit saying afterwards that he'd enjoyed it.

There was a bit of a flare-up in that game, the upshot of which was that Jerry copped a one-match suspension and missed our home game against Australia. It was hard to accept after what happened to Byron in Cape Town. It puzzled me that the judiciary could have no problem with Matfield knocking a guy out and, as it turned out, putting him out of the rest of the tournament, but could ban Jerry for getting involved in a dust-up in which no significant damage was done. He got a hard time about it, though, because he ended up scrapping with Jaco van der Westhuyzen who's about five foot nothing. I was telling him, 'That's it: you've ruined your tough man persona now.'

Before we went away on tour we talked about the so-called throat-slitting gesture at the end of 'Kapa O Pango'. It had caused controversy here so it was a sure bet that we'd be criticised for it in Europe. Some people accepted our explanation of it but others didn't buy it at all, arguing that it was inappropriate in this day and age. I could see where they were coming from and after we'd done it a couple of times I realised we were going to have trouble with it. I felt it was fine to do it at home because the majority of New Zealanders understood what it meant: that we operated on that cutting edge where we were either heroes or zeros. And that's true. The All Blacks have to live with the public expectation that we should win every game and do so handsomely, playing spectacular rugby and winning by a big margin. When that doesn't happen, we get criticised and when we actually lose, doom and gloom descend and the criticism turns vitriolic. I did wonder, though, if it was a good idea to take it overseas where there wouldn't be that comprehension. We decided we'd just see what happened. We only used it for the English game and it created a stir. Before we came home we talked to Derek about changing it. His view was that the criticism reflected a lack of knowledge and understanding, so why should we change it to placate people who didn't understand? Which was true, but I didn't think we could ignore the reality that in this world of ours that particular gesture means a lot of different things to different people.

'Kapa' began with Richie, Aaron Mauger and Gilbert Enoka telling Derek what we were about and what was important to us — the blackness of the jersey, pride in the jersey, the silver fern. Derek put that into words and devised the actions. Derek and his wife Rose believed they owned it and were allowing us to use it. That was fine by us but we didn't want anyone else using it. There was a concern that the new haka would be commercialised as had happened to an extent with 'Ka Mate'. Inevitably, I suppose, commercialism reared its head. I couldn't help thinking that once the discussion started focusing on questions of ownership and remuneration, we were getting away from the rationale for creating a new haka in the first place. But I didn't begrudge Derek raising those issues because I knew that was the way of the world: if you create something good, everyone wants a piece of it. That had happened with the old haka and the NZRU must take some of the blame for that.

Within a week of us performing it for the first time, Rose saw it being parodied, in India of all places, on the internet. A group consisting of me, Darren Shand, Gilbert Enoka, Derek and Rose was set up to act as the guardians of 'Kapa O Pango' and safeguard the essence and context of it. We wanted to keep track of who was using it and how, and to make sure that it was used in the right context. That's a hard, if not impossible, thing to do; a more realistic goal was to stop people making money from it. After a lot of discussion and some questioning of both parties' motivations, we reached clarification and common ground. I'm still part of the guardianship group which involves monitoring both Derek's side of things and NZRU and All Black activities.

It was an interesting reflection of changing times that the leadership group drove 'Kapa O Pango' but ran into resistance from the younger guys and had to work through a process to get them on side. That was a far cry from how things were done when I started. Back then it was autocratic: the older guys would say, 'This is what we're doing' and the rest of us would go along with it, whether we liked it or not. In the All Black context the guys who were laying down the law were the players who were winning us games and were at the forefront of everything we did rugby-wise, so it seemed natural to follow them. In some of the other teams I was in, that wasn't necessarily the case and if, on top of that, what you were being told to do was stupid you just lost respect for the old guard. After I'd been in the Hurricanes for a while, I was always challenging the older guys; I wasn't often taken to task for it but sometimes it didn't go down well. If you've got the runs on the board, people have a reason to follow you; they know that if you say something, you're going to deliver. Without that it's just, 'I'm older than you so you have to do what I say.' It all comes back to what you do on the field; that's where you gain respect. I've never liked being told what to do, especially by someone who didn't practise what they preached or when what we were being told to do wasn't what was best for us.

Before we left on the 2004 end-of-year tour, I told Graham Henry that I was of a mind to retire after the Lions series. The personal disappointment of the 2003 World Cup had left me feeling deprived. For four years I'd focused on setting the World Cup ledger straight and when that was taken away from me I had nothing to look forward to. Then the Lions appeared on the radar. I reassessed and set a new goal: to play against the Lions and do well against them. To that point the captaincy had been a bit of a mixed bag for me so I indicated to Graham that the Lions would probably be it for me. He said the NZRU was working on having a test against Wales added to the 2005 end-of-year tour which would create the opportunity for a grand slam. We agreed to put it on the back-burner for a while and see what happened.

The subject came up again when we went to South Africa after the Lions series. The Wales match still wasn't confirmed but Graham pretty much assured me it would happen and suggested a grand slam tour would be a good way to finish. He went on to talk about the 2007 World Cup, the glittering prize. I agreed that if the grand slam was on, it would be a good note to go out on but that would definitely be it; I wouldn't carry on beyond that. I said I'd been playing for a long time, I'd spent a lot of time away from my family, and I didn't think I could do it any more. My family had sacrificed a lot to enable me to play rugby and it was time for me to sacrifice something for them. My kids deserved more of their father. For a moment it looked as if Graham was going to put forward a counter-argument but then he said, 'Well, okay, I can't argue with that.' I was thinking, geez, don't you really want me? But that's the kind of person Graham is: he grasped the issue and that was that. 'You're right,' he said. 'The one thing you can't get back is time, I won't ask you again.'

In the course of the discussion Graham indicated that they were going to try something different in selection policy; that was the first inkling of what became known as rotation. I could understand the thinking and I would have learned to live with it if I'd had to, but deep down I wouldn't have liked being handled that way. I just wanted to play and if I couldn't play then I didn't really want to be there. I suppose it just reinforced the fact that the timing was right.

I didn't feel as if I was leaving them in the lurch. I couldn't have kept going because I didn't feel as committed as I should have been and that would have been increasingly reflected in my performances. In the Lions series I played some of my best rugby in the black jersey because I was hugely motivated to give it everything I had. It was the biggest event in rugby outside the World Cup so the eyes of the rugby world were on us.

On the end-of-year tour I felt like I was just hanging in there, waiting for the curtain to fall. I think they were only picking me because I was captain, or perhaps Graham felt sorry for me. I only played well in the England game and again it was because we'd targeted it as the big test of the tour. And we were right. Those are the games you love: your backs are against the wall and you just have to dig in and guts it out. You lift when there's a lot at stake and you can sense the opposition and their crowd starting to believe that it's going to be their day. You also see the character of the players around you. But that was the only game in which I played to my standards: in the other games I made errors that I hadn't really made before, partly because I knew my race was almost run and partly because I was worrying about how I'd break the news to the team.

I didn't think I deserved to play in the Scotland test. The coaches must have thought about putting someone else in there but they asked me to play my last game in the All Black jersey, for which I was very thankful. After the game I asked the team to stick around in the changing-room which meant they all had to wait for me because, as usual, I was the last one to get changed. Then I got up and told them it had been a tough couple of weeks for me because I'd decided to retire from international rugby.

The only one I'd told privately was Jerry. He's a good friend and we've been through some tough times. I also knew that the knowledge wouldn't affect him; he doesn't get emotional about things. I had other good friends in the team, especially the Wellington boys — Ma'a Nonu, Neemia Tialata, Piri Weepu and Rodney So'oialo — but I didn't want to bother them with it or put them off their games. Everyone was a bit taken aback; I was choking back tears and guys were coming up to say how much they'd enjoyed playing with me and so on. It was the feedback from other players that always affected me the most, having guys say it was great to play alongside me or thanking me for what I'd done for them. Your ability to affect and influence your team-mates in a positive way is your legacy. That's what you leave behind.

I always made an effort with young players in the belief that if I passed on my knowledge and experience to them, they could avoid my mistakes. (Jerry says he wants to make them; I just shrug and say okay.) Even so, I was surprised at their reaction. Ma'a, Neemia and Piri went off and stood by themselves and I could see that they were down. I think it was a bit of shock, magnified by the fact that I hadn't told them in advance. I didn't know what to say to them really. I hadn't wanted to affect their games but in hindsight I should have told them. Neemia, Piri and I grew up in the same place; I've known them since they were little kids and we have a close bond.

It was important to get the timing right. I didn't want to go into another year to see if I could still summon the desire and, on the other hand, I wanted to give the coaches plenty of time to replace me, although they'd already done a lot of planning. It always makes me laugh when I hear people saying how are we going to replace so and so? All Blacks know that players come and go but the jersey remains. How you play during your time in the jersey is how you'll be remembered. There will always be another player coming through. At the moment there's Ma'a, Conrad Smith and Isaia Toeava, who was the pick of the centres in the 2007 Super 14, and there'll be others along soon. After Joe Stanley came Frank Bunce, after Frank came Alama Ieremia, after Alama came me, and now there'll be someone else. There always will be. We're a rugby country, so even though we're losing players overseas there'll always be new guys coming through. How many stars of the future were in the team that won the Under 19 World Cup this year? What's critical is how we bring them through: the most important job in New Zealand rugby is nurturing our young talent and making sure the All Blacks of the future get the right tutelage.

I've seen the fickleness of the public and the media. One minute you're irreplaceable, next minute they're baying for you to get out of the way so a new wonder-boy can set the world on fire. I've seen how the new broom coach can sweep clean. Wayne Smith was growing a group of players for the 2003 World Cup until the NZRU board decided he wasn't tough-minded enough; they got rid of him and brought in a new coach who took a different tack on a range of things. We all have a view on how things should be done and who's best equipped to do them; sometimes circumstances work in your favour or you can force your way into the mix, but there may be times when you just don't fit and you're gone.

The public loves a winner. When you're winning, everyone wants to be your friend; when you're losing, you suddenly become invisible. Now we're seeing that even winning isn't necessarily enough. Some recent All Black victories have been more or less viewed as failures because the manner and margin weren't up to expectations. And as the Crusaders have discovered, when you're highly successful year after year, your supporters can get very choosy about which games they'll bother to turn up to.

My parents were happy that I was giving up because I'd been in the game a long time and had a young family and they could see that I was starting to get injured quite a lot. Their view was that I'd done what I could for my country and they were happy for me to stay home and look after my family. My sisters were very supportive too.

There'd been some media speculation which I just had to stonewall because I don't do things through a newspaper. It got to the stage where I was just lying to them but I think they were used to that. I didn't want to tell them because I wanted to announce it at the time of my choosing but they kept asking so I didn't have any reservations about lying, just as it doesn't seem to bother them when the boot's on the other foot. Journalists understand the game: they'll just keep asking the same questions and getting the same non-answers or evasions. What they get angry about is missing out on the scoop. Wynne Gray broke the story in the *New Zealand Herald* — I don't know how — which really pissed me off, but not half as much as it pissed off the *Dominion Post*. An Auckland paper scooping the Wellington paper on the Wellington boy's retirement didn't go down well. I purposely delayed the public announcement until the New Year just to spin it out, make Wynne sweat a bit, and keep them guessing.

There was a theory going around that I was going to sit out 2006 and come back for the World Cup. Sean Fitzpatrick was asking, did he jump or was he pushed? People can believe what they want to believe; their perceptions and criticisms have no impact on me. Like most people, I want to have control over the big, life-changing decisions so I wanted to be the one who decided when I finished rather than have someone else make that decision for me.

← PLAYBACK

GILBERT ENOKA

Gilbert Enoka *is the All Blacks mental skills coach.*

I was involved with the All Blacks when Wayne Smith was coach and Tana was your typical New Zealand rugby player who played hard on Saturday, drank hard and partied after the game, then looked to refuel and do it all again the following week. John Mitchell phased me out but I came back into the All Blacks when Graham Henry came on board. In the last two games of the 2004 Tri-Nations we got dumped. When the coaches and selectors were debriefing they did a considerable amount of soul-searching and identified two things that needed to change if the team was going to be successful: the group lacked real and inspirational leadership that made a difference to individuals and it lacked self-reliance. The professional era was breeding this player who was basically given everything at an early age and didn't have to fend for himself in any way, then all of a sudden we threw them out on the rugby field and they had to make decisions in a contest which is a bit like life and death.

My role as mental skills coach was to tackle leadership and suggest a process going forward. I'd learnt through my involvement in other sports that the authoritarian, hierarchical, dictatorial leadership style was not the way forward in the current environment: Generation Y strongly seeks collaborative leadership and involvement in the decision-making and things that affect them, so the only way forward for us was to follow a model of shared responsibility. We adopted that model and the coaches selected players who they felt were good performers and reasonably certain selections. The environment at that time was that if the coach lost a game, then the

'We're the best-prepared Lions team in history; what could possibly go wrong?' Lions captain Brian O'Driscoll displays confident body language at a breakfast function prior to the tumultuous 2005 series.

Tana and Rochelle with Prince William at the conclusion of the Lions series in 2005.

One down, two to go: the defeated Lions applaud Tana and the All Blacks off Jade Stadium at the end of the first test.

Someone to watch over me: Anton Oliver looks on sternly as Tana fronts the press in a belated attempt to combat the media smear campaign orchestrated by the Lions management in the wake of the O'Driscoll incident.

After the Lions' week-long media onslaught and storming start to the second test in Wellington, this try signalled an emphatic turning of the tide. The All Blacks went on to trounce the visitors 48–18.

That's what happens when you grab a tiger by the tail: Lions players, including acting captain Gareth Thomas (right), look on ruefully as Tana salutes the Westpac Stadium crowd after the series-clinching win.

'Let's send them home with nothing.' An exuberant Rodney So'oialo congratulates Tana after one of his two tries in the third test against the Lions at Eden Park.

The victorious captain speaks after the All Blacks' 3–0 whitewash of the Lions at Eden Park, watched by Lions manager Bill Beaumont (far left), Prime Minister Helen Clark (third from left), and beside her NZRU President John Graham.

The All Blacks unveil their new haka Kapa O Pango before kick-off against the Springboks at Carisbrook in 2005.

Mission accomplished: Tana has his hands on the silverware after the final Tri-Nations game of 2005, against the Wallabies at Eden Park.

A low-flying Doug Howlett admires Tana's try against England at Twickenham in 2005 when the All Blacks overcame a flurry of yellow cards to win 23–19.

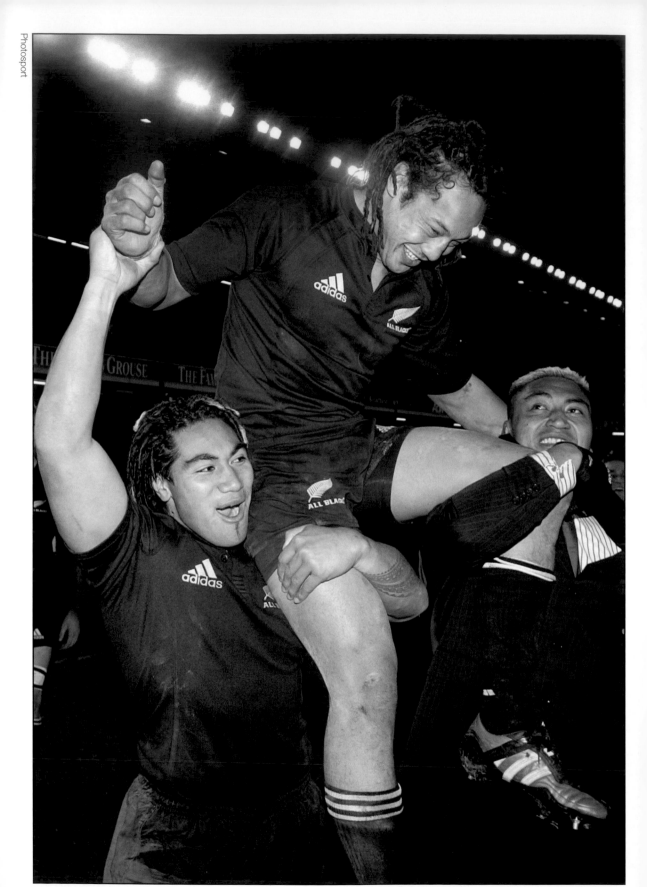

What a way to go: Ma'a Nonu (left) and Jerry Collins chair the Grand Slam-winning captain off Murrayfield.

pressure was on him. The players were just going from game to game because there was no certainty for anybody. The whole culture was one of uncertainty and people who had injuries would almost play injured so that they wouldn't give someone else a chance of taking their jersey. What Tana and Ted [Graham Henry] did was actually give a group of players a high degree of certainty. We had to grow them first as people because we felt that if we did that, they'd become better players, and if they became better players, then the team would become better. We met five times between the end of the Tri-Nations and the end-of-year tour. The players gave up their Sundays and we provided personal development activities for each of them. The leadership group has evolved and metamorphosed two or three times since, but the principle of shared leadership has been a core philosophy in the way this All Black team is managed.

Within the leadership group everything was up for grabs. There were no sacred cows. We found that the All Blacks were becoming trapped in tradition and were getting bagged by ex-players who were trying to keep the game back in their era. We had to resist those temptations and cut our own track. We challenged those people who were wanting us to have fish and chips after games and a dozen beers in the sheds before we left.

One of the first things we did was promote the concept of vulnerability. People have this image of the All Blacks being these macho characters who don't feel pain, who don't feel fear, who don't feel discomfort, and what we had to do was break through that outer barrier and get people talking about it. What we've done really is break out of the mind-set that you're a weak person if you talk about your fears. These talented individuals feel just like normal people and we spent a lot of time talking about the challenges of being an All Black, the effect of rugby on their families and on themselves, and we found that the more people shared, the more we were able to strengthen them from the inside.

We did lots of work on understanding the context of sport. The game finishes, someone pours a beer and says drink it, and people drink it because of the peer pressure that exists in the environment, even though from a principled point of view they may not want to do that. The environment had been such that they were more likely to cave in and be what other people wanted them to be, rather than actually being who they were, so we did a lot of work on individual choice and decision-making.

At every session we had some sort of personal development skill. We assessed their current leadership abilities, we identified areas of development that they needed personally, and then we put in place programmes that addressed issues on a team level but looked at developing them on a personal level. Brian Lochore, in his wisdom, just sat back and didn't say much until one day he said, 'In the end I truly believe that better people make better All Blacks.' To this day, that's been our philosophy. Each of the players had portfolios, areas of responsibility like media, training, entertainment, standards and alcohol, and they were responsible for the operation and functioning of that portfolio. They basically managed the interface between the team and management on those matters.

Unlike a lot of teams, this group is not afraid of fronting issues. The way we operate today, a lot of people find it very difficult to say, 'This is who I am and this is what I want' to people they love and care about, and a lot of my role is to bring things to the front so we can discuss and challenge. Quite often there's a high degree of personal discomfort associated with these discussions but there's also a high degree of progress made in the backwash. If you are saying one thing but doing something else in this environment, you can expect someone to get on your case.

We've learnt that we have to be comfortable being uncomfortable. The coral grows strongest in the roughest waters. The times when we sit back and feel comfortable and don't look at things are the times that we miss the edge that goes with quality performance. Failing is part of sport and we've lost some games. We have a target and some days we may come up short. We're teaching these guys that you don't have to be 100 per cent to get the job done. We can win with our B game and on a given day, in a given contest, someone may be better than us. This is not Disneyland.

Philosophically — and this is a philosophy of mine — what we're aiming to do with these athletes is both short term and long term. We want these players to be happy, healthy and really positive contributors in the All Black environment — adding to the jersey, adding to the legacy, adding to the nation through what they do whilst they have the jersey. Long term we've got to spit them out the other end being happy and healthy and positive contributors to society. There are many professional rugby players and other sports people who get spat out the other end with nothing. We're talking here about a person's character and standards and helping them to identify what they are and making sure that they live that every day.

If we produce citizens who come through the All Black experience with their personal and professional KPIs [key performance indicators] aligned, whose characters are defined by living those particular standards, they're going to make positive contributions to society as well. It's a bit of a sociological model but we're teaching these guys that rugby is what they do, it's not who they are. It's when people get their identity solely from rugby that the problems occur — the excessive drinking, the excessive socialising, the excessive adoration that comes along. 'Rugby's what I do, it's not who I am' is a core philosophy in the way we manage this.

After Tana had the video incident in Christchurch I said let's work out who you are and what you're doing and live that every day and get strength from it. I tried to bring him back to that centre and as he got a clearer definition of who he was and actually began to live that, he released another level of potential. He entered the conveyor belt with tons of talent but very little self-esteem and presence, but he became a man of remarkable mana. On that day in Dunedin when he led 'Kapa O Pango' he embraced the nation and connected with the nation in a way that no political party could ever do. He was truly inspirational.

At the centre of Tana's leadership is the fact that he didn't mince words, he didn't beat around the bush. He told it straight and people respected that quality. Watching him operate in the leadership group, very seldom did he contribute hugely through conversation but he was brilliant at getting a feel for what needed to be said, saying it when it needed to be said, and saying it in the manner in which it needed to be delivered. He had to deal with some reasonably challenging internal components. That time in Cardiff he had to look his mates in the eye and say, 'That's not up to what we expect, guys.' If we played lousy, he said so. If we weren't up to the mark, he stated it, and if people weren't pulling their weight, he wasn't afraid to put them in their place.

He never lost sight of those core elements of what it meant to be an All Black — he was very loyal to what's gone before him. His legacy has basically been to define what it means to be a New Zealander and an All Black. Tana's own transition through the All Blacks was one of a depleted individual who grew himself to such an extent that he could grow other people. He grew other people to such an extent that he's left a legacy in his era.

I see his next step as being an extremely challenging one for him because he's going straight into coaching in a foreign country. He's in a position where he can influence so many things because of what he's created as a rugby player and I think he'll end up being some sort of icon ambassador connected to a cause he truly believes in. If he's doing something that he's not connected to, he's as loose as a goose; if he believes in the cause and is genuinely connected to it, he can move mountains. His biggest challenge is to find out what that cause is.

A Sometimes Mighty Wind

In 2000 the Hurricanes shifted gears coaching-wise with Graham Mourie, a very good technician, taking over from the old-school Frank Oliver. As you'd expect, Graham was very good with loose forwards; he was full of advice and ideas and contributed a lot to the development of Jerry Collins in particular. Bryan 'Beegee' Williams came on board as the backs coach. As a former great player and highly successful coach of Auckland, he came in with a lot of respect, but soon found himself behind the eight ball. Information technology had taken analysis to a whole new level; the computer systems were up and running in Palmerston North churning out detailed information and feedback on all the teams. Perhaps because Beegee's recent coaching experience had been with Manu Samoa, he wasn't really up to speed with this new dimension of the game. I felt for him but we rugby players aren't very patient people.

At first we cut him some slack but when things didn't change the players started putting it on him and getting a bit cheeky. Having had the benefit of Wayne Smith's technical nous with the All Blacks the previous year, I felt like I'd taken a step back. I suppose it just shows how quickly the game evolves: every year there are new techniques for exploiting little weaknesses and even comparatively minor law changes give rise to dozens of new drills designed to exploit them. At the moment there's huge emphasis on designing new drills and developing new techniques to increase effectiveness in the tackled ball area. Frankly, Beegee and I struggled professionally: I wanted to be a better player, so I was always challenging him. I always want to learn and if I feel that the person I'm supposed to be learning from isn't much of a teacher, I'll tell them so and try to find someone who is. I had a lot of respect for what Beegee had achieved and he had a good heart and did things for the right reasons, but he lacked a little in the technical area. It was tough for a number of us but you can only make fun of someone for so long before you start thinking well, that's enough; why don't you just tell him instead of just going behind his back?

Early on I'd signalled that if the birth of my second child coincided with the trip to South Africa, I'd be staying home. As the trip approached there were actually three of us — me, Filo Tiatia and Gordon Slater — whose wives were expecting children around the same time. We beat the Waratahs in Sydney despite being reduced to 13 players — I suppose the cynics would have said that the Hurricanes of that era had plenty of experience of playing without the full complement. That victory put us in with a chance of making the semis but my wife was due to give birth the following week and Gordy's wife was due the week after that. Filo's child wasn't due for a few weeks so he decided to go to South Africa while Gordy and I flew home. We needed one win from our two games but lost the first one. Gordy's baby arrived, so he jumped on a plane; ours hadn't arrived, so I stayed. The final, vital match was against the Bulls, the last-placed team who hadn't won a game all season, but there's a first time for everything. The Hurricanes missed out on the semis and our baby was born about the time the team got back from South Africa.

There was a lot of discussion in the media about whether I should have gone. It fascinates me the way people want to debate and dissect things that don't concern them. Obviously missing out on the semis was a real disappointment for the boys. I shared that disappointment but I never felt that it was my fault. I wanted to be there for the birth of my child; that was far more important than any game.

At that time Wellington was trying to recruit players from other provinces for the NPC, but they didn't want to come. We were after All Blacks but they didn't see Wellington as the place to be, rugby-wise. To bolster our propping stocks, we brought in Kevin Yates from England and Morne van der Merwe from South Africa. It was obviously a short-term measure for both parties: we needed to shore up our scrum and they were looking for extra experience and conditioning. We had a really good team that year with me, Jonah Lomu and Christian Cullen at the back, Jason O'Halloran and Alama Ieremia in the midfield, the old hands Kupu Vanisi and Filo Tiatia alongside the young guns Rodney So'oialo and Jerry Collins in the loose forwards, Dion Waller and Inoke Afeaki at lock, and Norm Hewitt, our captain, up front between the imported props.

We lost badly to North Harbour. On the Monday morning, instead of doing yoga or whatever, we had one of those sit downs where you get it all out in the open. Dave Rennie and Graham Mourie were the coaches and Graham in particular really wanted us to play a structured game-plan. Whenever he talked he'd say, 'If you watch the Brumbies' or 'If you watch the Crusaders'; after a while it wore thin and turned a lot of us off to the point where we stopped listening to him. Technically it was another matter: as a video analyst Graham was up there with the best because he could recognise patterns within a team's overall game and identify where we could hurt them.

We told the coaches that we wanted to keep it simple, ease back on the structure, and get back to the game that came naturally to us: ruck and run — get the ball, give it some air, hit them here, hit them somewhere else. The coaches went along with it, saying if that was the way we wanted to play, go ahead. And we did: we scored a lot tries from 60, 70, 80 metres out: someone would break and get a pass away and we'd be right on top of it.

In the semi-final we played Auckland, which had been our bogey team during my time, at Eden Park. Alama was injured so Dave Rennie decided to give me a run at centre. I'd played there for Petone for a few years, outside Jason, and we'd always beaten Dave's club, Upper Hutt, even when he was coaching them. I was a bit nervous about it but delighted to be in my first NPC semi-final. Before kick-off I asked the referee, Steve Walsh, if it was a legitimate try if you forced the ball against the base of the goalpost. He gave me a bit of a look and confirmed that it was. Late in the game, as I went over for a try, I slid the ball up against the base of the goalpost. I was pretty pleased with myself so when Walsh put up his hand to award the try, I jumped up and tried to high-five him, but he yanked his hand away. Carlos Spencer reckoned I was a cheeky bugger and Robin Brooke agreed with him.

Alama was fit for the final but the coaches decided to stick with the same team, so he came off the bench. Filo wasn't fit which was a huge disappointment for him. He was always getting injured and, being a close mate, I was always giving him a hard time about it. The final was at Jade

Stadium and Canterbury was pretty much the Crusaders team that had won the Super 12 three years in a row, so they were raging-hot favourites. No-one had expected us to make the final so we had nothing to lose and no pressure of expectation. We had a simple game-plan: get involved, disrupt them and use our backs. My most vivid memory of the game is Jonah's try: he palmed off the Fijian winger Marika Vunibaka, who was quick enough to come back for another go, but the big guy just carried him over on his back. We got out to a big lead but Canterbury came storming back as they always do and we had to dig in or, in Dion Waller's case, slap down. It was a great feeling to win the championship after such a long gap — and in my case, in my seventh year of playing for my province — a big fillip for Wellington rugby, and the best possible way to send off Alama and Filo.

All but one of our five front-rowers got injured, so Norm Hewitt played on with a broken arm, which some people, including a Minister of the Crown, thought was setting a bad example. That's the kind of guy he was: a bit of a hard nut, a real competitor, one of the last of the old school. You could understand him not wanting to come off given how long he'd sat on the bench waiting in vain for Sean Fitzpatrick to get crocked and give him a chance.

In his book, Norm described the Jade Stadium faithful as redneck and abusive. I never found them that way. They just loved rugby. At games I tended to notice the kids in the crowd and they love who they love but don't get personal about it unless they're copying their parents. Having said that, I'd hate to be an Aucklander playing down there. After the game, it was a different matter: if you went out, you definitely felt a degree of hostility but that was generally alcohol-related.

The Hurricanes had another mediocre Super 12 in 2001. We'd lost some senior players and I'd lost friends like Alama and Filo. It had all started to get a bit much: we used to train at the Porirua Police College, which meant staying out there all day. After training we'd have a video session, then do it all over again after lunch. Lethargy would set in so the afternoon sessions were never much good. The afternoon sun would stream into the meeting room; we'd be lying on the floor watching the video presentation and the combination of sun and boredom often sent us off to sleep. It was a good facility because it had everything you could need, but they were long days and it was a bit of a hike out there for everyone except Jerry.

2001 was my first full year as a centre and I didn't think I made such a good fist of it with the Hurricanes. Dave Rennie gave me a lot of help during the NPC; I was just getting to know the position so I used him to look at my game and tell me how I was going and what I needed to do. He was a source of good advice and someone I had a lot of respect for so I was pleased when he became the Hurricanes backs coach in 2002. Ellis Meachem had come on board as Dave's NPC assistant coach. He was a local who'd done a lot of age grade coaching and they brought in a group of young guys, some of whom are really starting to come through now. They did a good job but the results weren't flash and they both got the axe, which seemed pretty tough because they were developing a team.

There was no stand-out candidate to replace Graham Mourie as Hurricanes coach. In 2002, the Taranaki NPC coach Colin Cooper had been assistant coach at the Crusaders, who were undefeated. I didn't know him personally but the Taranaki guys in the Hurricanes squad really rated him, so when Hurricanes CEO Malcolm Holmes asked me to give Colin a ring as part of the campaign to woo him away from the Crusaders, I was happy to do my bit. Colin's a very loyal person so he was confronted with a tough choice between his two-year commitment to Robbie Deans and the Crusaders and his ties to the Taranaki players and the region.

Eventually Colin opted for the Hurricanes, brought in Murray Roulston as his assistant, and asked me to be captain. We didn't start the 2003 season well. It seemed to me that Colin, who's a quietly-spoken man anyway, had decided on a softly softly approach: rather than come in and lay down the law, he was seeking player input and wanted to get the players thinking. After our second loss, I told him that he needed to stamp his authority on the team. We'd had a coach who sought player input but whenever he asked for it, the same two people would put their hands up. I told Colin that this group of players wanted a coach who would just put his foot down and say this is how we're going to play it; if he did that, the players would get in behind him.

To his credit, he took that advice and the players responded. We won seven in a row and made the semis for the second time in our history, even though on paper we didn't have the same quality as other sides. Ma'a Nonu made a huge impact but our success was really based on having a lot of workers who did what they were told. The players latched on to whatever Colin said because they had so much respect for him. Talent-wise the side was nowhere near what it is now, but there was a willingness to work for each other and it's amazing what you can achieve when no-one cares who gets the credit. Sometimes I think talent doesn't matter all that much: if you have a team of workers who know their roles and fulfil them to the best of their abilities, who can do what they need to do when it's required of them, it makes the game so much simpler.

When I was offered the captaincy, the coaches raised the issue of my stance of not talking to TV3. I said it was up to them because I wasn't going to drop it: if that wasn't acceptable to them, so be it. I wasn't talking to *Sunday News* either because they'd run a story painting me in a bad light that was plain wrong.

After our unexpected success in 2003, the 2004 Super 12 was a big let-down. We went into our last game against the Crusaders drifting along near the foot of the table but determined to finish well and give our long-suffering fans a reason to look forward to the next season. We won but the result was overshadowed by the fall-out from Jerry Collins' hit on Chris Jack which left him in la-la land. As those kinds of tackles do, it lifted our guys and put some fear into the Crusaders. They had less to play for than we did and certainly weren't queuing up to run the ball at Jerry. Afterwards Deans called it a cheap shot, the media took their lead from that, and Jerry got suspended. I thought that was total rubbish. It seems it's fine for Jerry to flatten guys from other countries but unacceptable when he does it to a Kiwi or, God forbid, an All Black. Who are they trying to protect here? I also felt that if the boot had been on the other foot, nothing would have happened. The feeling in the Hurricanes' camp is that the officials treat us differently — i.e. more harshly — both on the field and in the disciplinary wash-up. I've made that point to a lot of people.

John Plumtree became the Wellington Lions coach in 2003 but I didn't really have anything to do with him because of the World Cup. I'd met him in 2002 when he was the All Blacks' video analyst. He lasted about two months: from what I heard, he thought he'd be doing some coaching but that didn't happen and he didn't enjoy spending long hours analysing footage. I got the impression that a lot of the Wellington players didn't really like his style. He was abrupt and abrasive and didn't mind ripping into players in front of everyone. You just can't do that these days; players resent being made to look fools in front of their friends and workmates. It doesn't just bring down the guy on the receiving end, it upsets all his mates who have seen it and they're going to rally around their mate rather than try to get in the coach's good books. So by berating one person, the coach alienates four or five others and then it just grows.

When I joined the Lions after the 2004 Tri-Nations I saw it at first hand and felt it just wasn't right. The team did well, though, under Rodney So'oialo's captaincy. There was a core of experienced players with 'Rodders', Ma'a, Joe McDonnell, Jason Spice and David Holwell, and that was what kept the show together. It was a different story in 2005 with David and Spicey having moved on and Rodney coming back late from All Black duty. They just didn't have the same kind of leadership, so there was pressure on the coaches to do more.

I played only a couple of games but I had a meeting with John Plumtree to pass on what I'd heard from the players and what I thought we needed to do looking ahead to the next year. It had got to the stage where people expected me to do that and I didn't have a problem with it because of my seniority and the fact that I'd learned the importance of communicating. If you don't say anything, nothing changes. I found that out quite early and try to live by it now. Nothing may change as a result of you speaking up but at least you can say, 'I told you; I said my piece but you weren't willing to listen or deal with it.' I had a good rapport with John. He's a passionate rugby man but he'd burned players. I wasn't comfortable with the way he sometimes talked to people or his willingness to tell all and sundry what he saw as his next step. I believe that if you put your head down and work hard and if you're the right man for the job, you'll probably get it; I'm not sure self-promotion is the way to go, particularly in the New Zealand rugby environment. Everyone knew that John wanted to be the next Hurricanes coach, but Colin wasn't doing a bad job so there wasn't likely to be a vacancy any time soon. Over time John evolved and became a better coach. He learnt a lot about the individuals and realised that you can't get offside with the players. In the end, success is dependent on the players going out there and implementing the coach's plan, so it makes sense to establish a rapport with them and work with them rather than against them.

In 2005 I played my 100th game for the Hurricanes. It was against the Blues, whom we'd never beaten, at Eden Park and we had to win to make the semis. It was a very big thing for me, and the boys really got behind me. Jerry said, 'Don't worry, boss, we'll get this one for you.' It was a tough game; I just remember jumping on the loose ball whenever I could as we tried to guts out a win. When the final whistle went there was relief that we'd won, coupled with the satisfaction of finally beating the Blues.

The NZRU presented me with a mere and a plaque and the Hurricanes franchise gave me a really cool book of photographs and comments from guys I'd played with and against. We had a few speeches and beers in the changing-rooms before heading back to the hotel for a court session. Normally at these things you have a sip of your beer and make a comment that might only be a few words. The nominated subject was yours truly and some guys just went on and on. Andrew Hore and Joe Ward, who were in charge of proceedings, were rolling their eyes and looking at their watches. After an hour we'd only got through half the team. The Samoan boys, who usually prefer to giggle in the background, did a traditional dance for me and put a lei around my neck, which was a big honour. They asked me to lead a song: one of my favourite songs and, more to the point, one that I know all the words to is 'Don't They Know It's Christmas' by Live Aid; I sang the whole thing. There was other stuff planned, but Andrew said we didn't have time for anything else. The team gave me a Big Save shopping voucher which I gave to my wife; I assumed that was the idea. The boys were keen to go out but my family had come up for the game so I went back to the hotel to spend what was left of the night with them.

It was a good year for the Hurricanes thanks to the coaches' planning. The young players they'd shown faith in had matured and come to terms with the kind of game we wanted to play. Unfortunately we came to grief in a big way in the semi-final against the Crusaders.

In 2006, Super 12 became Super 14. It would be fair to say that I wasn't giddy with excitement at the prospect of two more games and an extra week in South Africa. In fact the thought of retiring altogether was quite attractive. I talked to friends and family about it because without the lure of the All Blacks I was struggling for motivation. It just felt like here we go again. At that stage going overseas wasn't on the radar — I was just going to give up rugby and find another job. On the other hand, I had two years to run on my contract with the New Zealand Rugby Union and Wellington wanted me to fulfil my side of the bargain by finishing well and staying loyal. Colin Cooper was keen for me to stick around and help with the leadership. We talked about a reduced workload but that fell through when there were a few injuries, notably Conrad Smith breaking his leg. I didn't play my best rugby. I was looking to bow out, which in hindsight meant that I wasn't giving everything I had to the jersey. I got up for some games and played at my old level but there were other games when I didn't really want to be there. At training, I tried to contribute by giving Colin as much input as I could and backing up the coaches. Coaches sometimes struggle to gain the players' respect and I think I've got a good sense of when a coach needs a bit of a backing.

The players are more inclined to follow the lead of a player they respect and that was one of my primary roles.

I injured my knee in South Africa and was out for a few weeks. It was the same knee I'd hurt in 2003 and I was running out of ligaments to hold it together. When I came back I was down on confidence, as well as lacking motivation, and my performances reflected my state of mind. I wasn't playing up to my standards: I wasn't taking pressure passes, I was dropping balls that I didn't normally drop, and I didn't have the confidence to run the same lines. While I was off the pace, our forward pack was maturing into a force to be reckoned with. We hadn't had a dominant pack since 1997 but now in addition to Jerry and Rodney, we had the likes of Chris Masoe, Andrew Hore, Paul Tito and Neemia Tialata. We won the must-win games. We went over to Sydney for the last round-robin game with a home semi at stake and played some of our best rugby, defending strongly to shut them out. The semi-final itself was a similar kind of game and in the final minutes we just got hold of the ball and kept it, creating mauls and rucks to wind the clock down. It's the sign of a mature side that it can do the tough work when it comes to the crunch. We had good discipline and the players understood their roles and were happy in them.

I would've backed us to win the final against the Crusaders on a good night but once the fog descended, the plans went out the window and we struggled to adjust to a situation in which you couldn't even rely on basic rugby instincts. At ground level you could still see quite a bit but you couldn't tell if a kick had gone out or not. In the second half I thought I'd kicked it out but next thing Rico Gear emerged out of the fog with the ball under his arm and I was like, what the hell was that? The slippery ball didn't help and the game just became an arm wrestle with both sides trying to play field position. Neemia hurt his knee and was scrumming on one leg, which seriously reduced his effectiveness, although he showed what a tough young man he is by staying on. Piri Weepu's head knock was another major blow. They'd been key players for us and we needed them to be at their best, but those knocks handicapped them. In the end, the game turned on one missed tackle. It was disappointing but that's the Crusaders for you: they apply pressure and wait for you to break. We made basic errors and gave away silly penalties when we were on attack, which enabled them to relieve the pressure and put it back on us. It was just disappointing to get that far and come second but they adjusted to the conditions better and made the most of their chances.

In our round-robin game against the Crusaders, which I missed because of injury, there were a couple of incidents that created a stir and gave rise to claims of bad blood between the Wellington and Canterbury All Blacks. We had a lot of respect for Canterbury and the Crusaders; we admired their success and had the mind-set that when you played the best, you had to front up with your A game so the guys really fired up. When you're in that hyped-up state of wanting to do everything you can for your team, you're pretty much ready to rumble and it just takes one little trigger to set things off. That's what happened in that game: there was a huge amount made of the incident when Neemia Tialata had Richie McCaw by the throat, but knowing Neemia I'm sure there was nothing more to it than the heat of the moment. That was what I told Richie after the game and that was what Neemia told him when they talked about it in the All Blacks camp. Richie's a menace because he's so good on the ground and these things happen when you're out there trying to do your best.

On the Monday after the final the guys in the All Black and Junior All Black squads went into camp. Being an ex-All Black, I went home. I'd been given a fortnight off before starting training with the Wellington Lions so that we could have a family holiday on the Sunshine Coast, but both my daughters got chickenpox and couldn't travel overseas. The Wellington squad was going into camp so I figured if I couldn't go on holiday, I might as well go back to work.

I actually enjoyed it. It was the first time I'd had a training window before the provincial championship and been able to do consistent weight training. I actually made significant gains during those four weeks, setting personal bests speed and strength-wise, so I could understand where the All Black coaches were coming from with their rest and reconditioning programme. The last pre-season training window I'd had was in 1998 when there was no end-of-year tour because of the following year's World Cup and I got a lot fitter then too, achieving a base fitness which held me in good stead. I can remember telling Richie my weights and times and assuring him that he too could have a body like mine.

I wasn't sure I wanted to captain the Lions and looked around for another candidate but John Plumtree's view was that I'd been doing most of the talking so I might as well be captain. I was fortunate that Colin and John and even Graham Henry, to an extent, gave me a lot of say in what we did. Perhaps they realised that I was going to have my say anyway, so why resist the inevitable?

Our All Blacks came back keen and wanting to play. I'd like to think that I've set an example of loyalty to Wellington, to who we are and where we're from, that's now being carried on by the next generation of Wellington All Blacks. I also encouraged them to make sure they spoke up if they felt things weren't going well or the administrators weren't delivering on their commitments, so that Wellington could maintain progress and keep pace with the best.

In the last couple of years I became a player who listened very carefully to his body. I could sense when I was and wasn't going to play well and I worked out that I could probably play three games at a reasonable level, but then fatigue would set in and a fourth game on the trot would be a bridge too far. I played one of my better games of the year in the semi-final against Auckland at Eden Park but I took a few hits and it left me physically drained. I was sore, particularly my shoulders, throughout the following week. That's not an excuse for the way I played in the final in Hamilton but in light of what I'd come to understand about my body's powers of recovery, it shouldn't have come as a surprise. I played my worst game of the competition, letting in two tries. I felt that I'd let the team down and lost us the final. That awful memory was what drove me when I went to play in France: I didn't want to have another game like that. I also used it as motivation when we played the Chiefs in 2007.

Earlier, history had repeated itself: with Steve Walsh refereeing, we lost a Ranfurly Shield challenge against Canterbury in the final minutes. Over the years I've been criticised for my demeanour with referees because I wasn't one of your polite, ingratiating 'Is everything alright, sir?' type captains. I was more the 'What are they doing? How come they're getting away with that?' type. I was pretty direct if something was wrong and expected my questions to be answered. It was an aspect of my leadership that I had to work on when I became All Black captain, but I became very frustrated in my last couple of seasons with Wellington and the Hurricanes, to the point where I didn't really care if it showed. I believed we were being refereed on reputation rather than on what was actually happening, sometimes to a ridiculous extent. Walsh started it way back, Paul Honiss followed suit, and now most of them do it. We adjusted to referees as well as we could, but it becomes very difficult if they don't adjudicate consistently. I was on to Colin all the time; he'd tell me I had to manage the referee and I'd say, 'F**k the refs, they've got to do their job, they should be accountable.' I think Honiss and Walsh are two of the worst offenders. Earlier this year everyone was congratulating Honiss on refereeing 200 games; I couldn't believe that he'd been allowed to.

Before I went to France I talked to Colin about not picking me in 2007. It was World Cup year and we had two All Black midfielders who weren't in the reconditioning group, plus Tamati Ellison, a Junior All Black, and Tane Tuipuloto, who I rate as a very good player. I actually had a meeting with some NZRU officials to apply for dispensation not to go into the draft if the Hurricanes didn't pick me. I outlined the thinking behind what I'd said to Colin and explained that I didn't want to go into the draft because I had a 13-year-old son who was about to start secondary school and three very young daughters; I wasn't going to uproot them for three months and I wasn't prepared to be away from them for that time. I told them I'd retire rather than move to another franchise. They conceded I had some valid arguments but it had to go to another committee which included the All Black coaches. They knocked back my application on the grounds that I was a recent All Black and to give me dispensation would enable the Hurricanes to have more quality players because they wouldn't have to use up one of their protected spots. In the end, Colin selected me in his protected squad and Tane got picked up by the Chiefs, which worked out well for him because he made the Junior All Blacks.

Colin wanted me involved because he was losing so much leadership to the reconditioning programme. I said I'd help out as much as I could and be there if I was needed, but he had to promote the other three midfielders because they were the future. I didn't start the first game but Conrad got injured — he really has had terrible luck — so I was back out there again. As in 2006, I struggled for motivation. I was very keen to support the younger players and help out as much as I could with off-the-field stuff and at training, but it didn't work out that way. It probably doesn't reflect well on me, but I don't think I gave it 100 per cent every time I went out there. There were times when I just thought, oh, not again; do I have to do this? It seemed like my body was starting to protest too because I had niggly injuries that just wouldn't go away. I was having to manage myself to the extent of not training on Mondays and Tuesdays.

Obviously losing six forwards from what had been a dominant pack the year before had a major impact. The young guys stepped up in the early rounds but the physicality and intensity of Super 14 took its mental toll. The key to this competition is being able to back up week after week, which means talking yourself into sending your bruised body back into the fray.

With our leaders gone, we were without the guys who'd contributed a lot to the way we played. Paul Tito was outstanding but he could only do so much. We needed more leaders in the pack, but also lacked decision-makers in key backline positions: we had a youngster at 9, a 10 who wasn't playing as well as he can, and I was struggling with injuries. The malaise seeped into our training. I don't believe the coaching approach was right for the players we had. We suffered a few defeats and lost a bit of belief and confidence in what we were trying to do; guys were looking for motivation everywhere except within themselves and some players didn't perform as well as they had in 2006. We've seen players who, when given the opportunity, have stepped up to the mark and proved they can play at that level, but perhaps some others failed to make the case for themselves. Things mounted up, one bad thing led to another, and we just couldn't get ourselves out of it. But lessons will have been learnt: you've always got to be tinkering, trying to find ways to motivate and innovate and keep things fresh. I know the coach learnt a lot from it.

People said the competition was harder in 2007 but for me it was just same old, same old. The Sharks, though, definitely played better football than they have for a while. They had a good mix of young and old and looked invigorated by the new coaching set-up of Dick Muir and John Plumtree. As I said, innovation and fresh ideas do wonders for the players' state of mind. The Bulls had a couple of terrible years but they understood the problem and turned things around. When you look at the two finalists' line-ups, what strikes you is the fact that they've been together for a good while. Without our top 22, the New Zealand franchises mightn't have had the same calibre of player, but a lot of guys held their own which I think is a testament to our depth.

I wasn't really conscious that I was coming to the end of my time with the Hurricanes. Even when the talk first started, it didn't really dawn on me. Maybe I was waiting for a great wave of emotion but it never arrived. I was ready to go; in fact I'd suggested a couple of earlier games would be a good time to finish but had to stick it out. I was left out of the squad for our second to last game against the Highlanders. Colin asked me if that was okay; I said it was fine with me, Conrad and Tamati were the future, and I knew I'd be reinstated for the last game. But as I walked out of his office I realised that it was the first time since 1996 that I'd been left out when fit and available — and then it hit me. When I told my wife, she said, 'Well that's the way it is — you're almost gone.' As it happened, Conrad pulled out with a hamstring injury and I got the late call-up.

I had to do so much media stuff in that last week. I tried to get out of it, as I do. I'd hardly done any all season; whenever they asked for me I always said, 'No, man, I'm old news, I'm out of here,' which didn't please the media guys. But this time the Hurricanes media officer didn't let me off the hook: Luke

Andrews, Lome Fa'atau and Paul Tito were also finishing and they'd done their bit with the media; now it was my turn. One day I did an hour of media after training and just when I could see light at the end of the tunnel one of the reporters said to me, 'You know, you're going to have to do this all over again when you play your hundredth game for the Wellington Lions and finish with them.' There's nothing like two days of media interviews to dull your emotions so it really wasn't until I was on the bus going to the game that it all hit home: this was it; this was the last time I'd make this bus trip and see those supporters in their Hurricanes jerseys and Hurricanes hats and faces painted yellow and black. I always took a lot of joy and pride from seeing those supporters because I knew they were going to the park to watch us perform. To watch me.

Colin had asked me to present the jerseys. By this stage the emotion was welling up so I was concentrating on making sure that I didn't cry. I was telling myself, don't cry, pull yourself together, you fool. I had some quiet time in the toilet trying to get it together and decided I'd just say a few words, hand out the jerseys, and leave it at that. I told the boys that it was a great honour to hand out the jerseys, it had been an honour to have played with them, and it would be an honour to run out with them tonight. Then I handed the jerseys out, exchanged a few hugs, and prepared as I normally do. I felt I played well, particularly on defence, but as a team we had a shocker. We just couldn't keep things together. Maybe the emotion got to people. We'd had a pretty relaxed week because we didn't want to get too wound up but, for whatever reason, we saved our worst game for last and just played silly rugby. I was disappointed that we lost but it wasn't that empty, kicked-in-the-guts kind of disappointment because it wasn't that kind of year.

I was relieved to come off early because I was tired. I always looked up at the crowd and clapped them to thank them for coming out for us yet again but that night I felt for them and I hope that came across in my speech. I can't remember much of what I said apart from thanking the crowd and my sisters and cousins who always came along to support me. I'm thankful to everyone who has supported me but especially them because their support was unwavering.

Afterwards the team went out for a meal and my wife and I went into town to meet up with family and friends for a few drinks. The team always gets together on the Sunday after the last game but my recollection of what took place is hazy to put it mildly. There was an endless queue of guys lining up to buy me a drink and tell me what a great guy I was. Well, that's what it seemed like — maybe it was the same two or three on a loop. I don't drink much during the season but when it's over and you know you've got three or four weeks off, there's no better time. One thing I've discovered about myself is that I'm a hopeless drinker: some guys are marathon runners but I'm a sprinter. It was a good day. Well, it was alright. The next day was pretty awful. And the day after that.

A couple of days later we went through the review process and had the last official Hurricanes function, a meal at which the players give awards — player of the year, team man of the year — and the coaches pick the rookie of the year. These are the awards that mean the most because they're given by the guys who've trained with you and played alongside you and sat next to you on the bus and really know you as a rugby player and a person. The significance of the occasion didn't really hit me until we got home and Rochelle pointed out that it was my last official Hurricanes function. I'm not into regrets or looking back; what I've come to realise is that everything comes to an end and it was my time, a time of my choosing.

One thing about playing for Wellington and the Hurricanes is that we've never had the problem of the fickle supporter syndrome that comes from constant success. I think our supporters have appreciated the effort and achievement of getting into semi-finals and finals and for a while were probably happy with that. Because we've promised so much recently I think the public now expects a bit more. So do I. I expected us to have won a championship with the sides we've had.

The fans' loyalty was one reason why I loved playing for Wellington and the Hurricanes. They still turn up even when we're out of the running. We used to wonder why sometimes: why do they turn up when they're not getting as much out of it as we are, given that we love playing in front of a packed house? We understand why our families come along — because we beg them to — but what about the rest? I know you can't take it for granted but at the same time you can't say enough about it.

I think they just feel an affinity with the team. Part of that is down to the work that's been done right from the start to give the Hurricanes a strong regional identity and hopefully the franchise will continue to see the value of that. When we have the bye, the players split into groups and spend a day visiting the cities within our region, going to schools, and being seen by the people out there who support us. I've done quite a few in my time and while it can be a bit of a hassle you just grin and bear it because it's part of a bigger picture.

The brand of rugby we've played is another factor and the personnel have definitely helped. Why wouldn't you turn up to watch the likes of Christian

Cullen and Jonah Lomu? Now, there's an exciting blend, with quite a few All Blacks and youthful talent with the likes of Cory Jane and Hosea Gear, but in 2007 we promised a lot and didn't deliver much. It didn't really come together and that's the challenge for the coaches looking ahead to 2008.

A lot of it has to do with the environment. At the elite level everyone does the same training and everyone's physically and aerobically pretty much on the same level, so the mental side of things is critical. Coaches have to understand that. Sometimes they can get lost in trying to mould the player to themselves and their vision of the game — Graham Mourie was a case in point. Aussie McLean has come from Canterbury where he'd have five players offering suggestions when he asked, 'What shall we do here?' When he asks for input in Wellington, I go, 'Oh, why don't we do this move and that move?' and he just looks at me thinking, not you again.

I've told him and Colin that the players they've got here don't like that. They just want to be told what to do. If you tell them, 'We'll do this move,' they'll go, 'Yep, okay.' It's not that Pacific Islanders can't think for themselves but sometimes they just can't be bothered. And they've got a different way of learning. We learn by doing it; we don't learn in front of a blackboard because it reminds us of being at school and for some of us that's not a pleasant memory. You can be enthusiastic about learning — I certainly am — but if the learning environment is off-putting or discomforting, enthusiasm soon wanes. Some people learn from being told or having it written up on the blackboard and then there are those — the majority, I'd suggest — who learn by getting out on the training field and going through it until they get it. The key is to acknowledge that not everyone learns the same way. I have a real problem with people who say Pacific Islanders can't think for themselves or you can't have a Pacific Islander in a decision-making role. At the end of the day that's just racism.

A coach might want to play a particular style of game which doesn't suit one of his best players. Does he change the game to suit the player or vice versa? If he tries to move the player away from what he does best and make him do something that doesn't come naturally, what will happen? The chances are the player won't like it, he'll get disenchanted, he'll probably do it wrong, and end up losing confidence and form. A lot of coaches take a while to understand that.

At the elite level the coach's challenge is to understand his players. The trainer takes care of the athlete, ensuring that he's in peak physical condition.

The coach's job is to pick a core of players, establish what they do well, then create a game plan that suits their temperaments and physical attributes, rather than force them to play a style of game that doesn't come naturally to them. That involves changing ingrained habits, which takes time. If you just get a group of players three weeks before the competition starts there's no way you're going to be able to break them of their old habits and teach them new ones.

I felt that I could help in this area but it's quite a tricky path to negotiate and sometimes I had to step back to avoid encroaching on the coaches' roles and having the likes of Jerry give me crap about being one of the coaches. Colin and I had a mutual respect: he was very open to my advice and suggestions and vice versa, and I got involved in selection discussions and planning. But it got quite tough when I'd get back from the All Blacks' end-of-year tour and they'd want to involve me in the Hurricanes planning. It became very draining going to meetings before training and in 2004 I told Colin I needed a break and he needed to develop other leaders. With no disrespect to Rodney, who was being developed, I was the guy with the experience so they kept coming back to me.

I tried not to interrupt or override a coach unless I felt that what was being pushed was just wrong. That's not to say I didn't challenge them to explain why something had to be done a certain way or to consider alternatives. I've always been prone to doing that and as I accumulated All Black experience, that tendency became more pronounced. As it should have: why stand there with your mouth shut watching people go through a process of trial and error when you know from experience what the solution is?

As an All Black whenever you go back to your franchise or province you have to make sure of two things: that you pass on what you've learnt and that you play like an All Black. No matter how many levels you go down, people expect an All Black to play like an All Black. The biggest mistake you can make is to go down a level with the attitude that I'm an All Black now, this stuff doesn't really matter. You'll lose respect and eventually those sub-standard performances will count against you at the selection table. The toughest thing about becoming an All Black is the expectation, not just from the public and the media but from other players, including other All Blacks. I made sure young All Blacks understood that: if they had to go and play club rugby, I'd tell them, 'Mate, you make sure you go back as an All Black. That's what you are and always will be and you've got to live with that.'

No-one knows better than I do that it's not easy dropping down to club level and playing on a churned-up, muddy field in the suburbs in front of a handful of people who probably want to see you get your comeuppance. I liked to go back and play for Petone as a bit of a payback to the club and the people who've supported me. It took them a while to warm to me but they did eventually and I'm a fairly loyal person: one club, one province, one franchise. But it's really tough to get yourself up for it. I wouldn't say we're spoilt, but international grounds are pretty impressive as a rule and then you find yourself at somewhere like Ian Galloway Park where I had to play when I was coming back from a knee injury in 2001. I was worried about hurting it again, it was cold, the wind was whipping across the ground, and I was marking Ma'a Nonu. I'd rather have been at the dentist. I had a shocker: I kept drifting off Ma'a, leaving him to our second five. But I'd like to think that most of the time I 'put in' and lived up to what was expected of me.

I believe Wellington is one of the better unions in terms of their All Blacks and Super 14 players turning out for their clubs. I don't know how much it happens in other provinces. Jerry's allegiance to his club is legendary and Piri, Ma'a and Neemia go back whenever they get a chance, but top players who play club rugby are probably a dying breed. More and more the best young players come through the age grade representative teams and academy systems and go straight into provincial rugby and I sometimes get the impression that representative coaches would much rather have their players train than play for their clubs.

← PLAYBACK

FILO TIATIA

Former Wellington, Hurricanes and All Black loose forward **Filo Tiatia** *now plays for the Welsh club, Ospreys.*

I met Tana when he was playing for the Wellington Colts and I was in my first season with the As. We had a court session after we'd played Canterbury in Christchurch and 'Monkey' [Tana's older brother Mike] was the judge, so he couldn't leave the room until the session was completed. Tana and my wife were waiting for us in the bar. Cade had just been born and we celebrated that night. From that point on we were pretty close mates, always at each other's places for birthdays and barbecues. Obviously now that we're living overseas it makes it a lot harder but we're in regular contact. He's a good mate, a person you can rely on.

When I first met him he was confident and very polite, a young Samoan kid from Wainuiomata who basically just looked up to Monkey — they were mirror images — and a bit of a comedian who loved his music. But he was always learning and aware of his surroundings and able to adapt to anyone, and those qualities made him the person he is now.

He was one of the worst trainers I've ever met — he was never fit. He just basically played on talent and when he had ball in hand he was so expressive and competitive — he always wanted to have a crack and score. When Super rugby came in he made a decision that he was going to give it a crack; he got a personal trainer and crossed boundaries he'd never crossed before in terms of his endurance and mental fitness and became a totally different person.

For me to see this young, raw Samoan kid who just played on his natural ability change his work ethic was something I never expected. It was quite inspiring. He reaped the rewards of it: he was one of the top try scorers in the competition and went on to make the All Blacks, which was a credit to his hard work and self-belief. A lot of Polynesian players really admired that and looked up to it, not just the young guys but some of those who'd been around the block. When he became All Black captain it was one of the proudest moments in my association with him, but back then I could never have picked it. He's made a lot of people proud.

He's a Gemini and there are definitely two sides to him. On the field he's dynamic and physical with a great skill set — there are precious few like him in terms of how he plays the game. His statistics are bloody outstanding. Off the field he's a bloody comedian who loves to take the piss out of players. He's a bloody good dancer too, one of the best I've seen: he's fantastic to watch on the dance floor — he'll pull out all these moves and you just go, 'Wow.' He's also a human juke box. He loves his old school music: you'll be sitting in the car with him and some old song will come on and he'll know every word.

After his stint in Toulon, he and Rochelle and the kids came down here. We were walking around Swansea, Tana in a hoodie, and all these Welsh kids were coming up wanting to talk to him and have their photographs taken with him. He was so patient; he took time to have a little conversation with all of them.

He's made a few mistakes, as we all do, but he's learned from them. As the cliché goes, you have to fail in order to succeed and he's definitely done that and become a well-moulded person. He's had good people around him throughout his rugby career and he's picked up good qualities from them, and his parents have had a big role to play as well. He has good principles, he's a good family man; he'd do anything for Rochelle and his kids and his friends. He's not a bad bloke. Not a bad bloke at all.

Team Umaga

Christian Cullen has to be the greatest player I've played with. He had the knack of being in the right place at the right time. It wasn't luck; his timing was impeccable. He could sniff out where to be and just glide in from anywhere and he was one of the best support runners I've seen. In his early days he was fearless under the high ball and in taking the knocks and hitting the lines he did. Sometimes he'd hit a line between two big blokes who were renowned as hard tacklers, but he'd go for it because they weren't expecting him to hit it so hard and at such an angle. Cully wasn't the most talkative person, he just did things on instinct. The more I played with him, the more I picked that up and we worked well with each other. He's very competitive and has brilliant hand/eye coordination — he could just pick up a bat or a racquet or a cue and play anything. I had it over him on the golf course because I could get inside his head. If his ball went a little bit off line, I'd tell him that he wasn't hitting it very well. I'd challenge him — 'Do you want to bet on who gets closer to the flag?' — then have him on, insisting that I'd got closer. It would end up in an argument with him whacking his golf bag or chucking his club and me in fits of laughter. But he was definitely the better golfer.

Doug Howlett is the ultimate professional and all-round good guy. He made his Super 12 debut as a kid straight out of school in 1997 when he played for the Highlanders, then came to the Hurricanes the following year.

You could see then that he had all the makings of a great player: he was very conscientious, worked hard on his game, fitted in really well, and had speed, skill and guts. Like Cully, he was a brave player who put his body on the line. His journey from where he was then to where he is now is a testament to his self-belief and willingness to hang in there and keep working at his game and on his body. I've always thought he's the best winger in world rugby because he just never gives up; whenever he plays, he gives everything he's got, both on attack and defence. He's maturing into a good leader too; he's been around for a long time and gained a lot of knowledge.

The big guy, **Jonah Lomu**, was just a monster. He did things that no-one had seen a big man do before. I first came across him in the New Zealand Colts in 1994 and went the way of so many, having my face pushed into the ground as he ran past to score a try. He was a good team man who helped the younger players as much as he could. I'm not sure whether it was a good thing or not, but whenever we went on tour he'd come on the plane with big bags of lollies which he'd hand around. He's a very giving person, a really good man. If anyone needed anything, he was there to help out and more than anything I respected him for what he did for people off the field. I felt for him sometimes and got angry when I could see people taking advantage of him. Some of those he helped didn't need it; all they needed to do was open their wallets.

It was sad when his illness came back. The one thing about Jonah that frustrated me was that he never talked about it. You had to respect him for not wanting to make a song and dance about it, but it was frustrating. At the Hurricanes he wasn't training well and players were talking behind his back; being the captain I said to him, 'Mate, what's happening here? You're not doing it; you've got to get your game back.' A few days later he announced that he was sick again, which made me feel pretty bad. I know Colin Cooper had had a similar conversation with him. He didn't say anything because he didn't want sympathy but I felt that if he'd told us what was going on, we could have had some understanding. Being in the dark it just looked like he wasn't playing well and you wondered why not, when in fact it was physically impossible for him to do what he used to do. Given everything he's gone through, it was great to see him come back and play again.

My centre is **Frank Bunce**. I looked up to Buncey because he was tough and uncompromising — I like tough guys — and didn't give an inch to anyone. When I played with him he was second to none in the world. He was a good guy off the field, although it took a while to get to know him because he didn't let just anyone into his little circle. When I came into the team he looked after me and let me know what was required. I learnt a lot from watching Buncey play and train. He had a no-nonsense attitude to training: he was very quiet and just went about his business. When he was asked to contribute, he'd make some low-key comment about defence but you listened because he knew what he was talking about. It's funny to think that back then he didn't talk much, but now he's always talking on TV.

The second-five I most enjoyed playing outside was **Pita Alatini**. His career in the black jersey was cut short for reasons other than his on-field performance because his last year in the All Blacks was his best. He was a guy I trusted to do what was required on the inside, both on attack and defence, and someone I was very compatible with. We complemented each other: he was a silky, skilful player and I was the crash and bash merchant. He was the life of the party off the field, and had a knack of making me laugh. When things weren't going too well on the field, we'd have a bit of a joke and it would just get us back up.

Before the 2005 Lions series I'd never played with a first-five who had the complete game and I'd played with some good ones. In that series **Dan Carter** produced the most complete performance from a first-five that I've been involved with: kicking, running the game, running with the ball, and defence, which is a big part of it for me. Of all the first-fives I've played with only David Holwell was a better defender. As well as his skill set, he had the combination of maturity and youthful fearlessness. He was never overawed by the occasion and there'd always be a sly smile or a little wink at the camera because invariably he was on the big screen.

I really enjoyed playing outside Earl Va'a. We played a lot together in my league days — he also went on to play international rugby — and we combined really well, running a lot of plays together.

My halfback is **Piri Weepu**, another Wainuiomata boy — in fact he's Earl's nephew. Piri's got the skill set and he's another of these young guys who don't get overawed by the big occasion. He sees it as just another game; he looks forward to it; he feels it's his right to be there. He's got the skills, the heart and the ability to read the game and usually makes the right decision. Most important of all, I know he'll do what I tell him.

My number 8 is **Filo Tiatia**. We're good friends and have been through so much together — and that gets him in ahead of Rodney So'oialo. Filo's very much a family man and our wives are best friends so we spend a lot of time with them. Having been involved in some of his best games, I know what he could do. He's such a big man, an intimidator, and scored tries that I don't think other players could have scored. The constant theme of his career was injury. It used to make me laugh when I'd hear about him getting injured overseas. I'd ring him up to tell him that he had to realise he was getting old and didn't have to go as hard at training as he did in a game. But he only had one setting: full steam ahead. I liked to train but I didn't go out there to get hurt. It must have been a Wests Roosters thing because Alama Ieremia was exactly the same and he was always getting injured too. Filo was another player I could trust to do what was required if I asked him. He's a fiercely loyal person and a great team man who looks after his team-mates so wherever he goes he's loved by his team. I thought he should have played a lot more for the All Blacks. He mightn't have been everyone's cup of tea but he was big and strong and abrasive, although in the end I guess you come back to that injury curse.

The openside flanker has to be **Richie McCaw**. What can you say about him that hasn't already been said? You don't get anything but 100 per cent from this guy. I saw the leadership capabilities very early on. On our way home from his first tour a couple of guys were playing up on the plane; he came to me and said, 'Tana, do you think these guys should just sit down and be quiet because they're getting a bit rowdy?' I looked at him and thought, geez. By the time we got there they were asleep but it showed the quality of the guy and the fact that even on his first tour he knew what was required of All Blacks. On my first tour I wouldn't say anything to anybody. That's what you'll get from Richie: he'll do what's best for the team; there's no ego-stroking or hand-wringing at the thought of upsetting people. I operated the same way.

When Richie became All Black captain there was talk that he encountered some resistance from the Wellington players because as far as they were concerned he was stepping into shoes that didn't belong to him. It was really a non-issue. This sort of thing is always to be expected when there is a new captain appointed. A lot of the talk was to do with how the Wellington players saw me: I was very fortunate to have respect from the players based on how I'd played and how much I'd helped them, but also on the Samoan culture of respecting your elders. It was an age thing: Richie's their age and some of them had been through the grades with him, whereas I was nearly 10 years older and had been around them in a leadership capacity for a long time.

Taine Randell was younger than some of the players he captained and there was a lot of talk about what happened there. Sometimes it must be hard to captain players who are your age or older; you have to have a strong will. But respect is earned on the field so Richie has that aspect nailed down — he's already a great player — and it all settled down very quickly. Everyone's right in behind him now.

At six I'd never pick anyone but **Jerry Collins** — a good soldier, tough and loyal, who's looked after me a lot on and off the field. He wouldn't want people to know this, but he's also very intelligent. He likes people to think that he's a tough guy from Porirua because out there you get more respect for being tough than being intelligent. He's got a distinctive turn of phrase and was always coming up to me to ask if I'd heard his latest quotable quote. Sometimes I just thought, where the hell did you get that from?

People tend to be a bit wary of Jerry because he's a loner and very gruff and doesn't take much rubbish: he'll tell you how it is and sometimes he'll tell you in two words where to go and what to do. I could give him a hard time about anything and he'd just bite his lip, out of respect and because we're related. He had that, 'You're older than me and you're my cousin, otherwise . . .' kind of thing but I'd just say, 'Whatever.' When I retired from the All Blacks, there was some concern about who was going to handle him. I used to get a lot of 'Tana, can you talk to Jerry?' but sometimes you just think, well, mate, if he's not listening, do something about it. He's like everyone else: sometimes he needs to learn. I'm close to the guy but I wasn't his babysitter and I didn't want to have him saying to me, 'You know, you're starting to sound like the coaches,' or 'You're starting to sound like my mother,' although that wasn't so bad because she's really the only one he listens to. On the other hand, I was prepared to do what was best for the team which sometimes meant telling him that maybe he needed to slow down on this or pull his head in about that.

Jerry's a good man who looks after his family, but he is who he is. People want to change him, tell him what he should be, put him into their little mould, but he just says, 'I don't want to be like that, I want to be who I am.' You've got to respect that.

One of my locks would be **Craig Simms** who was the Petone captain when I joined the club. Everyone there was very good to me but for the captain to welcome me with open arms made it so much better. In one game we weren't playing well so he got us all together and said if things didn't improve he was going to smack someone; he didn't care if it was them or us. Things got a lot better after that. He was tough, he was a toiler, he was always there in the rucks, and won his lineout ball. He was a bit of a string bean which was perhaps the reason he didn't go further, but he had a very big heart.

Robin Brooke, Ali Williams, Chris Jack, Norm Maxwell and **Keith Robinson** can fight it out for the other locking spot. Robin Brooke was one of the few older guys to whom I could really relate when I first made the All Blacks. Unlike the other senior players, he'd always go out for a drink with the young guys. You wouldn't find a more skilful lock but he was also tough and quite uncompromising in the way he played.

Jacko's the prototype of the modern lock: he can kick, catch the ball with one hand, run with the ball, and use it skilfully. He did some great things in the All Black jersey when I was playing. Ditto Ali Williams, another very skilful player: when he's focused on his job, he's brilliant. He's also quite a lot tougher than I first thought he was, if not quite as tough as he thought he was. He was always happy to tell you what he could do, which would make me laugh. We're good friends; I gave him a hard time and he liked giving me a hard time in return.

Norm Maxwell was a great team man who always put his body on the line despite not having the most robust of physiques, while Keith Robinson's as tough as they come. I've never seen a lock stand out as much as Robbo did in the series again England in 2004: he was out wide running with the ball, he was cleaning out, he was winning lineout ball, he was in their faces the whole time, and he didn't mind it one bit. In those two games he showed what kind of player he is: the uncompromising hard man, the grafter who does all the little things that need to be done, but can get around the track because he's so fit. He's going to be an important part of the All Blacks. Before we met the Queen on the 2002 tour, we were instructed on matters of protocol and specifically told to greet her by saying, 'Hello, Ma'am.' Robbo said, 'How're you going?' and started talking about dogs. I was thinking, Oh, my gosh, but I shouldn't have expected any different. That's who he is and he doesn't sway from that no matter who you are.

To be honest I don't really know what props do in there, so I'll go with guys I know, and I've known **Neemia Tialata** since he was a little kid. I know where he's come from and what he's done to get where he is. This year I've seen a maturity in him; you couldn't get boo from him for the first few years but now he's leading the talk on the scrums. I really enjoy watching someone I knew when he was a cheeky little bugger develop and flourish and make his mark. He can play both sides of the scrum and clearly has the potential to fill the void left by Carl Hayman who has played outstandingly on the tighthead side in recent years.

My tighthead, though, is another cousin, **Olo Brown.** Other players were always telling stories about Olo's strength at scrum-time. The call would be, 'Drop it an inch, Olo; drop it two inches.' He had the strength to lower the scrum at will thereby putting pressure on the opposition loosehead prop who would want to keep it up and dominate. His strength was just legendary. Being my cousin and a bit older, he kept a watchful eye on me and made sure I wasn't stuffing up. His family have been great supporters of mine.

I've watched Tony Woodcock develop into the premier loosehead. He's a very solid man, one of the most solid I've bumped into. When I was holding bags at training and the young guys were coming through, I used to give them an extra shove as they hit the bag. When I tried to do that to Woody, I hurt myself. He doesn't look that hard but he's like granite. It's that farming pedigree.

Carl Hoeft was a good scrummager — or so I was told — and a good team man. He had this dog called 'Killer' so I assumed it must be a pit bull or a rottweiler or something big and mean. It turned out to be a dainty, yappy little thing, a chihuahua or something. I started laughing and he just looked at me and said, 'Don't you laugh at my dog.' I thought he was joking but he was deadly serious. I had to say sorry. Everyone used to give him a hard time: he'd tell these jokes which amused him no end, but no-one else found them funny.

At hooker I'd go with **Anton Oliver**, another uncompromising player who's done the yards and at his best is a great scrummaging hooker. Besides, with so many Island boys in there, we need some white guys to do the work. I admire his knowledge and ability to keep calm in tough situations. He's also a good friend who's taught me a lot. The transformation of Keven Mealamu from the quiet boy of 2002 who was all about running with the ball to the multi-dimensional player and leader he is now is amazing. I doubt there's anyone, anywhere with a bad word to say about Keven. And if there is, it's only because they're jealous.

I had great respect for Sean Fitzpatrick, particularly for his ability to control the team and control a game. Everyone else would get flustered — the opposition and the referee — but not him. I loved his little digs and the way he'd wait for a reaction; you knew you were watching a real operator at work. He could manipulate players; guys would complain about how much he talked but it was just a part of the game that he was so much better at than they were. In a Wellington-Auckland game I got pulled into a ruck by my hair. I jumped up ready to swing at someone but saw it was Fitzy. Someone was yelling at me, 'Smack him, smack him,' but I just thought, it's Sean Fitzpatrick. Obviously I did nothing; I suppose I was overawed. He was a good man off the field but best of all he didn't ask me to put money into any of his schemes.

In this day and age you don't have much interaction with opposition players which is disappointing. As soon as you finish a game, you start preparing for the next one by having ice baths or doing other forms of recovery to get yourself in shape to train properly on Monday. That really cuts into the after-match window and the opportunity to meet the opposition. Former All Blacks from the 1960s and 70s like Andy Leslie and Brian Lochore have always got an old opponent from Wales or wherever coming over to stay with them and when they're in Europe they're always catching up with guys they played against. All Blacks just don't get to spend much time with opponents, especially the northern hemisphere teams. You might bump into them at the pub later that night but it's not as if you're striking up friendships.

I get on well with George Gregan and always catch up with him after a game. After we played the Brumbies this year we went out for a beer and a chat about what was going on in our lives and he was saying how impressed one of his young team-mates was when he heard I was coming in to pick George up. Sadly, I don't think the majority of players coming into the game now have the personal skills to socialise with and get to know their opponents. They don't want to get out of their little groups and their comfort zones and it's not really encouraged because the focus immediately switches to the next game. George is a very knowledgeable and worldly character and one of the nicest guys I've come across in rugby. New Zealanders tend to have a jaundiced view of him, seeing him as a yapper and a nuisance, but he's just a fierce competitor out there.

I got on well with the Irish boys — the likes of Geordan Murphy and Ronan O'Gara. Gareth Thomas is a colossus on the field but off it he's a nice guy who enjoys a laugh and a beer. John Smit's a top bloke. The way he talks, you'd swear butter wouldn't melt in his mouth, but that's why he's a good captain — he keeps the referees under control. When I started out I had a lot of time for the likes of Ben Tune and Chris Whitaker and always had a chat with them. My two toughest opponents were Stirling Mortlock and Daniel Herbert — big, strong men and such hard runners. It's all comes from respect: you talk to them because you respect them and you respect them because they always came at you hard. At Toulon I got to know Dan Luger and Rob Henderson who's a bit of a larrikin and a real laugh. But George is the one I keep in contact with; we're always calling or texting to see what the other is up to.

I don't have any enemies but whether that cuts both ways I'm not sure. I imagine I've said and done things on the field that opponents have taken a while to get over. I once marked a debutant who only lasted 15 minutes. 'Is that it?' I said. 'You're a disgrace.' But he came back and had the better of me in a later game so I probably provided him with motivation. Most of my on-field clashes were with forwards who roughed me up and I reacted by getting in their faces. I didn't go hunting, following them around hoping for a chance to kick them or anything like that; I just wanted us to give them a hiding so I could rub it in. I once got rucked in the face — I'm sure it was on purpose — but then we scored three quick tries and I gave it to the guy as he was trudging back to the posts: 'Yeah, you fat bastard, get back under there.' I'm not averse to giving a bit of lip and I have a long memory: if people wronged me, I tried to get them back, allhough not physically because I wasn't going to beat forwards up. Anyway, having me laughing at them and telling them they're hopeless as they go back to their changing-room after a loss hurt a lot more than a half-arsed punch or a sneaky little stomp.

What sledging there is comes mainly from the older guys. As a young player you're just trying to concentrate on the game but as you get older you're more inclined to make the odd comment when the opposition makes a mistake, just to remind them that it didn't go unnoticed: 'That's your second time, don't do it again.' But when the game's finished, that's it; what happens on the field, stays on the field. You deal with it there and if it's not dealt with, tough — them's the breaks. You win some and you lose some. If anything, you don't blame the player who did it, you blame the referee for not picking it up.

That's very much the New Zealand attitude. I was perplexed by the carry-on over the Brian O'Driscoll incident because I was thinking, geez man, this is what happens in this game so what's all the fuss about? Get over it. But I try to look for the good in others and from what we heard, he was being manipulated by people with a wider agenda. We responded in the best possible way by smashing them in the next game and sending them home with their tails between their legs. Our relationship now is what it is but I don't hold a grudge and if I saw him tomorrow I'd say hello.

Brian was placed at my table at the post-test dinner in Auckland but didn't turn up. They said he was sick but whether he really was crook or just couldn't be bothered or didn't want to sit next to me, who knows? His partner turned up but didn't stay for long. Prince William came over and said hello which made my wife very happy. Jonny Wilkinson, a total gentleman, come over and we wished each other the best. I had a yarn with Will Greenwood who retired after that tour. I see he's popped up in the commentary box as most retirees do. The Irish wings Shane Horgan and Dennis Hickie were at our table and made no bones about the fact that they were off to Sydney to get on the piss which seemed worth mentioning in my speech.

When they decided to play the tsunami game in 2005, George Gregan and Rod Macqueen rang me to get my support. It was a matter of giving the exercise enough credibility to encourage good players to participate. The game was a way for rugby to make a contribution to a good cause so I was all for it. Linking up with Rod and George also had a lot of appeal: I'd read Rod's book and knew what he'd done with the Wallabies and I was keen to play with Georgie, having played against him so often. Phil Waugh and Chris Latham were the other Aussies and John Smit, Schalk Burger and Victor Matfield were the South African contingent. Some of the European clubs wouldn't release their best players, which was disappointing, but they assembled a more than useful team.

We certainly weren't short of captains: we had the captains of South Africa, Australia, New Zealand, Samoa and Fiji. We were also meant to have the Tongan captain but Inoke Afeaki couldn't make it. Ian Jones helped Rod with the coaching and Morne du Plessis, the former Springbok captain and a good man, was our manager.

When you play against Matfield you're always trying to devise plans to counter his lineout prowess. Rod and John Smit had had some advance discussions on lineout calls and when the forwards had their first meeting John wrote the calls up on a board. The code involved matching numbers and letters and left most of the guys completely confused. Semo Sititi told me afterwards that just as he was coming to the conclusion that we'd never get the ball, Victor came in. He took one look at the blackboard and said, 'John, if I run here, chuck it to me; if I run over there, chuck it to me.' And that was what happened; those were our lineout tactics. George and I agreed it was good to play with him for a change because he's such a bloody nuisance to play against. He's a good guy, too.

The game itself was something of an anti-climax for me because I tweaked my quad in the warm-up and the first time I tried to take off something went and that was that. Brian Lima had been in Samoa training for sevens so no-one had seen him for a while, but he was outstanding — the 'Chiropractor' of old.

It was great to play alongside guys I'd played against so often and it made me realise that all rugby-playing countries have a pretty similar rugby culture: everyone trains hard and enjoys a beer and a good time. You could understand why Rod Macqueen was so successful: he got on really well with the players and pretty much left us to our own devices, which is a good skill for a coach to have. It was a really enjoyable and very social week. Andrew Mehrtens decided that we should have an annual reunion and volunteered to organise it but we're still waiting for the phone call.

← PLAYBACK

JERRY COLLINS

Tana and I are related on my mother's side. His mother and mine come from the same village on Savai'i. They're cousins — cousins of cousins. Everyone in Samoa is related.

I grew up in Porirua East and he's from Wainui. I suppose the problems are the same and the perceptions are the same. Geographically they're different but the principles in terms of the social climate are the same. Most of it's working class. We didn't see much of each other before we started playing together — Tana's eight years older than me so when he was starting out, I was still in intermediate school. I saw enough of him on TV playing for Wainuiomata and Wellington. But once you jump on the rugby bandwagon, the only way to catch up is to join in.

When I first played with him I wasn't in awe of him. I'd seen him play on TV and saw that he was a proud person, but the last thing you want to do is play with someone who doesn't think they're good enough to play with you. I could never play centre, but I could damn well do what I was doing to the best of my ability and try to get the best out of myself. If some young players were in awe of him that was instead of having the attitude of, what do I have to offer him? what can I bring to the table for everybody to see? they were making sure they were always one step behind him.

Respect runs both ways. I'm not there to waste anyone's time; I didn't look to Tana to salvage anything for us and I wasn't looking for his praise. As a player, when you're standing in a room with a guy like Tana, you've got to bring your game to match his, or better it, because you're playing under him, and the last thing you want to do is disappoint not only him, but the other fellas by not bringing what you have. I never looked to him for reassurance because, I suppose, you'd be thinking that the guys playing under him should have just as much self-belief as he does. Playing for Wellington, there weren't many guys like that; over the years we were lucky to have three or four guys in our team who really, truly believed that they couldn't lose.

I'm not really into carrying on other people's legacies. One of the greatest honours in my rugby career is to have played under him, but most important is to have played alongside him. There's no way in hell that any of us could carry on that kind of legacy. I suppose once the fanfare's died down and we get over it, probably a good six or seven years down the track, you'll get some other bloke forging a legacy. Before Tana, there's a good 10- or 15-year gap to guys like Murray Mexted and that era. The late 1990s and the early 2000s would probably be Tana's era. The next era will come in the next 15 years.

As captain, Tana spoke to me the same way he would normally. If there was something wrong out on the field with the All Black forwards, he kind of waltzed over and swore at me like normal. It never changed and I never took it personally. Some guys can talk to me like that; not everybody. If the captain of the Wellington team came over and said, 'Jerry, what the f**k's going on? Sort the forwards out,' in that tone of voice, I'd turn around and say, 'What did you say?' He never changed: on the field, even when the pressure was on, he spoke to me the same way as he would in a normal sense.

When you become captain of the All Blacks, it's natural to go to people you're used to going to and talking that way. Playing for the All Blacks once, one of the guys said to me, 'Don't you get upset when he talks to you like that and shouts at you like that?' I said, 'No, he's been doing that my whole career, it's something I'm used to.' It shows you're a good player if there are eight guys he could say that to and he chooses you to sort out the problem.

He's had his fair share of ups and downs, the stuff that happens to normal people, your family issues and your off-field issues and stuff like that. Every real person can relate to that. I suppose if you try to better yourself as a person, you end up playing better rugby and your team benefits from that. You never felt sorry for him or kind of sad because he left: if someone wants to say that's enough, then good on them. A lot of people in New Zealand forget that there's more to life than playing rugby.

I think that when you're playing rugby probably one of the greatest things is the need to be yourself. You can take all the good things in yourself and use them and make sure you use them at the right time. Sometimes you get it wrong and use them at the wrong time, but 90 per cent of the time you get it right.

You play against guys and you play with guys and if you take away the skill factor and the ability factor, you see it in the eyes. Tana's got it; he's one of those guys who doesn't flinch even if the team's down by 60 points and I suppose that's the kind of player you very rarely get to play with. You're probably lucky to play with two or three players like that in your career.

This Sporting Life

Everything changed when rugby went professional. Probably the single biggest change was actually being paid to train. Guys who were used to filling in training around their jobs and sometimes even having to make financial sacrifices to play the game suddenly found themselves getting paid to do what they loved doing.

The second biggest change was in meeting the demands of sponsors and the media. Some of us struggled with the media duties — having to talk about the team's performance, your own performance, and what you made of the opposition. We had to learn on the job and I'm sure there were a lot of mistakes, for instance with regard to what you should and shouldn't say to avoid giving the opposition information or motivation. I learnt how to play the media game, which basically means not being too honest. Sometimes you really just want to tell it like it is but you've got to remember that it won't necessarily come out in the media exactly as you said it. I got quite good at talking in circles. Sometimes I'd confuse myself and wonder if I'd made any sense and I'm sure the media picked that up. At other times I chose my moments to speak my mind. I was more brutally honest about our performances than the opposition's because I knew I could control the repercussions.

As I've already touched on, I've had my battles with the media, especially TV3. Having had to relent on TV3 when I became All Black captain, I blacklisted them again in early 2006 just after I'd retired from international rugby. The first Super 14 game was the Hurricanes against the Blues, a repeat of the first-ever Super 12 game back in 1996. I wasn't doing any interviews about stepping down from the All Blacks: as far as I was concerned, I'd made the announcement, I'd done the press conference, it was done and dusted and time to move on. That's the way I am: once something's over and done with, I'm not interested in dwelling on it. Now I was just a member of the Hurricanes and it wasn't about me, it was about the team.

Our media guy told me that John Campbell wanted to do a piece harking back to that first Super 12 game which took place in Palmerston North. I played in that game and Jason Eaton, who was still at school, was a spectator so that was the hook; the focus wasn't really going to be on me as much as the game and Jason. I didn't really want to do it but it was such a good idea that I agreed. When the time came, Campbell came over to thank me; he said he really understood where I was coming from because, 'I know what it's like to be papped' — as in pursued and photographed by the paparazzi. I didn't say much — 'Okay, yeah, nice' — as he went on to assure me that it was mainly about Jason and what happened in 1996 and just one part of a bigger story involving similar pieces from up and down the country.

A week or so later I was watching television at home when TV3 ran a promo for an exclusive interview with Tana Umaga. In fact, it wasn't anything of the sort, so anyone who tuned in expecting an in-depth interview would have been disappointed. I was angry, though, because it was quite contrary to the detail and spirit of what had been presented to me and their assurances that they understood my misgivings. I got my agent to ring TV3 to convey my disappointment but they didn't seem to care. It was like, 'Oh well, that's just the way it is.' To me that meant we were back to square one. At first, TV3 indicated that they'd like to repair the breach but I wasn't interested and I don't suppose they were too bothered about it given that I was on the way out.

The other outfit I've blacklisted is *Sunday News*. This goes back to the infamous stripper incident at Norm Hewitt's house in 1999. As Christian Cullen said in his book, I wasn't there when whatever happened happened; I'd been there earlier but left about 10 pm. When the story broke, *Sunday News* claimed I'd been interviewed by the police and the New Zealand Rugby Union. I was never interviewed by the police; that was just plain wrong. When some NZRU guys came to our training base, I was called into a meeting, but Christian told them there was no reason for me to be involved because

I wasn't even there and didn't know anything about it. That was the extent of the 'interview'. Apparently *Sunday News* is still rehashing that incident, even though the sports editor, John Matheson, wrote Cully's book.

Some people in the media have no sense of responsibility or accountability: they plaster something all over the front page and if they get it wrong, they bury a three-line apology on page 32.

Other papers have been in my bad books for various reasons but in those cases it's been faced up to, dealt with, and things have got back to normal. I understand the media's role and requirements; I acknowledge that if you've had a bad game, you can expect to be blasted. I don't believe you shouldn't talk to a journalist just because he gave you a bit of a lashing over your performance — if you played badly, that's what's going to happen. Sometimes, though, they get the facts wrong but refuse to acknowledge their mistake or provide redress.

I've heard coaches and media liaison people talk about controlling the media, but they can't do it. They try but they never succeed. It makes me laugh: they say let's have a meeting with the media, as if having a cup of tea and a cosy little chat with them today is going to influence what they write about us next week. They don't care; in the end they'll write what they want, secure in the knowledge that they'll always have the last word. Everyone I've heard talk about controlling the media or improving relations with them has ended up getting angry with them. I don't know how you fix it. The players often say, 'Let's just cut them, let's do no media,' but apparently you can't do that.

In the end they're just chasing the story and trying to get it before anyone else does. That's their job, just as our job is to play rugby. Some of them are good, some stick to the facts, and some know what they're talking about; they can see what teams are trying to achieve and take that into account. Others can probably see that, too, but they know that controversy sells. Again, I don't know what you do about that. Sometimes it's just the people: in Wellington we've had good reporters who keep it on a rugby level but there are those whom you can never please and a few whose reporting is often just a thinly-veiled personal attack.

Even now I'm uncomfortable with the so-called 'networking with sponsors'. I'm not one for small talk; I'll exchange pleasantries and nod a lot, then as soon as I can I'll do the, 'I've got to go over there now.' If you ever go to one of these functions you'll find a group of rugby players who are meant to be mingling huddled in a corner talking to each other. The Pacific Island boys in particular tend to congregate in corners. For a lot of rugby players mingling with strangers and taking an interest in someone else's day just doesn't come naturally; it's an element of professional rugby that was and still is really hard for them to come to grips with. They'd much rather be out there doing what they do best.

Some players — Byron Kelleher is a prime example — are good at it but most struggle when they're ushered into a room full of strangers and pretty much left to their own devices. Over the years different people have supplied us with stock lines and conversational gambits to break the ice. I don't know if anyone else ever used them but I certainly didn't. Apart from the fact that they were invariably corny, it was just delaying the inevitable: sooner or later you had to speak for yourself.

On the 2002 end-of-year tour I found myself at loggerheads with the NZRU for the first, but certainly not the last, time. After a European tour we usually did a promotional exercise for adidas. In 2000, the whole team went to the adidas factory in Nuremburg to have a look around and meet the people who make the boots. I had to stay on the following year and in 2002 they asked me to stay on again. I suggested they get someone else; I'd done it two tours in a row and this time I really wanted to get home to my family. During the last week in Wales I told the coaches I didn't want to do it; they weren't bothered and the manager Tony Thorpe indicated that the team management would back my stance. Then the pressure came on from the NZRU: obviously adidas had specified which players they wanted. I was annoyed that it had been left so late and there was a week of phone-tag involving me, my agent and Tony. NZRU deputy CEO Steve Tew turned up and told me I had to stay; I replied that it was my turn not to stay and I was going home. They back-tracked and asked me to stay on just for one day: they'd do my shoot on the Monday morning after the last test and I could fly out on Monday afternoon. On the advice of my agent I agreed to that.

After that I always seemed to be battling with the NZRU. Their commercial guys were always telling me I had to do this and they needed me for that; their attitude seemed to be: just do it. They never seemed to think it through and recognise that there were other factors to be taken into consideration. Perhaps because the marketing guys weren't rugby people, they seemed to find it hard to get their heads around the fact that we were rugby players, not actors. They expected us to know our lines and do things that didn't come naturally to us and which most of us weren't comfortable doing.

Me becoming All Black captain was the NZRU marketing team's worst nightmare. Sometimes I'd say, 'No, the team doesn't want to do that.' Or, 'No, I don't think that's a good idea.' Or just plain, 'No.' Eventually we brought someone into the process who could give the marketing people the players' perspective and advise them on what the individual players would and wouldn't be comfortable with. To take an obvious example: some players didn't mind taking their shirts off for the camera but others did and for some reason they tended to go for the ones who didn't. It was the same with having to speak lines in ads: some players simply weren't comfortable doing it. It was really just a matter of approaching things collaboratively, instead of them presenting us with a fait accompli and saying, 'Just do it.' We wanted them to understand that some of the things they were insisting on didn't feel right to us. We wanted it to be as natural as possible so we came across as being ourselves; we didn't want to be portrayed as something we weren't or made to look stupid. You don't get to be an All Black without having a certain amount of ego and a lot of pride, so it stands to reason that you're not going to welcome a scenario that demeans you or damages your reputation as an individual or as an All Black.

The other thing about the marketing and promotion world is that nothing ever happens on time. We'd be told we had to be somewhere at 8 am but then wouldn't actually do anything until noon. The 2004 All Blacks poster which showed us on a beach in the haka stance is a case in point. We waited around for two hours; the tide was coming in and the photographer was saying, 'Guys, we're just waiting for the sun,' because he wanted a sunset look. I could hear the guys behind me grumbling, grumbling, grumbling so I said to the photographer, 'Mate, you've got five minutes. That's it, then we're off.' He looked at me and I could tell he was thinking that's not the way it works, pal; I've got you till I've finished with you. They always seemed to want to drag things out but we'd trained earlier that day and the guys were tired and hungry so I really put the pressure on.

After that we got some photographers who understood that dragging things out didn't necessarily ensure a better outcome so they needed to make sure that they were on the job right from the start. We pressed the NZRU's marketing team to put heat on the people making the TV ads and posters to get their timing down pat so that when we got there, they'd be ready to go. The less time spent mucking around, the less whinging. When you make guys who don't like doing it in the first place twiddle their thumbs for a few hours, what do you think is going to happen when you tell them, 'Okay, now let's have a nice big smile'? There'll be no smile, just, 'Hurry up, we want to get out of here.' We understood our role in marketing the game but they had to understand that it wasn't natural for us or something we'd do out of choice.

We just wanted people to be organised. We're expected to be organised: players get dropped or disciplined if they're not in the right place at the right time, so aren't we entitled to expect the same degree of professionalism that's demanded of us? Having said that, I did come to appreciate how much work goes into a 30-second or even a 15-second commercial and it gave me a new respect for the people who work on them. There are an unbelievable number of people working behind the scenes. I met some good people making these ads, which was just as well given how bloody long they take. We did a lot of stuff around the Lions series and by then they were starting to get it right, but to be honest I think the NZRU marketing department was happy to see the back of me.

After the 2004 end-of-year tour we had to stay on to do the 'last man standing' advertisement for the upcoming Lions series. The concept was a game of bull-rush involving All Blacks and British and Irish players. The guys making the clip wanted it to look real so they were pressing us to put in some big hits. My man was Gareth Cooper, the Welsh half back: I was letting him go past me and tackling him from the side, but the director wanted me to smash him. He asked for a real big collision and I had to tell him there was no way we were going to do that. I didn't want to hurt the guy or look as if I was trying to waste him and he wasn't going to want people sitting in front of their TVs all over Britain laughing at an ad showing him being cleaned up by an All Black. As I said, we're proud people. All Black against All Black is another matter: we can handle that; we can waste each other and have a laugh about it. Ditto Lion against Lion. That was the strong feeling I'd picked up from both groups of players. The director wasn't happy about it but he wasn't going to get what he wanted so he had to listen to our suggestions. In the end, they settled for Richie McCaw flattening Byron Kelleher. On the first take Byron stepped Richie and went past him, but they didn't use that.

As a professional rugby player you often hear, 'You're getting paid a fortune so what's the problem?' It's like any other job: you have your good days and your bad days and the odd day when you really don't want to be at work, but with the added pressure of public expectation. Everyone expects the All Blacks to win and it seems that since we started getting paid, that expectation has ratcheted up a few notches. In my last couple of years we worked hard to alleviate that pressure of expectation, to try to take the public out of it. We understood what they wanted from us but we also knew we couldn't please all of the people all of the time — I learnt that a long time ago. I tried to do my best but I wasn't going to beat myself up if I failed to please everyone because you can never do that. We figured that if we could put pressure on ourselves to perform on and off the field as a team and as individuals then we wouldn't feel the public pressure as much.

When I hear people criticise the behaviour of young rugby players I sometimes feel that we're being held to a higher standard than the rest of society. If I ask why a 19-year-old rugby player shouldn't behave the way other 19-year-olds do, I'm often told that he should know better. Why? Because he's making some money? Because he's a role model? He's still 19; he's still going to make mistakes. In my view, anyone who thinks a 19-year-old rugby player should be a role model in anything but the most superficial sense has got a strange outlook on life.

I accept that rugby players do become role models, as was the case with me. But people need to understand that there's a difference between a role model and a saint. I'm not perfect; I'm going to make mistakes. Most young men and women make mistakes, but that doesn't make them bad people. After that incident in Christchurch, the coaches told me that I'd make mistakes and do silly things but in the end I was still a good person. I believe I'm a good person and a good parent and a role model to my kids first and foremost.

I've struggled with the role model thing because sometimes I just don't want to be one. I ask myself, who am I to tell younger players that they shouldn't drink when I drink and have done silly things as a result. When I was young I was a bit of a rat-bag and got into trouble, but as I grew up I learnt from those mistakes. I went from feeling sorry for the people I hurt and paying for the wrongs I did to knowing what was right and what was wrong. But it's a long process — perhaps a lifelong process — and I still make mistakes because I'm still finding out about myself and trying to be the person I want to be, not the person other people want me to be. I've always fought for the right to be myself, to be an individual, to be independent; I've always resisted being pigeon-holed. I understand there's a balance between what I want to do and what I need to do, but that can still involve an internal struggle.

You can't live up to other people's expectations all the time because sometimes they're completely unreasonable. One week you're great, you've won the game; next week you're useless. I can't accept the mind-set that you're a good guy when you're winning and a bad guy when you're not and it all revolves around results. I'm either a good guy or I'm not.

Within the All Blacks we came to understand that you've got to be true to yourself. Gilbert Enoka was big on that and it became a real positive. We have these expectations, these outside influences, pointing us in a certain direction and trying to tell us who we've got to be, but you've got to be yourself. I took that on board to the point where I'd speak up if I thought something wasn't right for us or right for me. The realisation that I didn't have to keep fighting with myself helped transform me into the person I wanted to be and made me a better person. I try to remain that person and keep my feet on the ground. My wife and sisters monitor that closely.

At the leadership meetings everyone said I was one of the few players who could tell it like it is and get away with it. I could tell a player, 'You stuffed up' and they'd take it. I've been like that at every level I've played. Every team has its rules. They might call them values or something else but they're the rules and the better the team, the fewer the rules. You don't want grey areas; you want things to be black and white so you're never in two minds over whether you're breaking a rule or not. When I was captain I had to deal with players who'd broken rules and I didn't hold back: 'Why did you do that? Who do you think you are? You were there when we signed off on these rules.' Now and again I wondered where I got off barking at guys, but I had the support of the other leaders who told me it was the right thing to do and I was the right person to do it.

Sometimes you just need to get the word out. Players can't keep their mouths shut and they're quick to tell their team-mates when they've had a rocket. That sets the precedent, which is what you want. If rules are broken, something has to be done about it otherwise the players will very quickly draw the conclusion that the rules aren't for real and they can do the same thing without paying a price. Every so often they need a reality check: uh-oh, we're back in front of that guy again; he won't let us get away with it. When I was captain, that guy was mostly me and after I stepped down players seemed to delight in reminding me of the times I told them off. I'd always say I couldn't remember and they'd go, 'This is what you said, word for word.' I'd shake my head and say, 'Geez, that was a bit harsh.' They knew I was finishing and didn't want to miss the opportunity to remind me how I'd come down on them. But that's how I was: deal with it, bang, it's done. Besides, better me yelling at them than having the coach tell them they're this or they're that or they're out.

The tricky part is accommodating individuality and different personalities within the team environment. As we all know, there's no 'i' in team, but it's not that simple in real life. For me, once again, the litmus test is performance: if you're doing the job on Saturday, then it doesn't really matter what you get up to during the week, as long as it isn't outrageous and you're not overdoing it. Some people want to know what everyone's doing and are very quick to make judgements, but you have to be able to accommodate a degree of difference. On the other hand, if an individual gets into the habit of having big nights out during the week and his performance levels drop off to the detriment of the team, he can't complain if his coaches and team-mates make a connection between the two and put it on him to change his ways.

Players aren't all the same. It's like pre-game routines: some players don't talk, some don't like being talked to, some can't shut up, and some bang their heads against a wall. Andrew Mehrtens joked around whereas the likes of Ian Jones were very solemn. I liked having a bit of a joke. If you're too tense and hyped up, you go out there and rush around at 100 miles an hour making mistakes and achieving nothing; you try to do it all instead of just doing your job to the best of your ability. You need to be relaxed and focused on your role, so it's a matter of doing whatever gets you into that state.

Players need to be able to relax because you can't be wired up all the time. You'll get fatigued and run down, which leads to inconsistency. You have to acquire the ability to switch off so that when work's finished you go and do something else. Obviously it's easier to do that if you have real interests outside rugby. In my case, that's my family, and when I was with them I wouldn't give rugby a thought. Legendary Brisbane Broncos coach Wayne Bennett is a strong believer that players should have something outside the game that's more than a hobby, for instance some kind of training or study or even a part-time job, so that rugby's not the be-all and end-all. People for whom rugby is the be-all and end-all tend to come to regard training as a bit of a chore, and when something becomes a chore you switch to auto-pilot and look to cut corners.

I like having my own space and being a bit anonymous so I've never enjoyed being seen as public property. Some people do but I'm definitely not one of them. I understand that a certain amount of intrusion goes with the territory but I don't have to like it. I'm not sure the general public understands just how tough living in the fish bowl is for high-profile players and their families. You go out for a meal with your wife or family and parents are sending their kids over to get an autograph. I don't like parents pushing their kids on me; a lot of the time you can see the kids are shy and really don't want to be doing it and it doesn't make me feel great when someone hands me their baby who promptly starts crying. It's a running joke among rugby players that they always apologise: 'Sorry to bother you but . . .' You think, well if you're really sorry, you probably shouldn't be over here. I'm used to it but my family isn't. My wife gets understandably frustrated if people intrude when we're trying to have some time to ourselves. Generally people just yell at you and say hello so you say hello back and keep walking. That's fine: it takes one second out of your day.

My son Cade won't walk beside me, which I find tough; he walks behind me or in front of me. He's been there throughout my whole career so my absences have been particularly tough on him. One of the reasons I gave up international rugby was my desire to spend more time with him. He's a teenager now and I want to watch him play football and do other things and be involved in his life as he grows up. There's no substitute for time spent with your kids and you tend to rue what you've missed rather than look forward to what you'll have.

He and I were down at the park with my Canadian brother-in-law and his kids. The boys were having kicks at goal and my brother-in-law was telling Cade how to do it. Now my brother-in-law's a great guy and a sportsman but he's never played rugby and I could see that he wasn't teaching Cade properly so I went over to show him the right way to do it. He just looked and me and said, 'That's not what Uncle said.' I thought, geez I know a little bit about this game. It was a combination of me being away a lot and him not wanting to be pigeon-holed as my son. He's very independent and wants to make his own way in life, which I respect and approve of, but something like that gives you a jolt: you know you can help and you want to help but he doesn't want your help. It cut deep and it wasn't long after that that I decided to give it away. He's older now and wants to do his own thing, which is fine, but I'm there to support him and do what I can. Maybe one day he'll want to listen to what I say.

It's good that people feel they can approach All Blacks and we've worked hard to be seen as approachable. Rather than putting ourselves on a pedestal, All Blacks want to be seen as coming from the people and belonging to them.

January 2006: flanked by the All Black coaches, from left Wayne Smith, Graham Henry, and Steve Hansen, Tana ends months of speculation by announcing his retirement from international rugby.

The bitter taste of defeat: Jerry Collins, Tana, and Joe McDonnell show their disappointment after the Hurricanes' loss to the Crusaders in the fog-wreathed final of the 2006 Super 14.

Just a face in the crowd: Tana and Cade watch the All Blacks do battle with France in Paris in 2006.

Here come the men in black: Tana leaves the stage after being presented with a leadership award by Richie McCaw at the 2007 Halberg Awards.

Bonjour, je m'appelle Tana: making his presence felt for his French club Toulon.

We're with him: Toulon's drawcard overlooks the crowd at the club's 22–16 home victory over Lyon in October 2006.

Tana is chaired off Westpac Stadium by John Schwalger (left) and Ma'a Nonu after his final appearance for the Hurricanes in May 2007.

The ties that bind: Wainuiomata boys Piri Weepu (left), Tana and Neemia Tialata signal that home is where the heart is.

The long goodbye: bidding farewell to the Hurricanes faithful after his last Super 14 match.

Playing his 100th and last game for his beloved Wellington, against Manawatu at the Westpac Stadium, 11 August 2007.

The family man with Rochelle, son Cade, and daughters Anise (on Rochelle's knee), Lily-Kate (on Tana's back) and Gabrielle.

I'd never want anyone to find the All Blacks unapproachable, but there's always that potential contradiction in wanting to be seen as approachable but then resenting it when people take you at your word. It's partly a matter of the public being sensitive enough to realise that All Blacks need to be able to have private time in public otherwise they'll become hermits, prisoners in their homes and hotel rooms. Having a meal with your family or a night out with your wife or partner is obviously private time and you'd hope people would see it as such and realise it's not such a good time to intrude. Some don't, but that's more reflection on them than the wider community. It's annoying but you just smile, do your little bit, and move on.

With a number of All Blacks heading overseas after the World Cup, it's been suggested that the current coaching regime is putting players under more pressure than ever before. There's obviously pressure, but not just from these coaches; most of it is pressure that's built up over the 20 years since we last won the World Cup. A lot of planning has gone into developing a strategy to win this World Cup; the players have been involved in that — as they wanted to be — but at times the coaches' meticulousness and attention to detail has been a challenge for them. They've been involved in a lot of meetings which aren't necessarily a player's cup of tea; I think it's really got to some players but they actively sought that level of involvement and the opportunity to have their say on whatever was being implemented. It's all for the betterment of the team: the younger players are aware that when things are put forward, the leadership group has had an input and knowing that increases their buy-in.

Obviously, playing in a World Cup is a good way to end an All Black career, although I don't think New Zealand rugby's seen the last of some of these guys. There's no doubt some of them want time out from living in the fish bowl: wherever All Blacks go, there are people wanting a piece of them and sometimes it becomes quite smothering. But at the end of the day, you can't go past the financial appeal of playing overseas. The money on offer has gone through the roof and professional sportspeople are all too well aware that their time is limited, so there's an obvious incentive to make hay while the sun shines. Most of these guys, especially those with young families, are making business decisions as well as life decisions.

I don't think we've got a crisis on our hands because quite a few experienced players are sticking around and we've got great depth of talent. New Zealand is rugby. Whenever I watch my son play I see talented kids. We need to improve our identification and nurturing of this talent whilst maintaining the balance: we've also got to promote education because not every talented kid will make it as a professional rugby player. Everyone wants to live the dream but sometimes it just doesn't work out, no matter how hard you try. I was one of the fortunate ones who landed on their feet, because I didn't have anything to fall back on. The one area where I was really on my son's case was education; I don't have to be now because he enjoys it. As I keep telling him, he's my investment.

When I talk to young players I tell them to save the money they make in their first year and put it towards buying a house because as long as they've got a house, they've got an asset. In this country the average professional rugby career lasts three years and in one to two years you can save enough money to buy a house. All the young guys I've been closely involved with have done that, but the average pro rugby player blows most of what he earns in his first year. Then it dawns on him that he's got lots of clothes and is going out all the time but he's spending $200 to $300 a week to keep that nice car he bought on the road and he's still living with Mum and Dad. I know houses are expensive and for some reason rugby players are always moaning about spending money, but it gives you some leverage.

As I said earlier, the Samoan culture is to look after family and I try to help out my immediate family, my parents and my siblings as much as possible. I don't look after cousins I don't know, which is probably where I get offside with other Samoans. Mum and Dad are always being asked for money because everyone knows who their son is. I tell them that's not my concern. They are my concern; they looked after me and I'll make sure they have everything they need for the rest of their lives. My parents, sisters and brother all looked after me at different times and it's important that I repay them for what they've done for me.

Professional rugby players in the southern hemisphere spend a lot of time on the road, especially the South Africans. I enjoyed it at first but in the end it really got to me; after you've been to South Africa 20 times the novelty wears off and it's not somewhere I'd recommend anyway. I like animals as much as the next person but I don't want to sleep in the wild. It's not just the overseas travel: if you play a test in Dunedin or Christchurch or Auckland, you're there for the week. Some years I spent more time away from home within New Zealand than overseas. The travel just got too much for me. I enjoyed it less and less, to the point where I hardly ever went out. I'd seen the sights and I'm not an arty person so I didn't go to museums; the last couple of times I was Paris, I stayed in my room and read books. I always took away a lot of books and the management would bring books they'd read so there were plenty to choose from. I read heaps of them, mostly escapist stuff. People would ask if I wanted to tag along on their outings but I'd say, 'Nah, I've been there,' and just sit in my room reading. I hate to think what my phone bills were because I'd ring home every day for five or ten minutes, just to say hello, how was your day. If there's a benefit to all this travel it's that it really makes you appreciate New Zealand. In places like Rome and Paris there's history all around you, but there's also insane traffic and crowds everywhere you go, while in South Africa the poverty's in your face. I would long to get home where it's safe and green. I even missed Wellington's wind.

Being away from home so much is very tough on the family you leave behind, especially when there are children to be looked after. We were very fortunate to have supportive families close by; in fact that's one of the major reasons we stayed. Even being away as much as I was, I always knew that my family was safe and well looked after: Rochelle only had to pick up the phone and she'd have her family or my family on the doorstep to look after the kids if she had to do something or needed some time out. We were quite spoilt in that respect. There were various opportunities to go overseas but we placed a high value on that support and on our children having the opportunity to know their grandparents and cousins. My brother Mike lives in the UK and Rochelle has brothers and sisters living overseas: talking to them and our expatriate friends it's clear that they miss their families and are very conscious that their kids aren't having that interaction with their cousins.

Being away that much puts pressure on relationships. In my case it got to the stage where that pressure on my home life was just too much and it was certainly a factor in my retirement. It's turned around now, so much so that that my wife doesn't mind me being away because it gives her a break. You get used to having your bed made and your meals cooked and not doing the dishes and it's very easy to slip into feet-up mode when you get home. It doesn't go down too well, so you get out of it pretty quickly.

With the Hurricanes and Wellington Lions we had the option of staying in the hotel the night before the game. I always grabbed it because it was the best night's sleep I had all week. Our kids come in around 7 am — if we're lucky. It's not so bad when you don't have much on but if you've got training in a couple of hours you'd love to sneak another half hour. We tell them to sleep a bit longer but they start talking and wriggling around and wanting to watch TV, so when the option was there to go into a hotel, I didn't have to be asked twice. I'd go to bed at 10 pm and wake up at 10 am and make up the week's sleep shortfall in one night.

I wouldn't change anything with the kids, though. Whenever I went away there'd be tears and, 'Where are you going, Dad? You're always going to rugby.' Now, they understand that I'm home most of the time and they're happy about it. Our seven-year-old daughter is particularly happy that I'm no longer too sore to do things with her.

← **PLAYBACK**

COLIN COOPER

Colin Cooper *has coached the Hurricanes since 2003.*

I had a successful year with the Crusaders in 2002 and really enjoyed it down there. When the Hurricanes job became available I was in the process of buying a property and was really keen to stay down there. Then Tana rang me. I didn't know him except as a player who I had a lot respect for but he rang me out of the blue and put the case for why I should come back. That was the difference really. There was a decision-making process to go through but that sort of tipped it in favour of coming back, a guy of that ilk telling me to come back to my own area and take on the challenge as a head coach. At that time the Hurricanes were in the process of losing a lot of players and had been a big user of the draft. He really convinced me to come back and I'm very pleased and happy I made that decision because I've certainly grown as a coach from my experience with him and doing this job. I was very lucky to have him and he's just added to my experience as a coach.

Whereas the Crusaders had basically similar players, similar views, similar backgrounds, the challenge of the Hurricanes is having so many different cultures within the group: Tongans, Samoans, Maori, farmers. Understanding each culture and bringing those cultures together as a working group is something that you've got to continue to work towards. It's just not going to happen in one or two years.

The other thing the Crusaders had was a lot of experience, a lot of leadership, a lot of All Blacks. The Hurricanes were totally different and harder for a coach, so it was huge for me to have the support of Tana who had a lot of respect among the team. Probably too much really, in the sense that players are in awe of him and when you're in awe of a person you don't challenge him. That comes back to the Maori and Polynesian culture of respecting elders.

In 2007, Tana was still playing well enough to be an All Black. If it was just purely down to having the ability to play for the All Blacks, he could still make it now. There's his strength, his ability to step off both feet, his distribution — which is the best around — and to cap that off his defence is way above any other player. Not only does he defend, he then gets back to his feet and attacks the ball, which was unique to him and now a lot of other players are following that trend. He overrides that law and he probably gets penalised too much, but it shows courage when a man readily puts his head in dark places.

The mark of Tana is that he felt this year that he should step aside because we have the philosophy that we want our players to become All Blacks and he no longer wanted to be an All Black. He also knew that I'd have to put one of my midfield players into the draft. I was able to convince him that I couldn't lose him on top of losing so much experience but he wanted to play the role of bringing these players through into the All Blacks.

What I've witnessed is that he's been a great example of professionalism to the players in this region, particularly the Polynesian players. Day in and day out he has to deal with a lot from Joe Public, particularly in South Africa and Australia, but you never see him moan and he's the last one signing autographs. He's always available to the players one on one, he always offers advice. As I said before, there was a downside that he's held in such awe in that it might have held people back. If there is a negative in my time with him, that's it, but that's the nature of our group. Maybe when Tana goes, someone else will speak up.

He's a tough character, physically and mentally, and he's so professional — that's why he's survived. Off the field, in his nutrition and rehabbing and recovery, he's a great example to younger players. He was always the first to training and the last to leave and he never slid away from contact; in fact, I'd have to pull him out of contact sessions. He might tell you that he takes the first opportunity to get out of contact at training but that wasn't the case in my time. He'd always commit to what everyone else was doing but sometimes you have to manage your players. They weren't very good conversations when I wouldn't allow him into contact sessions because he didn't like to be seen as being looked after. That's a great attitude, isn't it? I mean, it's every coach's dream to have a player with that attitude on top of the experience and quality.

I think he'll make a very good coach. It's totally different to being a player and only time and experience will show him that. I think he'll be quite tough because his standards and demands are very high. As a coach you need to read your soldiers and know what type of leadership you put across to that particular group. He's got to learn all that but I'm confident he'll adapt quickly. There's no doubt that he's got the skills, the technique and the clarity in terms of his understanding of game plans, and his rugby knowledge is very high so there won't be any issues there. A couple of seasons ago he felt that I should be looking for the next captain; he saw Rodney So'oialo as the person to step into his shoes and made way for him. He thinks like a coach.

One of my proudest moments in coaching the Hurricanes was presenting Tana with his last jersey. I'm very lucky and privileged and honoured to have worked alongside him.

Tomorrow the World

The first thing I'd say about our World Cup campaign is that it's in very good hands. I believe Graham Henry, Steve Hansen and Wayne Smith form an outstanding coaching set-up, the best I've come across. Wayne and Graham are very similar in their work ethic, attention to detail, and desire to get the best out of themselves and everyone else; Steve's also a hard worker but finds it easier to relax and knows the value of setting aside time to do that.

What they've learnt, I think, is that regardless of how hard they work, there's a limit to how much information they can successfully communicate to the players in the time available. Their instinct would be to keep churning out information, but there's a point at which the players have to say enough is enough because if they're overloaded, they won't remember any of it. If you give me 20 things to remember I'll probably remember the first point and the last point and not much in between so it's about prioritising, making sure you get the key points across, and having faith that the players will absorb them. Once again it goes back to the leadership group which enabled the coaches to get to know the players as individuals and establish a mutual trust. One of the key things they took from our feedback was the value of simplicity.

These coaches don't have closed minds. They're always thinking outside the square and challenging you, but not in a way that makes you feel inadequate or that you're being set up to fail. They're always looking at ways to improve and innovate, which is what players like. The game keeps changing and the other teams have looked at what you did last year; they've broken it down and analysed it to death so what worked then won't cut it now. You've got to strive to stay one step ahead because if you don't, you'll stagnate and be overtaken. Staying one step ahead is what these coaches are good at.

They also know their limitations, so while they're trying to better themselves, they're always open to input and help from players and specialists. Rather than taking the attitude that, 'I'm the forwards coach so leave scrummaging to me,' they're prepared to put their egos aside and utilise the knowledge and talent available for the betterment of the team. They've created an environment in which players are encouraged to come up with ideas and suggestions, and that in turn has had a positive influence on the way the players think about the game and their roles within it.

They've picked the right players, based on an understanding of the kind of game they want to play and of the players as individuals. They began the process of building depth early on, having realised that if you operate a first-choice fifteen backed up by guys who hardly ever get on the track, you can't expect the back-ups to step up to the same level if they're suddenly called upon at the knockout stage of the World Cup. You need a squad — rather than a team — of quality players and that's what they've developed. The squad's been together for a while now, which is another strength; they know each other and they know the coaches. The key is managing them and keeping them hungry and I'm sure these coaches know how to do that.

I fully supported the conditioning window even though it didn't pan out entirely according to plan because of injuries. That was just unlucky: injuries are part of the game and can happen at any time. We needed to be innovative because the way we've gone about it for the last four World Cups hasn't worked, but, for whatever reason, the rationale for the rotation system and the conditioning programme hasn't been accepted by some critics. Criticism is one thing, but some people seem to be itching for the opportunity to say, 'I told you so', which is a sad indictment.

It was more about mental freshness than physical conditioning. I'm sure the conditioning group went into the All Black environment with less Super 14 clutter in their minds and were therefore keen to take on whatever the coaches gave them. I think the public and media underestimate what's involved in making the transition from a Super 14 team to the All Blacks. If you make the semis and/or the finals, you will have had 15 or 16 intense weeks in that set-up but within a matter of days you've got to jettison everything you've learnt over that period and start again in a different organisation with different systems and different ways of doing things. Your franchise team might be a group who've been together and grown together over several seasons; you've got to know everyone's idiosyncrasies and likes and dislikes. Then you go into the All Black camp with another group of players, some of whom you mightn't know and some who might be reticent on account of being new boys. By the end of the Tri-Nations guys have had enough. That's why they have a break before coming into the Air New Zealand Cup when, of course, they've got to go through the process a third time.

Mental freshness is the key: the body always does what the mind tells it to do. What I've found is that if you come in thinking about being tired, you'll talk yourself into being tired, and vice versa. I often had coaches tell me that the players would take their lead from me: if I came in acting tired, they'd follow my example. The challenge then was to forget about the kids waking me up from a good sleep and throw the switch when I got to training so that as far as everyone knew I was a box of birds. I'd run around like I was 21 and then collapse when I got home. A lot of leadership is about perception: people attach a lot of importance to your mental state and demeanour; they notice if you act tired or don't have much to say, so you need to be able to turn yourself on and off. I acquired that ability quite early, so when I needed to be on, I was on, and when I didn't, I was right off.

One of the criticisms of the conditioning window was that it opened the door for the South Africans, who took a lot of confidence from having two teams in the Super 14 final. Well, perhaps they did, but having two teams in the final has proved a two-edged sword for us: the 1999 and 2003 Super 12 finals were all-New Zealand affairs but that didn't help us later in the year. Winning the Super 14 means you've already peaked once and as Graham Henry kept saying, he didn't want players peaking at the end of May. Besides, if Jake White was correct in saying that come the World Cup final, no-one will remember or care who won this year's Tri-Nations, then presumably the same applies to the Super 14.

A tournament is very different from a campaign. You don't want to lose in pool play because you want to take momentum and confidence into the knockout phase. It's the All Black way to try to beat everyone and beat them well, but perhaps you should hold back a little and unleash from the quarter-finals on, although that's easier said than done.

You have to be in the right frame of mind for sudden-death games. In 2003, we'd seen South Africa beating teams up so we knew we had to be at our mental peak to overcome them in the quarter-final. We did that, but it was a sapping game for us, physically and mentally; the guys were sore afterwards and when players are still trying to come right physically it detracts from their mental state. I noticed a difference in the preparation for the semi-final against Australia. The build-up to the quarter-final all started on the Monday, but going into semi-final week some guys couldn't train so the build-up didn't really start until the Wednesday. The intense focus on the Springboks wasn't really replicated, perhaps because we'd hammered the Wallabies in Sydney earlier in the year. Maybe there was a little bit of complacency and a little less attention paid to what they were going to bring to the game. I say 'maybe' because I was watching from the outside but the preparation seemed to leave us a little short, given the work the Australians had done on us and the way they played. They'd done their homework and they were fired up. Hopefully that lesson won't have been forgotten.

You hear suggestions that various teams have been foxing, holding things back in order to spring surprises at the World Cup. I don't really think that's realistic, although — and feel free to point out that I'm contradicting myself — I have a gut feeling that that's exactly what France is going to do. In the months leading into the World Cup you'd have to practise one thing at training and do something else in games, and that's difficult; you're not going to win your games doing that. It's more sensible to practise a range of game plans for different opposition and develop players who can adapt to and execute whichever plan you go with. One thing I've learnt is that you can spend a lot of time analysing an opponent and preparing on the basis of that analysis and, meanwhile, they're working on another game plan. Analysis is important, but you still have to have the ability to change your game because they might come out with something you haven't prepared for.

People are getting nervous about the Springboks and there's no denying that their rush defence has caused us problems in the last couple of years. I'm sure the All Black coaches have been working on ways to overcome it which will be implemented at the right time. There's a counter to everything: it's about timing and everyone knowing what to do. The rush defence is in quite wide use now so players are getting more used to it and teams are finding ways to beat it. Obviously if you rush up there's space in behind and teams have improved their kicking games with that in mind. The main thing is to back yourself to cope with it and trust what you've been practising at training. When things aren't going well the key is not to try to save the day with a flash of individual brilliance, but to concentrate harder on doing the basics well and carrying out what you've trained to do because that's what everyone knows and understands. Under pressure, players can revert to individualism and try to do other players' jobs, when in fact all you have to do is do your own job a fraction better.

It's actually a simpler game at the top level because you're playing with players of the highest calibre and like-minded people. The higher the level, the less you have to worry about anyone else, and the more you can concentrate on your own job. All you have to do is be there and because your team-mates expect you to be there, they'll know straightaway when you're not and bring it to your attention. At a lower level there are always players that you have to help along and sometimes cover for. I enjoyed not having to worry about anyone else: you just went out, did what you had to do, trusted your team-mates to do likewise, and made sure that you fitted into the plan.

Most debutants' overriding first impression of test rugby is that everything happens more quickly. Things are done quicker because of the high skill levels. The basics are done properly — the passing is usually spot on and everyone runs correct lines. If all those little things are done well, it increases the speed of the game. The collisions are bigger because the occasion gets the adrenaline pumping and jacks up the intensity levels to the point where big, strong men are hurling themselves into the fray with complete disregard for their own well-being. Obviously there's a price to be paid for that.

Those big occasions create additional pressure: players are aware of what's at stake and the potential consequences of making a mistake. I was probably a bit unusual because as far as I was concerned a mistake was a mistake whether I made it in a test, a Super 14 game, a provincial game, or a club match. Sydney, 2001: I thought I could have stopped Toutai Kefu scoring the match-winner but I didn't. Johannesburg, 2004: I missed an easy tackle on Marius Joubert who scored a try. Hamilton, 2006: two halfbacks ran through me to score tries. Petone, 2007: I dropped the first three balls I got. I don't see one as worse than the other; I just see a mistake that hurts and I remember it. I don't feel worse because I was playing for my country, I feel as bad because I've let my team down and dropped my standards. I'm quite proud of what I do and letting things slide through being slack is not what I'm about.

In fact, I probably got angrier with myself for making mistakes in club rugby. In the first place, I was an international player and everyone, especially my amateur team-mates, expected better of me; secondly, I would have talked to the team about the importance of doing the basics well. Once you start thinking, 'Well, okay, I made a mistake but it's just a club game; it doesn't mean much,' you're heading for trouble. If you're really honest with yourself and you want to be a quality player, you shouldn't accept making mistakes in any form of the game. You've got to have pride and set high standards for yourself. I was harder on myself than I was on others and I think that helped me when I became a captain. If a captain shrugs off his mistakes, how can he say something to his players when they make a mistake? What are they going to think? You can't gain respect that way.

You can never write the Aussies off. I know from first-hand experience that there's no such thing as a bad Aussie side. They've been through a rough patch, as everyone does, but sometimes on the day they can draw a lot out of each other and from their history of having come up and trumped sides that were perceived to be better. People who know a bit about rugby or have been involved at this level know better than to take anyone lightly, least of all the Australians. They've still got an action-packed side and they generally get up for the big games. They've got a mix of youth and players who've been there and know what it takes to win the World Cup. As a player, you hate picking up the paper and seeing patronising stuff about the awful Aussies and how they haven't got depth, haven't got a front row, haven't got a hope. It just gives them what they want: ammunition, especially when they play us. I have a problem with the so-called experts who write and spout this drivel. The sad thing is that a lot of people who might not know much about rugby probably take this stuff at face value and assume the All Blacks should flog the Wallabies every time.

After what happened in 1999, I'd never dismiss a French side. The first time they do it to you, you can call it an ambush but if they do it to you again, then you didn't learn the lesson and that's just stupidity on your part. I believe the French have the capability to do more than we've seen from them recently. They've got skill, they've got size, they've got all the ingredients for a dominating side, but they've been playing very simple rugby and not really chancing their arm. I love French rugby: I was a big fan of Phillipe Sella and Serge Blanco and the 15-man game France played in their era. What we saw at the end of 2006, however, wasn't the France of old who could play end to end and side to side and whose trademark was flowing rugby with interplay between backs and forwards. Instead, we saw English-style rugby — hit it up here, hit it up there, kick to the corner. But when you think about it, that's a simple game plan to play and if you are practising one way and playing another, that's the way you'd do it. That's my conspiracy theory.

It has to be said, though, that Blanco and Sella were very natural footballers and wonderful athletes whereas some of the current French backs seem a bit muscle-bound and robotic which suits the way they've played recently. Of course, that doesn't just apply to the French. The days of the under-80-kg player like Terry Wright are long gone; these days everyone has to bulk up. When Conrad Smith first played NPC he wasn't much more than 80 kg and I told him he needed to get into the gym. You need size to be able to take the knocks as well as give them. You have to have a bit of impact and impetus otherwise you'll keep falling off tackles and going backwards in tackles and the opposition will target you every time. If there's a choice between running up against a guy who's 100 kg or one who's 80 kg, you're always going to go down the lightweight's avenue. There's no hiding-place in rugby nowadays; everyone's looking for a weakness and if they sense one, he'll be targeted until he proves people wrong or gets dropped. But there has to be a balance: you can't get so big and muscular that you lack the agility and flexibility to execute basic rugby skills.

Everything's a collision in the modern game — tackles, rucks, mauls, scrums — and you've got to be able to handle it, week in and week out. If you're 80 kg you might be able to handle it for a while but you'll soon get sick of backing up week after week. That's why the selectors focus on the business end of Super 14, those last few games when teams still have a chance to make the semis and there's plenty on the line. That's when you find out what players are really like: have they got anything left? Can they still guts it out after 10 tough weeks?

The 2005 end-of-year tour coincided with the final submissions to the International Rugby Board from the countries seeking to host the 2011 World Cup. Well before the tour New Zealand Rugby Union Chief Executive Chris Moller and Chairman Jock Hobbs indicated that they were thinking of including the All Black captain in their presentation line-up. I pointed out that after the Brian O'Driscoll incident I wasn't exactly flavour of the month in Ireland — the IRB's headquarters are in Dublin — and suggested they'd be better off with Richie McCaw. (I was very good at promoting Richie as the ideal person to do all sorts of things.) They decided to put off the decision until the All Blacks got to Ireland and they could get a feel for whether it was a good idea or not.

We'd been in Ireland for all of half an hour when it became obvious that some people weren't inclined to let bygones be bygones. As we walked out of the airport terminal, this old guy started giving it to me, saying I was a disgrace and should be ashamed of myself. Some of the guys gathered around me and we just kept walking to the bus. Then, as I got out of a car outside a sports store in Dublin where an adidas promotion was being held, another old guy gave me lip and tried to get to me but the security people blocked him. I was thinking, geez, I've certainly got the older generation fired up. I was a bit apprehensive about the signing session, hoping that none of the locals took it into their heads to reach over and have a dig at me, but I needn't have worried. People were actually joking about it and some even thought it would be a laugh to get me to sign their copy of O'Driscoll's book.

At the dinner after the Irish test — in which neither of us played — a couple of Irish players told me they were embarrassed by the whole carry-on. One of them actually said he'd told Brian to pull his head in. It was good to hear because it confirmed that not everyone over there saw the incident and its aftermath in the same light. The IRB chairman Syd Millar said he'd heard I might be coming back for the bid. I told him, 'Well, if you say yes to us now, I won't have to.' He didn't think he could get away with that.

The decision was made to include me in the final presentation. The following day we went over to England; I flew back to Dublin after training on the Wednesday and went straight into a rehearsal in a hotel boardroom. You had a set amount of time to make your submission so everything had to go like clockwork. There was me, Colin 'Pinetree' Meads, Chris Moller, Jock Hobbs, and the NZRU staffers who'd been working on the bid proposal. The Prime Minister was arriving the next morning and going straight to IRB headquarters. I was told when I'd speak, shown the presentation DVD, and briefed on some of the lobbying of various IRB member countries that Jock and Chris had done. I was blown away by the attention to detail and given a crash course in the politics of international rugby. Jock had heard that one of the other bidders was putting it around that we'd done something underhand and Sir Brian 'BJ' Lochore was off down to the bar to gauge the mood and have a last-minute word in the ears of some delegates. To someone who hadn't seen any of this before, it was both amusing and enlightening.

They'd written a speech for me but I prefer to speak without notes because

I don't like looking up and down all the time. When I give speeches, I ask the organisers what they want me to talk about and come up with something appropriate from my experience. I draw from what I know; I can't say what other people want me to say if it doesn't feel right and represent who I am and what I believe. What they'd prepared for me wasn't me so I had room service and worked on my speech, putting their content into my own words. I talked to myself in the mirror until I had it absolutely clear in my mind because I knew it was a big deal. I wanted to do as good a job for the country as Chris and Jock and their team had done.

After breakfast the next morning we rehearsed again. The others said my revised speech was 'perfect,' which is what you like to hear. We walked down to IRB headquarters and waited in the holding room where I met François Pienaar, the captain of the 1995 World Cup-winning Springbok team, who was leading the South African delegation; he seemed very confident. The Prime Minister arrived. We were all a bit nervous, worrying about what could go wrong. I got a sense of what it must be like for politicians before a big vote; you've done the head count and are quietly confident that you've got certain people's votes in your pocket but then you find out that they've been enticed into the rival camp. It had been a long road for Chris and Jock. Jock, in particular, looked very stressed, as if he'd been let down; it turned out that the Australians had thrown their support behind Japan's bid. He was understandably upset: we're always hearing about the special relationship between New Zealand and Australia but that was the second time in the space of three years that they'd shafted us. Part of me couldn't help but be amused at this demonstration that you can't even trust your supposed closest mate.

We followed the South Africans. We walked in to find the 27 IRB delegates sitting around a horseshoe-shaped table looking at us expectantly. I wondered why there were all these booths down one side of the room, then noticed that some of the delegates had headphones on and realised they must be for translators. Jock spoke first and did a brilliant job. The Prime Minister went next, emphasising that the bid had the Government's backing. You'd never have known that she hadn't been at any of the rehearsals: she was very polished and her contribution fitted seamlessly into the overall presentation. Chris addressed the logistic and financial aspects — most of it was over my head but it certainly sounded impressive — and Pinetree talked about the old days. Then it was my turn.

I spoke not just from a New Zealand player's point of view but also as a

Pacific Islander, making the point that a World Cup in New Zealand wouldn't just be for Kiwis as it would be the closest the Pacific Islands would ever get to hosting the tournament. I'm a worrier and I always worried about my family when they came to see me play, especially in a foreign country, because I would be busy but I'd want to know how they were, where they were, and what they were doing. I made the point that players coming to New Zealand could rest assured that they and their families would be safe. I finished with something to the effect that it had been a long time since the World Cup was held in New Zealand and it was time it was played there again.

I was meant to take five minutes but I only took three. Apparently I was the only one of the 33 speakers who didn't use cue cards or notes, probably because my speech was the shortest. Even so, I was still quite proud of that. I got the thumbs up from the ladies in the translation booth so I figured I must've got my points across.

The Prime Minister was heading straight back to the airport so I hitched a ride with her security detail. On the way we dropped in at her Irish counterpart Bertie Ahern's office where I signed about 100 autographs, further evidence that perhaps I wasn't the man all of Ireland loved to hate after all. We drove out onto the tarmac right up to this room which was a sort of departure lounge for dignitaries and VIPs. I realised how little down-time the Prime Minister gets: for her, the bid was already history because she had to focus on the next meeting in the next country. She can't afford to get bogged down on one issue because there are issues coming at her all the time. Not wanting to be a nuisance, I found myself a quiet corner but she got me over to sit with her and made time for me before we went our separate ways.

When I retired from international rugby a reporter told me that there was a rumour I was going into politics. I just laughed and said: 'Are you serious?' Nothing against politicians but no thanks: politics is the art of compromise and compromise doesn't come easily to me. As All Black captain you have to steer clear of politics because you represent a lot of people who don't view you in a political light and haven't mandated you to endorse a particular party or cause. Businessman Lloyd Morrison asked me to get involved in the campaign to change our flag. I could understand where they were coming from on it but realised they didn't want Tana Umaga, private citizen; they wanted the All Black captain and you only have that status for a short time. I was also very aware that a lot of people have fought and died for this flag and I'd never want to be seen as disrespecting them.

I didn't find out that we'd been awarded the hosting rights until the next morning when I was back in London. I was really happy for Jock and Chris and their teams in Dublin and back at NZRU headquarters in Wellington because I'd seen how much work they'd put in and the stress they were under. It was fantastic to play a part in it, albeit a very small one. The challenge now is to make sure that we put on a superb event. I just hope we don't drag our feet and fight amongst ourselves; I hope New Zealanders see it as a wonderful opportunity to shine on the world stage rather than an inconvenience or a burden. As Jock said, now it's about making it work. The Lions tour was amazing but this is going to be on a much bigger scale and we've got to be ready.

← **PLAYBACK**

JOCK HOBBS

Former All Blacks captain **Jock Hobbs** *is Chairman of the New Zealand Rugby Union.*

The 2007 Rugby World Cup is a very important tournament. We would dearly like to win it and if we were to do so, it would certainly have a positive impact on rugby in this country and indeed on the country as a whole. But I also think there's a need for perspective. It's not our right to win it and despite the fact that I feel everything that could be done has been done, we may not, and if that were the case we'd need to manage that situation. No doubt there would be a period of grieving but we'd pick ourselves up and push on. There are always challenges and opportunities ahead.

There's certainly pressure and there's certainly a lot of expectation. I think the media and some sections of the public have this feeling that the sun won't break over New Zealand rugby unless we win it. I don't believe that. Of course there's a real risk that the expectation and pressure become so claustrophobic that everybody gets overwhelmed and overborne by it. It's important — it's a Rugby World Cup, it involves our All Blacks, it's our national game, it's bloody important; but it's not everything.

There's certainly a risk that the World Cup could cast too big a shadow over the game if we allow things just to continue on the path that international rugby is currently on. I think, however, there's the opportunity — and it needs to be grasped very much in the short term — to ensure that that doesn't happen. I'm talking in particular about ensuring that test matches in between World Cups have integrity and meaning and are important. That's absolutely crucial for New Zealand. If that's achieved, it will provide balance to the fourth year of Rugby World Cup, but there are some real dangers if it's not achieved. I think it's a wholly unsatisfactory situation to have a four-year cycle where you have a World Cup and in between you have a few friendly test matches. That, in my opinion, is disastrous.

There's this issue around what's become known as rotation, and criticism of its use, that I'm becoming increasingly annoyed and frustrated by because the All Blacks jersey is important. I know that our players wear it with a great deal of pride and aspire to the very highest playing standard as All Blacks. Every test is important and I have no doubt that we do our very best to win every test. To win every test in today's environment you've got to have a squad of about 30 players who are capable of playing international rugby and the only way you can do that is to give them the opportunity to play international rugby. In the past we used to have tours, we used to have Wednesday games and Saturday games, and players went from the Wednesday team to the Saturday team or the Saturday to the Wednesday; there was interchange and a test team was selected. We don't have that any more. We don't have tours, so the flip side to this whole issue is that, putting aside injury, you'd play the same 15 players through a 12- to 14-match annual test programme. That's just nonsense and it's not good for those players: it's not good in terms of their welfare, in terms of their performance, and in terms of them continuing to win test matches. So even though there has been this criticism and commentary around what's been dubbed rotation, I don't believe it's geared towards winning the Rugby World Cup; it's geared to ensuring that we continue with our outstanding record of winning test matches.

We don't focus on just one goal, we focus on test matches. We have a programme, obviously, and we need to be conscious of how we manage, prepare, plan and execute that programme, but on an annual basis we've got test matches and we want to win each one of those test matches.

In terms of bidding to host Rugby World Cup 2011, we had to do some preliminary work before making a final decision to go for it and pay what was a non-refundable deposit (if there's such a thing). The important part of that was securing Government support. If we were not able to secure Government support, in our view it certainly would have made it impossible to proceed, given the size of the tournament and the commitments required. Having secured the Government's support, and without a lot of preliminary work in terms of feasibility studies or the like, we felt that the New Zealand rugby community would like us to have a go — that was a driving force. If we're just talking about the decision to go for it, we didn't do a lot of work in the sense of seeking people's opinions. A, we had to get the Government onside and, B, we thought people would want us to have a go, given what had happened in 2003. It was a very compressed process from that point, which would have been around February 2005, through to the filing of our bid document on 13 May. During that period there was an enormous amount of work done by hugely committed individuals and Chris Moller went all the way to Dublin to file the bid document with the IRB leadership.

When we actually began talking to the international rugby community, the events of 2003 weren't really mentioned to any degree. I think there was an element, certainly not be overstated, that two or three countries felt uncomfortable, or at least disappointed or sad, for New Zealand over what had happened in 2003, and while that may not have been a prime driver in their decision-making, I think it still sat there.

Going into the final presentation process in Dublin, my feeling was that the first round of voting was going to be extremely close, but if we could get through the first round we had a real chance of winning because we were the second choice for a number of countries. The Australian decision [to back Japan] wasn't a bombshell because we were in discussion and dialogue with them over a long period of time. When I was finally, emphatically, told on the day of the vote that we weren't receiving Australia's vote, it wasn't a bombshell, but it was extremely disappointing.

Our position in world rugby and the importance of rugby to our nation was an important part of our message, but it wasn't the only part. It wasn't even the backbone to the presentation. In terms of the lead-up to the final presentation the emphasis had been on an outstanding experience for players, an outstanding experience for spectators and those who would watch from home given the high standard of our broadcasting, our proven record of delivering high calibre rugby events as demonstrated by the Lions tour, and the fact that it would be a commercial success and good for world rugby. It wasn't just on one platform, although our heritage, our history, and our past performance were certainly factors. We had to cover a huge range of issues.

We obviously had all the rugby aspects in terms of the playing facilities, the fact that people here in New Zealand would embrace it, that people who came to New Zealand for the Rugby World Cup would be soaked in rugby, and that it would be unique because of that. Of course, we also had to cover the commercial aspects and guarantee the fee. We could guarantee clean stadia six years in advance of the Rugby World Cup. We had to cover accommodation, transport and broadcasting. We covered how important rugby was in New Zealand and that New Zealanders actually contribute to rugby throughout the world; the World Cup would help New Zealand to continue to make a strong contribution to rugby worldwide. We pointed out that if Rugby World Cup 2011 was staged in New Zealand it would almost be a home tournament for the Pacific Islands because of their close proximity.

The way we planned it, our pitch began with the bid document which was an extensive document covering all of the necessary aspects of the tournament. We then waited on the IRB's analysis of the various bids and it was on the back of that that we went on a tour around the world, during which we tailored each presentation to whoever we were speaking to, right through to making sure that the colours used were their national colours and the video clips were tailored to what we believed were the advantages and benefits to that particular country to have a Rugby World Cup in New Zealand in 2011. We also pulled the good points out of this technical analysis and also if there were any negative points, such as accommodation, we dealt with those sorts of issues as well. So it was really the lock down of all of those sorts of issues throughout that tour and the presentations to each of those unions. The final presentation had to pull all that together for a different audience: the IRB Council.

Tana was always in the frame to be part of the presentation team but with the O'Driscoll affair and also the statements made by the Chairman of the IRB, we became concerned about whether Tana would want to be involved. So, after that world tour I got back up to the UK and had some time with him just to check that it was something he did want to do and was really committed to. There was no doubt at all — he really wanted to be involved and he wanted to do it really well.

We'd obviously provided Tana with a framework, the sort of things we wanted him to speak on. We had to have that structure because there were messages we had to get across. I could tell at the first rehearsal that he felt a little bit uncomfortable with it. Early the next morning we had our last rehearsal and he was outstanding. We were saying, 'Tana, if can you do that later this morning, that would be fantastic.' He'd obviously gone away that night and really thought about it and he wanted to do it in his own way and in his own words. He certainly did that and the difference from the night before to the next morning was considerable.

All of our material, whether hard copy documents or video, was just absolutely outstanding — world class and very powerful. We started with the 'Stadium of Four Million People' video, and then I spoke, followed by the Prime Minister. Having her there was the most emphatic statement you could make about the Government's support and she articulated that extremely well. We had Colin Meads to give a rugby perspective. We had Tana there to speak about it from a player's perspective — that New Zealand would deliver what was important to players in the tournament.

Importantly, Tana, with his Pacific Island heritage, was able to talk about how positive it would be for the Pacific Islands to have a Rugby World Cup in New Zealand. Chris Moller was able to cover the commercial issues. I summed up, and we finished with a very strong video with a player from every rugby playing nation we could muster, passing the ball from one to the next. The last recipient of the ball was a New Zealander, welcoming them all to New Zealand in 2011.

I think the majority of votes were mandated and organised prior to the presentation day. Having said that — and I'm very quick to say this — what the final presentation does if it's done well, and I think we did do it very well, is reassure those who have decided to commit that it's the right way to vote. Secondly, there will be some who have not yet made up their minds — they will be in the minority but still very important — and to swing two, three or four votes at that point can be absolutely vital.

Eden Park was always going to be a major project. It involves construction of a large stand and other construction work, so obviously there are risks associated with it, but we're a long way advanced from where we were 12 months ago. With respect to other matters, we've established the company which is charged with organising the planning and delivery of the tournament in association with Rugby World Cup Limited, with the two shareholders being the Government and the NZRU. It has a good board, we have a CEO in place who's working very well, we have several staff, and we have a master plan and budget already in place. I think we're tracking well. We've had the advantage of knowing where we stand six years in advance of the tournament, which is longer than has previously been the case, so that's been helpful. I'm very pleased with the progress that we've been able to make and so too are Rugby World Cup Limited and the IRB.

It's Not Tiddlywinks

When reviewing your own career statistics — 14 years of first-class rugby; 74 tests; 121 Super 12/14 games; 100 games for Wellington; one of only a handful of New Zealanders who've played more than 300 first-class games — makes you want to have a lie-down, you know it's time to give it away. And I guess it says something about the way rugby has changed over that time and the sort of society we live in that, after all that, some people will remember me as the man who stated the obvious — rugby isn't tiddlywinks — and donged a team-mate with a handbag.

The handbag affair just got blown way out of proportion. It was my birthday; we'd lost the Super 14 final and I decided to have a big night with the boys. We'd had a good night out and were just about to leave this bar when there was an incident involving Chris Masoe and another patron. I pulled Chris away. I was angry with him because I try to fly under the radar when I'm out but I knew I was going to get dragged into it. I gave him a blast, telling him that he just had to keep his mitts to himself, and reinforced the point by cuffing him over the head a couple of times with a handbag that happened to be within reach.

There might have been a shortage of common sense in that bar, but there was even less in the aftermath. We live in a day and age in which people crave their moment in the spotlight, even if it's by association — the 15 minutes of fame syndrome — and I suppose spending $22,000 on a headline-making handbag is one way of doing it. I don't know what the handbag's owner did with the money but I'd be a little disappointed if she didn't give some of it to charity.

I got a hard time about it. While we were warming up at one end of the field before the game against the Brumbies in Canberra this year, this kid kept yelling, 'Tana, where's your handbag?' Eventually I turned around and said, 'I think your dad bought it for 22 grand, to go with his dress.' Everyone around him started laughing and that was the last I heard from him. All my mates and every second person I ran into, even in France, would come out with some variation on, 'If I get a handbag, will you hit me with it?' It's truly amazing how these things take on a life of their own once the media's pumped a bit of air into them.

The irony of the infamous tiddlywinks call was that it was directed at Peter Marshall who was one of my favourite referees, although some people might say that's a contradiction in terms. There was an element of premeditation to the extent that I'd seen a few incidents and calls in various games which made me wonder what the hell was going on. I was thinking, the game's going soft: it's meant to be a contact sport but these refs think it's tiddlywinks. We were playing the Crusaders in Christchurch: Leon McDonald was running straight towards me — he was my man — and the Crusader with the ball dummied to pass to Leon so I just put a hit on him, knocking him backwards, and Peter Marshall penalised me. I know Leon didn't have the ball, but he was coming into the receiver's zone and the other guy just held the pass back; if I'd stood off and Leon had been given the ball, he probably would've been through. Bear in mind this is split-second stuff: it's not like watching the slow-motion replay and knowing what's going to happen; we all have impeccable judgement then. I did what I did, which I'd done on many other occasions, which had been done to me many times, which used to happen all the time, and got penalised for it. In my best confrontational style, I said my piece, which caused quite a stir. Peter had announced that he was quitting and a couple of weeks later one of the Australian refs asked me to sign a box of tiddlywinks that they were going to present him with.

It wasn't meant as a joke — it actually summed up my frustration over what I saw as a worrying trend in the game — but it came back to haunt me. Everyone started saying it to me. The first time I'd played Conrad Smith was in a club game against Old Boys University: he tried to run straight at me, but I bowled him over and was on my feet trying to rip the ball away. He wouldn't let it go; I was yelling, 'Release, release, release,' but the ref, Lyndon Bray, was slow to get there. By the time he finally arrived, three other players had come over the top of us and he penalised me for hands in the ruck. I went off — it was right in front of our posts — and as I trudged back one of their props said, 'It's not tiddlywinks, Tana'. I told him, 'Don't use my clichés, mate.' Now, of course, Conrad cheerfully admits that *he* should've been penalised, not me.

I think the reason it caused a stir at the time and has reverberated since is that it tapped into a widespread unease and frustration over refereeing decisions and touch judge interventions that seem at odds with the fact that rugby is a contact sport. It's almost as if they're trying to eliminate all the elements within rugby that used to make the game unique. You don't get rucked in Super 14 and there are times when you actually miss it a bit. When I first started playing club rugby, you'd show off your ruck marks with pride. I still don't need much encouragement to show the scars I've got on my back. One of them was courtesy of Richard Loe — I know that hardly makes me unique, but I was five metres away from the ball which must be almost out of the danger zone, even by Loey's standards. I didn't say anything, though; I just thought I'll take that, because you expected it.

That was what happened in those days and no-one moaned about it. I don't know if it's a reflection of social change and the fact that we live in a politically correct society in which risk is minimised, if not eliminated altogether. My view is that if you're not prepared to run the risk of getting hurt, you probably shouldn't be playing a contact sport, because injuries are inevitable when people keep banging into each other. Obviously players have to operate within boundaries and with the clear understanding that there are certain acts which simply aren't acceptable, but the lawmakers and referees also have to be able to see things in the context of the game. If someone's lying on the ball, do you just stand back and let them lie there? It's all very well to say, 'Let the referee deal with it,' but what if he doesn't? The sure answer is that they'll do it again at the next ruck. Besides, you only need to lie there for a couple of seconds to slow down the ball and ruin the flow.

In a club game this year I fell on the wrong side, accidentally of course, and heard this guy yelling, 'Yeah, yeah' as he rucked my back. It wasn't even that hard but he was obviously proud of himself; he was a tough guy. I get that a lot when I play club rugby. My wife hates me playing club rugby because

I'm always getting hit or punched off the ball; there's always someone trying to make a name for himself by taking me out or putting some dirt on me. Half the time I reckon they just want to get in a cheap shot so they can talk about it after the game. Besides, everyone knows I'm a nice guy and won't do anything about it. If they did it to Jerry Collins, on the other hand, he'd get up and chase them. He doesn't care.

That's just the way it is. When I was young I used to eyeball the best player in the other team because if I could stand out against him, I'd be getting somewhere. Setting myself those challenges made me lift and helped make me a better player.

Something needs to be done about the tackled ball law. People who don't follow soccer can watch a soccer match and understand what's going on, but people who've played and followed rugby all their lives often have no idea what the referee's going to rule when he blows up at the breakdown. In 1997, we played a good brand of rugby because the laws governing the breakdown were weighted towards the attacking team and you could be pretty sure of getting the ball back. But because of this apparent infatuation with the contest for possession — and maybe because we were too good on this side of the world — the law was changed. Now we have a contest alright, but the outcome is usually decided by the referee.

They've effectively banned rucking and the laws say no hands in the ruck so if you can't use your hands or your feet, what can you use? The fact is that everyone uses their hands: it's supposedly illegal but everyone does it and sometimes the referees let it go and sometimes they ping you. Logically they should either enforce the letter of the law and have no hands in the ruck, or change the law to allow players to use their hands.

Yet law changes can be a minefield. It's the way of the world that if you change the rules, people will adapt to the new landscape both positively and negatively, either by trying to extract a benefit or finding a way to nullify it. In rugby, every law change generates new skills, new tricks, new short cuts — that's the way the game evolves. I was always trying to find ways to play to the letter of the law and push the boundaries, and I certainly wasn't the only one. The net effect is that law changes often don't produce the desired and expected results because players and coaches adapt in ways the lawmakers didn't foresee.

The crucial thing is to preserve the essence of rugby, the elements that define it and differentiate it from any other game. I can't believe what I'm hearing when people suggest getting rid of lineouts or de-powering scrums. Why not just go the whole hog and play rugby league? The guiding principle for lawmakers should be to make the game simpler to play, watch and understand while preserving the essence of rugby.

A few years ago we lost a lot of good, experienced referees, the likes of Peter Marshall, Wayne Erickson and Paddy O'Brien. I was a big fan of Paddy until everyone started saying he was one of the best referees in the world; after that he went off the boil. Just like players, referees can believe their own press. To Paddy's credit, he came back and was hard done by in not getting the 2003 World Cup final. In my opinion the new referees coming through, especially in Australia and South Africa, lack the empathy and understanding of the game, which are hallmarks of quality referees. They need to be more accountable and the environment needs to be more competitive. If a ref has a poor game, he should slip back in the pecking order, as happens in the NRL. They should be in the same position as players: if you have a bad game this week, you probably won't be called upon next week and if you have too many bad games, you might be out of work next year.

I know referees get intimidated in South Africa, because I've seen it happen. It can't be much fun copping it from those crowds but it's a test of mettle and I've seen a couple of referees come up short. They just get scared; you can see them thinking, geez, do I really want to make that call because who knows what might happen. If players can see it, why can't the assessors and administrators? Why do referees who clearly haven't got what it takes get appointed to handle big games? At present the system doesn't inspire confidence. It should concern administrators that it's got to the stage where players and the public fear the worst when they learn that certain referees are going to be officiating because they expect them to have a significant influence on the course and outcome of the game. These days the referee's ego is often the biggest thing on the field. With Steve Walsh and Paul Honiss, it's all about them.

I was impressed with Bryce Lawrence in the 2006 Air New Zealand Cup. When he started he was a bit naïve and easy to manipulate, but he refereed well and deserved to get the final. But he was poor in our second Super 14 game this year and I thought, oh, he's going to go the same way. After the game I told him, 'Mate, when you watch the tape, you'll be so disappointed with your game.' A bit later, though, I watched the Crusaders-Chiefs game and he did a good job, getting the Crusaders for all the things that Paul Honiss had let them get away with when we'd played them the week before. In that game, Steve Walsh, who was running the touch, got Ma'a Nonu sin-binned for supposedly giving him a spray; it was just rubbish. As I've said, Colin Cooper was always urging me to manage the referee but after that game he saw where I was coming from. He put together a video clip of what Honiss had penalised us for but allowed the Crusaders to get away with and showed it at a coaching forum: the unanimous view was that Honiss had reffed the two sides differently.

Sometimes I probably didn't help myself or the team with the way I talked to referees but I didn't enjoy being told, 'You should respect my calls.' Respect can't be demanded; it has to be earned. There were plenty of games when things weren't going right for us, but I didn't say a word to the referee because it had nothing to do with him. We were the ones making the mistakes.

Our referees aren't as bad as their Australian counterparts, some of whom are atrocious. That's partly because they lost a lot of experienced refs within a short space of time — Stuart Dickinson used to be their worst, but now he's their best, so what does that tell you? It's important for our game that the standard of refereeing improves and we find good new people. I know it's a tough job but they are professionals in a professional environment.

The single international window is another thing that needs urgent attention. Everyone's playing too many games: the amount of test rugby and rugby in general is very hard on players and something has to give somewhere. The players are the product, but it seems to me that these days there's more quantity than quality. I was happy to get out before they expanded the Tri-Nations because it's just too much of the same old thing. The Lions series was exciting because of its novelty and all the hoopla and anticipation that surrounded it and to go from that back into the Tri-Nations was a real anti-climax. I know from talking to Georgie Gregan and company that the Australians and South Africans have a similar view: it's just the same thing year in, year out. There's no wow factor.

It's up to the International Rugby Board: instead of talking about it and commissioning more feasibility studies or shuffling it into the too-hard basket, they have to grasp the nettle. They're the leaders of our game so it's up to them to lead. I can understand why the European clubs are loath to release the players in whom they invest so much money to play in test matches on the other side of the world that often don't mean very much. I can also understand why the public finds it hard to get enthused about tests when they can see that the visiting team is nowhere near that country's best combination. An international window will require sacrifices and at the moment no-one wants to be the one making the sacrifice, so maybe the IRB will have to make a decision and say this is how it's going to be.

As a Pacific Islander, I have an interest in, and a concern for, Pacific Islands rugby. There are two issues: the nonsense the British media keeps pushing about New Zealand poaching players from the Pacific and the very real plight of rugby in the islands at both grassroots and international level. My parents emigrated from Samoa; I was born in New Zealand. There are some All Blacks who were born in the islands but came to New Zealand as children. Their parents brought them here for education, to give them the opportunity of having a better life than they had. My parents met in New Zealand. My mother worked up and down the country, picking fruit and doing odd jobs before becoming a nurse and my father worked in a factory to earn money to send back to his family in Samoa. They knew that education was a key for their children and wanted to send me to the best school, but couldn't afford it. My parents made sacrifices for their children; I may be a public success story, but a lot of that is due to them. All their children have benefited from the sacrifice they made by leaving their homes and families in Samoa to make a better life for their children in New Zealand.

Our parents sacrificed to give us opportunities and for some of us those opportunities were in rugby. A few became All Blacks: we had the opportunity to play for the best team in the world and earn a living doing it, and we took it. Wherever in the Pacific Islands you come from, when you've lived in New Zealand for any length of time the All Blacks are your first choice. I don't take these things lightly; I did it because I loved it and I knew that it would make my parents proud. Whether you're Pacific Islander, Maori or Pakeha, you want to make your people proud of you, especially those who looked after you and sacrificed for you when you were young. That's why I get angry when they go on about poaching.

The Brits have a crack at us over poaching because they can't have a crack at us over the way we play the game. The people who write that stuff should come down here and watch some club rugby. Or they could just take a look at their own soccer teams and Olympic track and field teams and boxers because they'd find plenty of examples of young people from immigrant communities who've seen sport as an opportunity. For some reason it's okay for them but not for us.

On the serious issue, I believe both New Zealand and the IRB need to do more for the Pacific Island nations: they're being slowly left behind, mainly because so many of their players play overseas. At the international level, they have guys coming together from all over the world — New Zealand, Britain, France and Japan — which makes it hard to develop continuity and cohesion. It also impacts on the development of the game in the islands because, to some extent, all national teams reflect the strength or otherwise of their country's grassroots game and domestic competitions.

We have a size problem in junior rugby. In schools and lower grade rugby the attitude often seems to be, 'Give it to the big kid and see how far he can go.' When these schoolboy stars who've been able to run roughshod over everyone because of their bulk and power come up against guys their own size, they're going to find it a much harder game: what worked for them at school won't work for them when they no longer have a physical edge. And because they didn't need to refine their game or develop skills when they were young, the chances are they'll end up being, in rugby terms, just another big lump. When I was growing up there were always kids who were able to dominate because of their physiques, but whether because they rested on their laurels or made certain choices, they didn't go any further.

The fundamentals have to be instilled around that 13 to 14 age, which requires coaching. I understand parents wanting to be involved in their children's sport but we need to realise that this is where future All Blacks come from. If we can give them the right tools at that age and they work hard honing them through their teens, imagine the players who'll be coming out of schools and going into the academies. At the moment the academies are getting players with impressive physical attributes but who have to be taught the fundamentals.

I see a lot of young players, even at Air New Zealand Cup level, who can't kick with both feet. I wouldn't boast about my kicking, but I could do it if I had to. The same applies to passing skills, the ability to draw and pass, and basic game sense — understanding where you should be and what you should do in a given situation. A lot of that comes with experience, but if we start them at 13, they're going to get there earlier. In soccer, the search for talent starts very early — they run academies for five-year-olds. I'm not saying we should go that far, but why can't we start at 13? In the last couple of years I've been involved with Ken Laban's pre-season leadership camps at which nine to 12-year-olds are taught not only fundamental rugby skills but also decision-making and what's required of a rugby player. Kids are like sponges: they soak up anything and everything. The question is, what are they learning?

These leadership camps are also designed to help and encourage parents and would-be coaches. Coaches need to be taught because they're the game's first point of contact with kids, and vice versa. I know many junior grade coaches are giving up their time and making sacrifices but they tend to fall into one of two categories: those who coach as they were coached when they were young and those who watch elite rugby and try to replicate it with kids who are just starting to learn the game. Both approaches have obvious flaws which makes it all the more important that club and school team coaches have access to up-to-the-minute drills and resources and are given a clear sense of what the union is looking for from coaches and players at the various age levels. Having said that, we should never lose sight of the enjoyment factor.

I believe Wellington has serious rugby talent and we just need to work hard at developing it. There's a module for teaching rugby skills, but it needs to be taken a step further because player numbers are declining. We need resource coaches to go into schools and promote the game. It comes back to those junior level coaches and the first point of contact which can have such a lasting influence on kids' development. If they learn bad habits, the academy coaches have to break them of those and start from scratch. The academies should be polishing gems, not weaning promising but untutored players off bad habits and teaching the fundamentals.

We also need to beware of pampering our young stars. Everyone talks about mental hardness, but where do they get it from if everything's done for them? Jerry Collins is hard because of his upbringing and some people are just naturally ultra-competitive, but if you've had to work for things, you're less likely to accept having them taken away from you. In those last 10 minutes of a tough, tight game the motivation to drag a bit extra out of your body can only come from within.

Once I'd made the decision to give up international rugby, I started to think seriously about what I would do after I'd retired from rugby altogether. An approach from Graham Mourie led to my first experience of community work. He's involved with Graeme Dingle in Project K, a programme for kids who may be going off the rails: they put them through a kind of Outward Bound course doing things like white water rafting, rock climbing and abseiling. It's good to have a go at things that are outside your routine and comfort zone.

When I was sponsored by Canterbury I tried rock climbing during a photo shoot at the Anakiwa outdoor pursuits centre: I got about a metre off the ground and couldn't go any further. (I'm not great with heights, but normally not that bad.) The instructor was telling me to move this foot there but I just froze. Eventually I defrosted and actually did it and took some confidence from knowing that I'd faced my fear and pushed through it.

Coming from the same sort of background as a lot of the kids they were targeting, I was keen to get involved. My one stipulation was that they started up a programme in Wainuiomata, which they agreed to do. My participation primarily involved putting my name to it and being there at the opening, but I made an effort to get to see the kids.

As well as the outdoors stuff, there's a mentoring programme and a community service element. It was good to give something back to the community and pass on some knowledge and, although I haven't done as much as I'd like, I'm still involved.

I wasn't interested in being associated with products and activities that I don't like and don't believe are good for kids, such as fast food and alcohol. Getting involved in Government initiatives was an attractive option and education was a particularly good fit given the age of my kids. The fact that the Ministry of Education's Team Up campaign to encourage parents to get involved with their children's learning was targeting Pacific Island families with working parents also struck a chord. Like many of their generation, my parents thought that education happened between the time you left for school and when you got home in the afternoon and after that you helped around the house. Now we know that parents have really got to promote learning in the home from early childhood and emphasise the importance of homework by helping out and showing an interest. Like many parents, we've learned that nothing encourages your kids to work hard and strive to do well like Mum and Dad taking an interest.

The feedback over the last year has been really encouraging and the campaign is having an effect. I think it works because people see me as being normal. I've experienced the downside of having a high profile with things like the handbag incident, but this campaign is the upside and makes it all worthwhile. I've recently become involved with Tourism New Zealand to promote tourism around the 2011 World Cup through an internet-based campaign. Again, it's not hard for me: I'm a proud New Zealander and a strong advocate for this country because I love everything about the place.

I was on the public speaking circuit for a few months because I was getting so many requests and it pays pretty well, but I didn't like it. Apparently I wasn't too bad but there are only so many stories you can tell. Wayne Smith told me that he went to two functions at which Sir Richard Hadlee spoke and heard the same stories at both.

Everybody does it; that's the way it works. After the 2005 end-of-year tour, I heard Will Carling speak. He told this story about getting into a taxi: the taxi driver studies him in his rear vision mirror for a while then says, 'Okay mate, give us a clue.' And Carling says, 'Well, actually I'm Will Carling; you might have heard of me — I played rugby and captained England . . .' The taxi driver butts in: 'No, mate, I just want to know where you're going.' I thought it was a pretty good story until I met a woman at one of these functions who wanted to pass on this wonderful story she'd heard Sean Fitzpatrick tell. Apparently he got into this taxi and the driver checked him out in the rear-view mirror: 'Go on, mate,' he said, 'give us a clue . . .'

I'd had lots of offers to go overseas, but I'd never given them much thought. I didn't want to uproot the family, I wanted to see out my contract with the New Zealand Rugby Union and finish playing rugby here, and I didn't want to go to the UK because of the weather and the number of games they play. If I was going to go anywhere it would have been to France but I always kept coming back to the same issues. Then I got the offer to go to Toulon for two months, which fell mainly in the summer holidays. I couldn't believe it; it meant I could take the family and treat it like an extended holiday for them. We asked the kids' teachers if it was a good idea to take them out of school and whether they should take work to do, but they all said the same: that just going and experiencing the culture would be a great education.

I went over a week before the family to get things sorted out, arriving in Toulon on the Thursday after the Air New Zealand Cup final. My agent had told me that there was no danger of me having to play that first weekend because they couldn't get through all the red tape — the medical certification and documentation — in one day. Well, as soon as I got off the plane, I had doctors all over me, then I was whisked off to a magistrate to get a visa and a work permit. Places stayed open especially so everything could be done in one day, including meeting the team and having a training session, and, of course, I ended up playing. The standard of rugby wasn't very high compared to Super 14 and the Air New Zealand Cup and I went okay, although I didn't do much — I only got the ball a few times. However, I did manage to score a try and, frankly, you can't do much better than that when it comes to persuading the locals that bringing you all that way for such a short time wasn't such a bad idea after all. I found out later that the club had jacked up the ticket prices — tripled them in some areas of the ground — so with a full house of 14,000 or so, they'd pretty much recouped their outlay straight away.

At the pre-match get-together in the club vice-president's restaurant we were served a three-course meal. I was saying, 'Geez, this is amazing — is it always like this?' The other English-speaking players told me they usually just got croissants with jam and a cup of coffee so they were hoping this was a sign of things to come now that I was there. The following week it was back to croissants. Luckily, I got a heads-up during the week and took the precaution of having a big meal beforehand.

Training was like being stuck in a time warp: two hours in the morning with contact; two hours in the afternoon with more contact. If you ask the guys I've played with in the last three years, they'll tell you I only did contact when I really, really had to; the rest of the time I'd move to the wing or hold a tackle pad. We were playing games against reserves and fringe players: obviously, if you're not in the first team, those games are opportunities to make an impression; if you are in the first team, they're opportunities to get hurt. After we'd been shown up by the reserves a few times I announced that actually I didn't do contact and that was the end of it.

I waited two or three weeks before I started making suggestions. I didn't want to take over, but I'm a competitive person and I felt we'd do better if we put the accent on quality rather than quantity. The other players, both the French guys and the imports, were very keen to know what we were doing down here and also put pressure on me to change the way we were training: 'You've got to talk to them, they'll listen to you.' I was conscious of striking a balance between not rocking the boat too much and making sure that things that needed to be changed were changed because they really weren't doing very well. They were down around eighth or ninth on the table when I arrived and in the top three when I left.

The second game was dire, an old-style attritional game with the forward packs rumbling away and lots of kicking, but I managed to score the winning try. It was a bit of a fluke but the French are very expressive and their relief was matched by their gratitude. I couldn't have wished for a better start, but I didn't score another try while I was there. I played seven games, missing one through injury. We lost that one at home, which simply isn't meant to happen.

There's a real home and away mentality in French club rugby: when you're at home everyone's fired up and champing at the bit to get out there; when you're away the intensity drops off and everyone's a bit relaxed; it's like we're going to lose anyway so why bust a gut? My first away game was Toulon's first win away from home all season. That made everyone very happy.

Toulon is a proud rugby town, a former power in French rugby which has slipped down to the second division. As a kid I remember reading about the great Toulouse-Toulon rivalry and I'd often wondered what had become of Toulon as the likes of Stade Français, Perpignan and Biarritz emerged as challengers to Toulouse. Eric Champ is one of Toulon's favourite sons; I remember him as a tough bugger, and a pretty fiery one. I met him, but the wild Harpo Marx hair I was expecting has been replaced by a conventional hairstyle. Eric Melville, the first South African to play for France, was a Toulon player, as was the former French halfback Jerome Gallion. The club's most famous player is the flanker André Herrero whom Colin Meads rated as one of the finest footballers, back or forward, he ever played against.

Although they've fallen from the heights, the Toulon public has remained faithful. Only one club in the 14-strong first division is better supported. It reminded me of Wellington in that even though they're not doing all that well, the support is still there and so is the expectation, which is great because you don't want mediocrity to be acceptable. When we lost at home the crowd started up this loud whistling as the players came off. I was sitting in the stand wondering what it meant, whether in fact it was a good thing, but one of the English-speaking players set me straight: it's like booing. It can't have been a pleasant feeling but we didn't play well and you could understand how the crowd felt.

The money comes from the club's owner, Mourad Boudjellal. He's a real success story — an Algerian immigrant in a country where they haven't always been looked upon favourably who's made his fortune and now wants to do something for the town. He's not a big rugby man in the sense of having a deep knowledge of the game, but he sees his investment in the club as a way of giving something back to the community. We used to speak through an interpreter. He's a proud Frenchman who loves Toulon and is also proud of his Algerian heritage.

When I played in Paris, the family came up for a few days. We went to the Palace of Versailles and Notre Dame and the Eiffel Tower. The visit to the Louvre just happened to fall on the day that I had to train. I don't know how many times I've been to Paris, but I've never been to the Louvre; I'm not an art lover like Anton Oliver. Cade was fascinated by the Mona Lisa. His friend told him that the Mona Lisa can see you wherever you are in the room so he tried to find a spot where she couldn't see him. He makes me laugh: nothing is great, it's just okay. At the top of the Eiffel Tower he said, 'It's alright; a bit high.' He and I went to watch the All Blacks at the Stade de France. I tried to sneak in incognito in a beanie and hoodie but it didn't work. The haka really brought out my emotions, as it always does. It wasn't so much a matter of wanting to get out there as being conscious of being a proud New Zealander and that that was our team out there.

In 1998, I learnt that if you think you've got this game sussed, you're going to be left behind because it will have moved on in the time it takes to write this sentence. You've got to keep working on your game; you've got to keep learning. I've learnt a lot from coaches and other players. As I keep telling young players, you can learn something from everyone you come in contact with, be it good or bad. You take what's good and file away the bad so that if you encounter it again, you'll recognise it and know how to deal with it.

When you come across guys who think they've made it, you just have to shake your head. I've tried to help a lot of players but, as they say, you can lead a horse to water but you can't make it drink. They say, 'Yeah, yeah, yeah,' then go off and make the very mistake you tried to warn them about. I say, 'Why don't you just not do that?' or 'Look, that's what got me into trouble,' and they say, 'Hey, you got to make mistakes, now I want to make them.' I sit back and think: can you hear yourself? Then there are others who get it, who take everything on board. A lot of it is to do with their backgrounds: some will take advice, some won't. You can't force it.

I've seen a lot of players get to a certain level and be happy with it; they cruise and get those second year blues. I did it myself. The player who doesn't think he's made it and therefore keeps working is the one who'll progress; he'll consolidate and find consistency and set new goals. That also applies to life outside rugby — I'm a better father now than when I was 20 because I was able to learn and adapt. I'm extremely fortunate to be married to Rochelle who's been very understanding. After Cade was born, I said to her, 'Rugby's number one at the moment; you're number two, and my family's number three.' I felt rugby had to be the priority because I had goals to achieve, but also because it helped put food on the table and I didn't want to blow this chance as I'd blown the rugby league opportunity with Newcastle. She accepted that, but looking back on it, if I'd been in her shoes I would've told me to eff off. Later, the pecking order changed and I gave up international rugby for my family. My wife and kids are number one now, which is as it should be.

It took me a while to figure it out. I became so focused on rugby because I really wanted to achieve — it was all about making money and making the All Blacks. But when I'd achieved those things, I realised the main reason I played was because I enjoyed it. I liked playing and I liked having a laugh with the guys and a few drinks when the time was right. But things change. I can't keep pushing my body and I don't really want to. There are other things I want to do, other challenges. I get to watch my kids play sport and be a more hands-on father and I enjoy that. I still can't cook, though.

What I've learnt is that in rugby, as in life, nothing lasts forever and you can't take anything for granted. I'm a big believer in karma: what goes around comes around, maybe not tomorrow or the next day but eventually. You can't keep having good luck; at some stage it's going to go against you. I had a great run with injury but when it mattered most, when I wanted to prove myself on the biggest stage and in the most important event in rugby, I injured my knee and had to sit and watch.

I've been here all my life and my family and I are very comfortable in our surroundings and circumstances, but I'm looking forward to starting a new chapter of my life in Toulon. The timing is right: I needed a change and a new challenge. Can I succeed as a coach? Can I handle being out of my comfort zone? And, of course, there are financial considerations. It's an opportunity to secure my children's futures, which is what I've always wanted to do. My parents left their country and found a new life because they wanted to do the best for their kids and I'm doing the same for mine. They're going to have a good start to life, just like I did. I promised them that.

← PLAYBACK

Mike Umaga

*Tana's older brother **Mike** lives in Kenilworth, Warwickshire, England and is head coach of National Division Two club Nuneaton.*

I'm seven years older, but he was always very competitive and wanted to beat his older brother, but it was a big gap to bridge. Before he came along it was just me against the sisters. I knew my place and when he came along, he knew his place, too.

They were very protective and were a big influence on how we grew up.

When he made the Junior Kiwis you could see there was something special about him. You just knew that if he was given direction, he'd cope with it. Playing together for Petone, I'd be at fullback and often I'd stand back and watch him do things that just freaked me out. He was already getting there then. The Petone coaches Frank Walker and Richard 'Hoey' Whittington were really good coaches and good people. They took time out to help Tana and me and give us a sense of belonging, and it was because of that environment that I had no qualms about encouraging Tana to come to Petone.

He always had the skills. When Frank Bunce went and they were looking for a replacement, he was probably the best centre then, but they looked at everyone else instead. Tana had everything you need in a midfielder. People talk about presence: you have something other players can't match; you walk on the field and you don't necessarily have to do anything but everyone knows you're there. Tana had that. Looking at the All Blacks going into the World Cup, they've got more than enough in most areas, but I think they're missing that presence in midfield.

Watching it on TV from afar I could see him getting closer and closer and I'd be thinking, just make him captain; don't piss around with this senior player and vice-captain stuff, make him captain. He should have been captain earlier; they missed out on a couple of years of him.

I remember the night he rang me up. It was quite late and I lay down on the floor in my lounge because we normally talk for a while. He's usually pretty quiet on the phone and he starts off, 'Hey, bro, Graham Henry asked me to be captain.' I started jumping around and he told me, 'Calm down, I don't know if I want to take it on. It's not just the prestige, there are other things to think about.' I said, 'Whatever. Listen, buddy, just let me have my moment of jumping around the house.' At that time, New Zealand needed a leader; they needed someone who the players would look up to and who would take them forward.

It had a big effect on the whole country. I was never actually in New Zealand when he was captain so I was looking in from the outside and I didn't realise how big an effect Tana being captain had, especially on our people, until I came down to New Zealand in February this year. It was one of the proudest moments a brother could have.

It will be nice having him and his family a lot closer — we've missed each other big time. And it's going to be good having a holiday house in the south of France. It's all coming together.

He had a good run. Mum and Dad instilled those family values deep in us — they're a big part of who we are so I understand where he's coming from. In February he was like an old lion prowling around — 'What am I going to do? What do I want to do?'

All those years he said he'd never come over to Europe and I'd say, 'Never say never, mate.' So he goes to Toulon and finds somewhere that suits him and I said, 'There you go.'

Of course, I taught him everything he knows. I've used that line quite a bit over the years. In fact, he's very much a self-taught man although he's had good people around him — Mum and Dad and our sisters and Rochelle.

← PLAYBACK

Tauese and Falefasa Umaga

Tana's mother **Tauese** *and father* **Paegauo Falefasa Ropati** *live in Wainuiomata.*

Tauese: I have a story behind my name: I was born premature at only seven months and my mum named me Tauese meaning 'Miscounted'. She said I was the size of two cupped hands. I came over here in 1952 and we met here. Our parents wanted us to come home for our wedding so we went back to Samoa in 1959 to get married.

Falefasa: I come from a very low family from Samoa. My beautiful wife comes from a very big family on the island of Savai'i. Most of her brothers and sisters are well-known people in Samoa because they're very well-educated — they all got scholarships — so I found the best woman in the world to marry.

Tauese: Our families wanted us to stay but I didn't like it. I found living there very hard and was thinking when I have children, how am I going to put them through school with no money? So after two months we decided to come back. We came back here and worked and helped our families in Samoa. We were bringing all our nieces and nephews and cousins from there. We had a really interesting life living in New Zealand and the seed was blossoming with the children.

We bought a little house in Petone when we first arrived in Wellington, then we found it was too small for our family when all the girls were born. We came to Gawler Grove in Wainuiomata — I bought the section myself — and that home is where my children grew up. Later we made it six bedrooms because at the time there were my four children and two of my brother's children that I put into schools. We stayed there until last year. All our children have their own places so Tana said we'd better sell it. This is his house so we live here with free rent.

Falefasa: He's a good boy, he's been a great help to us. He always wants to help with money.

Tauese: Tana and I always had a sort of easy relationship. He'd take what I said and I'd take what he said. I don't think I ever had any trouble with Tana, not as a mother. Sometimes he was reluctant to do things that weren't fair and I'd just take it as it goes and then later on we'd have a smooth relationship. Once the children were on their own feet, I didn't bother them but I'm welcome at their houses and I do whatever I can to help. I don't do anything for them now but my prayers go with them. I believe in that. Since Tana's been married and had a family, he's trying to help us so our relationship has carried on around that. Because we're churchgoers we like Tana to come to our church. Sometimes he does, sometimes he comes reluctantly, but I leave it at that: when he wants to come, he wants to come, if he doesn't, he doesn't. But I appreciate it and I support him in my prayer. Even now we're saying prayers for Tana every night. Whenever I know he's away or going somewhere, he goes with my prayers — that's my help for him.

Tana's never refused anything we've asked him to do, although you have to explain what it's for. He's a very good boy and we don't have any arguments. Sometimes he has accepted what we say reluctantly but even then he'd do it.

When my boys were young there were street kids in the area. I didn't like that, so at five years old I introduced Tana to rugby. He started as a number 8 — it was the time of [Murray] Mexted. Tana put his head in the first scrum and turned around and said to me, 'Mum, it hurts.' And I said, 'Put your head down.' He was very reluctant at the time, probably because it was cold. I used to do night duty and I'd come home on Saturday morning to take the two boys to rugby and Tana would say, 'Mum, it's too cold, I don't want to go.' I'd just say, 'Come on, come on.' That was my support for them and later on they really enjoyed it, but if it hadn't been for me pushing them, they probably wouldn't have played at all. His brother actually liked it but Tana was the hard one to push because of the cold and because they put him in the forwards, and he didn't like that. He still doesn't like the cold. My main concern was to get them away from the street kids, to do something for themselves instead of mucking around in the streets. Later on he got interested in rugby league. He just wanted to see what it was like and then he came back.

I was very happy when Tana became the All Black captain. I praised the Lord that my son was the captain. You know, as Samoans we never thought he'd get that far. We came here because we wanted our children to be well-educated — that was the most important thing — and also to open up avenues for them to play sport, so with Tana becoming captain we just praised the Lord that one of our children was able to do that job.

Falefasa: We don't want to show off; we just sit back quietly.

Tauese: Now Tana's eager to go to France. It will be an opportunity to see another place, different people, different customs. It's a learning experience.

Falefasa: It's good for him what he's doing now because he's got that spirit to help other people play rugby.

Tauese: I'm really proud of Tana and Michael and my girls. I have a feeling of: who am I that I produced these children who made news around the world?

For the Record

Compiled by Geoff Miller

#	Date	Team	Opponent	Venue	Score	Tries	Points of Interest	Position
1994								
1	27/4/94	Wellington	Canterbury	Christchurch	20–31			Wing
2	30/4/94	Wellington	ACT	Canberra	29–25	2		Wing
3	17/5/94	Wellington	Taranaki	Wellington	38–34			Wing
4	25/5/94	Wellington	Horowhenua	Otaki	85–0	1		Wing
5	6/6/94	Wellington	Manawatu	Wellington	42–7			Wing
6	21/6/94	Wellington	Hawke's Bay	Wellington	27–17	1		Wing
7	28/6/94	Wellington	South Africa	Wellington	26–36	1		Wing
8	31/7/94	NZ Under 21	NSW Country Under 21	Port Macquarie	76–3	4		Wing
9	3/8/94	NZ Under 21	NSW U 21 Development XV	Sydney	60–10	1		Wing
10	6/8/94	NZ Under 21	Australia Under 21	Sydney	41–31			Wing
11	13/8/94	Wellington	Nelson Bays	Nelson	55–13	1		Wing
12	21/8/94	Wellington	Counties	Pukekohe	3–29			Wing
13	27/8/94	Wellington	Waikato	Wellington	30–23	1		Wing
14	3/9/94	Wellington	Otago	Dunedin	14–31			Wing

#	Date	Team	Opponent	Venue	Score	Tries	Points of Interest	Position
15	10/9/94	Wellington	Auckland	Wellington	30–52	1		Wing
16	17/9/94	Wellington	King Country	Taumarunui	31–22	1		Wing
17	24/9/94	Wellington	Canterbury	Wellington	37–28	2		Wing
18	2/10/94	Wellington	North Harbour	Takapuna	17–43	1		Wing
1995								
19	17/5/95	Wellington	Wairarapa Bush	Masterton	43–26	1		Centre
20	24/5/95	Wellington	Taranaki	New Plymouth	45–38	2		Wing
21	5/6/95	Wellington	Manawatu	Palmerston North	36–22	1		Wing
22	26/7/95	Wellington	Nelson Bays	Wellington	94–12	1		Wing
23	1/8/95	Wellington	Bay of Plenty	Rotorua	30–20	1		Wing
24	5/8/95	Wellington	Auckland	Auckland	10–13			Wing
25	12/8/95	Wellington	North Harbour	Wellington	26–17			Wing
26	19/8/95	Wellington	Southland	Invercargill	21–16			Wing
27	26/8/95	Wellington	Otago	Wellington	19–33			Wing
28	10/9/95	Wellington	Canterbury	Christchurch	17–66	1	Ranfurly Shield	Wing
29	17/9/95	Wellington	King Country	Wellington	36–16			Wing
30	23/9/95	Wellington	Waikato	Hamilton	28–36	3		Wing
31	30/9/95	Wellington	Counties	Wellington	8–33			Centre
1996								
32	1/3/96	Hurricanes	Blues	Palmerston North	28–36			Wing
33	9/3/96	Hurricanes	Brumbies	Canberra	28–35			Wing
34	15/3/96	Hurricanes	Transvaal	Napier	32–16	1		Wing
35	24/3/96	Hurricanes	Reds	Wellington	25–32			Wing
36	30/3/96	Hurricanes	Highlanders	Dunedin	44–15			Wing
37	6/4/96	Hurricanes	Natal	Wellington	27–43	1		Wing
38	14/4/96	Hurricanes	Crusaders	New Plymouth	13–36			Wing
39	23/4/96	Hurricanes	Western Province	Cape Town	25–35			Wing
40	27/4/96	Hurricanes	Northern Transvaal	Pretoria	20–38	1		Wing
41	4/5/96	Hurricanes	Chiefs	Rotorua	23–15			Wing
42	10/5/96	Hurricanes	Waratahs	Sydney	25–52	1		Wing
43	26/5/96	Wellington	Samoa	Wellington	52–30			Wing
44	3/6/96	Wellington	Manawatu	Wellington	59–34	1		Wing

#	Date	Team	Opponent	Venue	Score	Tries	Points of Interest	Position
45	24/7/96	Wellington	Canterbury	Christchurch	25–16	1		Fullback
46	10/8/96	Wellington	NSW Country	Nowra	44–5			Fullback
47	13/8/96	Wellington	ACT	Canberra	37–31	1		Fullback
48	17/8/96	Wellington	Taranaki	Wellington	36–20	1		Fullback
49	24/8/96	Wellington	King Country	Taupo	41–19	2		Fullback
50	1/9/96	Wellington	Canterbury	Wellington	29–28			Fullback
51	7/9/96	Wellington	North Harbour	Takapuna	14–36			Fullback
52	14/9/96	Wellington	Bay of Plenty	Wellington	45–36	1		Fullback
53	21/9/96	Wellington	Auckland	Wellington	33–44			Fullback
54	29/9/96	Wellington	Waikato	Wellington	20–18			Fullback
55	5/10/96	Wellington	Counties Manukau	Pukekohe	22–40			Fullback
56	12/10/96	Wellington	Otago	Dunedin	10–18			Fullback
1997								
57	28/2/97	Hurricanes	Chiefs	Palmerston North	18–23	1		Wing
58	7/3/97	Hurricanes	Crusaders	Christchurch	17–19			Wing
59	16/3/97	Hurricanes	Northern Transvaal	New Plymouth	64–32	3		Wing
60	29/3/97	Hurricanes	Gauteng	Johannesburg	37–35			Wing
61	4/4/97	Hurricanes	Natal	Durban	24–29	1		Wing
62	12/4/97	Hurricanes	Reds	Brisbane	47–29	1		Wing
63	20/4/97	Hurricanes	Free State	Wellington	59–30	1		Wing
64	26/4/97	Hurricanes	Highlanders	Wellington	60–34	3		Wing
65	2/5/97	Hurricanes	Waratahs	Napier	19–3			Wing
66	10/5/97	Hurricanes	Blues	Auckland	42–45	2		Wing
67	18/5/97	Hurricanes	Brumbies	Wellington	29–35			Wing
68	24/5/97	Hurricanes	Brumbies	Canberra	20–33		Super 12 semi-final	Wing
69	8/6/97	NZ Barbarians	New Zealand A	Rotorua	29–22		All Black trial	Substitute
70	14/6/97	New Zealand	Fiji	Albany	71–5	1		Wing
71	21/6/97	New Zealand	Argentina	Wellington	93–8	2		Wing
72	28/6/97	New Zealand	Argentina	Hamilton	62–10	1		Wing
73	5/7/97	New Zealand	Australia	Christchurch	30–13			Wing
74	19/7/97	New Zealand	South Africa	Johannesburg	35–32			Wing
75	9/8/97	New Zealand	South Africa	Auckland	55–35	1		Wing

#	Date	Team	Opponent	Venue	Score	Tries	Points of Interest	Position
76	14/9/97	Wellington	Otago	Wellington	27–32	2		Wing
77	20/9/97	Wellington	Taranaki	New Plymouth	42–33	1		Wing
78	27/9/97	Wellington	Waikato	Hamilton	14–41			Wing
79	5/10/97	Wellington	Southland	Wellington	17–10			Wing
80	11/10/97	Wellington	Auckland	Auckland	42–44			Wing
81	11/11/97	New Zealand	Wales A	Pontypridd	51–8			Wing
82	18/11/97	New Zealand	Emerging England	Huddersfield	59–22			Wing
83	25/11/97	New Zealand	England Rugby Partnership XV	Bristol	18–11			Wing
84	2/12/97	New Zealand	England A	Leicester	30–19	1		Wing
1998								
85	27/2/98	Hurricanes	Stormers	Cape Town	45–31			Wing
86	6/3/98	Hurricanes	Bulls	Pretoria	37–19			Wing
87	13/3/98	Hurricanes	Chiefs	Hamilton	22–19	1		Wing
88	22/3/98	Hurricanes	Reds	Wellington	33–41	1		Wing
89	29/3/98	Hurricanes	Sharks	Palmerston North	23–39			Wing
90	3/4/98	Hurricanes	Cats	New Plymouth	30–15	1		Wing
91	19/4/98	Hurricanes	Highlanders	Dunedin	8–29			Wing
92	24/4/98	Hurricanes	Brumbies	Canberra	32–39			Wing
93	1/5/98	Hurricanes	Crusaders	Napier	17–37			Wing
94	9/5/98	Hurricanes	Waratahs	Sydney	32–26			Wing
95	16/5/98	Hurricanes	Blues	Wellington	34–45	1		Wing
96	8/6/98	NZ Barbarians	New Zealand A	Albany	55–14	2	All Black trial	Wing
97	13/6/98	New Zealand A	England	Hamilton	18–10			Substitute
98	28/6/98	New Zealand A	Tonga	Wanganui	60–7	1		Wing
99	11/7/98	New Zealand A	Samoa	Apia	28–15			Wing
100	31/7/98	Wellington	Wanganui	Wanganui	26–8			Wing
101	7/8/98	Wellington	Otago	Dunedin	22–47			Wing
102	15/8/98	Wellington	Southland	Invercargill	12–13			Wing
103	22/8/98	Wellington	North Harbour	Albany	28–19	2		Wing
104	29/8/98	Wellington	Canterbury	Wellington	28–40			Wing
105	6/9/98	Wellington	Taranaki	Wellington	29–18	1		Wing

#	Date	Team	Opponent	Venue	Score	Tries	Points of Interest	Position
106	12/9/98	Wellington	Waikato	Wellington	42–29	1		Wing
107	19/9/98	Wellington	Auckland	Wellington	16–27			Wing
108	25/9/98	Wellington	Otago	Dunedin	10–82			Wing
109	10/10/98	Wellington	Northland	Wellington	35–27			Wing
1999								
110	27/2/99	Hurricanes	Reds	Brisbane	0–11			Wing
111	7/3/99	Hurricanes	Stormers	Wellington	27–44			Wing
112	13/3/99	Hurricanes	Bulls	Palmerston North	37–18	1		Wing
113	19/3/99	Hurricanes	Crusaders	Christchurch	18–18			Wing
114	27/3/99	Hurricanes	Cats	Bloemfontein	27–43	1		Wing
115	3/4/99	Hurricanes	Sharks	East London	34–18	1		Wing
116	10/4/99	Hurricanes	Blues	Auckland	7–23			Wing
117	16/4/99	Hurricanes	Chiefs	New Plymouth	21–24			Wing
118	25/4/99	Hurricanes	Brumbies	Wellington	13–21			Wing
119	15/5/99	Hurricanes	Highlanders	Wellington	21–19			Wing
120	11/6/99	New Zealand	New Zealand A	Dunedin	22–11			Wing
121	18/6/99	New Zealand	Samoa	Albany	71–13	2		Wing
122	26/6/99	New Zealand	France	Wellington	54–7	3		Wing
123	10/7/99	New Zealand	South Africa	Dunedin	28–0			Wing
124	24/7/99	New Zealand	Australia	Auckland	34–15			Wing
125	7/8/99	New Zealand	South Africa	Pretoria	34–18			Wing
126	28/8/99	New Zealand	Australia	Sydney	7–28			Wing
127	3/10/99	New Zealand	Tonga	Bristol	45–9		World Cup	Wing
128	9/10/99	New Zealand	England	London	30–16		World Cup	Wing
129	24/10/99	New Zealand	Scotland	Edinburgh	30–18	2	World Cup	Wing
130	31/10/99	New Zealand	France	London	31–43		World Cup	Wing
131	4/11/99	New Zealand	South Africa	Cardiff	18–22		World Cup	Wing
2000								
132	29/2/00	Hurricanes	Sharks	Wellington	40–23			Wing
133	4/3/00	Hurricanes	Reds	New Plymouth	43–25	3		Wing
134	11/3/00	Hurricanes	Highlanders	Dunedin	19–35		Red card	Wing
135	25/3/00	Hurricanes	Cats	Palmerston North	29–23	2		Wing

#	Date	Team	Opponent	Venue	Score	Tries	Points of Interest	Position
136	31/3/00	Hurricanes	Blues	Wellington	14–25			Wing
137	7/4/00	Hurricanes	Crusaders	Wellington	28–22			Wing
138	21/4/00	Hurricanes	Brumbies	Canberra	28–47			Wing
139	29/4/00	Hurricanes	Waratahs	Sydney	27–20			Centre
140	16/6/00	New Zealand	Tonga	Albany	102–0	2		Wing
141	24/6/00	New Zealand	Scotland	Dunedin	69–20	2		Wing
142	1/7/00	New Zealand	Scotland	Auckland	48–14	2		Wing
143	15/7/00	New Zealand	Australia	Sydney	39–35	1		Wing
144	22/7/00	New Zealand	South Africa	Christchurch	25–12			Wing
145	5/8/00	New Zealand	Australia	Wellington	23–24			Wing
146	19/8/00	New Zealand	South Africa	Johannesburg	40–46	2		Wing
147	8/9/00	Wellington	Auckland	Wellington	19–24			Wing
148	16/9/00	Wellington	North Harbour	Albany	7–24			Wing
149	24/9/00	Wellington	Counties Manukau	Pukekohe	45–29	1		Wing
150	30/9/00	Wellington	Southland	Invercargill	28–21	1		Wing
151	7/10/00	Wellington	Waikato	Wellington	48–23	1		Wing
152	13/10/00	Wellington	Auckland	Auckland	48–23	1	NPC semi-final	Centre
153	21/10/00	Wellington	Canterbury	Christchurch	34–29		NPC final	Centre
154	11/11/00	New Zealand	France	Paris	39–26			Centre
155	18/11/00	New Zealand	France	Marseilles	33–42			Centre
156	25/11/00	New Zealand	Italy	Genoa	56–19			Centre
2001								
157	24/2/01	Hurricanes	Reds	Brisbane	18–27	1		Centre
158	3/3/01	Hurricanes	Bulls	Wellington	26–20			Centre
159	9/3/01	Hurricanes	Stormers	Wellington	15–27			Centre
160	17/3/01	Hurricanes	Sharks	Durban	21–39	1		Centre
161	23/3/01	Hurricanes	Cats	Bloemfontein	15–18			Centre
162	31/3/01	Hurricanes	Crusaders	Christchurch	41–29	1		Centre
163	6/4/01	Hurricanes	Brumbies	Wellington	34–19			Centre
164	14/4/01	Hurricanes	Highlanders	Napier	35–33			Centre
165	27/4/01	Hurricanes	Waratahs	New Plymouth	42–17			Centre
166	11/5/01	Hurricanes	Blues	Auckland	17–36			Centre

#	Date	Team	Opponent	Venue	Score	Tries	Points of Interest	Position
167	16/6/01	New Zealand	Samoa	Albany	50–6			Centre
168	23/6/01	New Zealand	Argentina	Christchurch	67–19	1		Centre
169	30/6/01	New Zealand	France	Wellington	37–12			Centre
170	21/7/01	New Zealand	South Africa	Cape Town	12–3			Centre
171	11/8/01	New Zealand	Australia	Dunedin	15–23			Centre
172	25/8/01	New Zealand	South Africa	Auckland	26–15			Centre
173	1/9/01	New Zealand	Australia	Sydney	26–29			Centre
174	15/9/01	Wellington	Counties Manukau	Wellington	47–0			Centre
175	21/9/01	Wellington	Northland	Whangarei	37–16	1		Centre
176	29/9/01	Wellington	Canterbury	Christchurch	29–31		Ranfurly Shield	Centre
177	6/10/01	Wellington	Auckland	Auckland	13–26	1		Centre
178	12/10/01	Wellington	North Harbour	Wellington	35–31	1		Centre
179	20/10/01	Wellington	Otago	Wellington	10–28			Centre
180	17/11/01	New Zealand	Ireland	Dublin	40–29			Centre
181	24/11/01	New Zealand	Scotland	Edinburgh	37–6	1		Centre
182	1/12/01	New Zealand	Argentina	Buenos Aires	24–20			Centre
2002								
183	22/2/02	Hurricanes	Blues	Wellington	7–60			Centre
184	2/3/02	Hurricanes	Bulls	Pretoria	37–18	1		Centre
185	15/3/02	Hurricanes	Sharks	Wellington	40–17			Centre
186	22/3/02	Hurricanes	Cats	Wellington	30–21	1		Centre
187	30/3/02	Hurricanes	Reds	Palmerston North	22–18			Centre
188	5/4/02	Hurricanes	Highlanders	Dunedin	10–19			Centre
189	14/4/02	Hurricanes	Brumbies	Canberra	20–13			Centre
190	27/4/02	Hurricanes	Waratahs	Sydney	13–19			Centre
191	4/5/02	Hurricanes	Crusaders	Wellington	20–48			Centre
192	15/6/02	New Zealand	Ireland	Dunedin	15–6			Centre
193	21/6/02	NZ Barbarians	NZ Maori	Albany	37–22	1		Wing
194	29/6/02	New Zealand	Fiji	Wellington	68–18			Wing
195	20/7/02	New Zealand	South Africa	Wellington	41–20			Substitute
196	3/8/02	New Zealand	Australia	Sydney	14–16			Centre
197	10/8/02	New Zealand	South Africa	Durban	30–23	1		Centre

#	Date	Team	Opponent	Venue	Score	Tries	Points of Interest	Position
198	24/8/02	Wellington	Southland	Invercargill	20–22			Centre
199	30/8/02	Wellington	Northland	Wellington	51–18	1		Centre
200	7/9/02	Wellington	North Harbour	Albany	19–17	1		Centre
201	14/9/02	Wellington	Waikato	Wellington	35–49	1		Centre
202	22/9/02	Wellington	Taranaki	Wellington	46–17	1		Centre
203	27/9/02	Wellington	Otago	Dunedin	20–21			Centre
204	6/10/02	Wellington	Bay of Plenty	Tauranga	74–20	2		Centre
205	12/10/02	Wellington	Auckland	Wellington	27–47			Centre
206	9/11/02	New Zealand	England	London	28–31			Centre
207	15/11/02	New Zealand	France	Paris	20–20	1		Centre
208	22/11/02	New Zealand	Wales	Cardiff	43–17			Second-five
2003								
209	22/2/03	Hurricanes	Crusaders	Christchurch	21–37			Centre
210	1/3/03	Hurricanes	Bulls	Napier	34–46			Centre
211	7/3/03	Hurricanes	Stormers	Wellington	33–18			Second-five
212	14/3/03	Hurricanes	Sharks	Durban	35–20	1		Second-five
213	22/3/03	Hurricanes	Cats	Bloemfontein	28–21	2		Second-five
214	29/3/03	Hurricanes	Chiefs	Wellington	24–14			Second-five
215	4/4/03	Hurricanes	Reds	Brisbane	26–23	1		Second-five
216	11/4/03	Hurricanes	Waratahs	Wellington	42–26			Second-five
217	19/4/03	Hurricanes	Highlanders	New Plymouth	37–15			Second-five
218	3/5/03	Hurricanes	Brumbies	Wellington	27–35			Second-five
219	9/5/03	Hurricanes	Blues	Auckland	17–29	1		Centre
220	16/5/03	Hurricanes	Crusaders	Christchurch	16–39		Super 12 semi-final	Second-five
221	14/6/03	New Zealand	England	Wellington	13–15			Second-five
222	21/6/03	New Zealand	Wales	Hamilton	55–3	1		Centre
223	28/6/03	New Zealand	France	Christchurch	31–23			Centre
224	19/7/03	New Zealand	South Africa	Pretoria	52–16			Centre
225	26/7/03	New Zealand	Australia	Sydney	50–21	1		Centre
226	9/8/03	New Zealand	South Africa	Dunedin	19–11			Centre
227	16/8/03	New Zealand	Australia	Auckland	21–17			Centre
228	11/10/03	New Zealand	Italy	Melbourne	70–7		World Cup	Centre

#	Date	Team	Opponent	Venue	Score	Tries	Points of Interest	Position
2004								
229	22/2/04	Hurricanes	Chiefs	Hamilton	7–19			Centre
230	28/2/04	Hurricanes	Bulls	Pretoria	19–40			Centre
231	7/3/04	Hurricanes	Stormers	Cape Town	25–19			Centre
232	3/4/04	Hurricanes	Reds	Wellington	29–12			Second-five
233	17/4/04	Hurricanes	Waratahs	Sydney	31–49	1		Centre
234	24/4/04	Hurricanes	Highlanders	Dunedin	14–26			Second-five
235	1/5/04	Hurricanes	Brumbies	Canberra	25–46			Centre
236	8/5/04	Hurricanes	Crusaders	Wellington	37–20	1		Centre
237	1/6/04	Probables	Possibles	Auckland	29–27		All Black trial	Centre
238	12/6/04	New Zealand	England	Dunedin	36–3			Centre
239	19/6/04	New Zealand	England	Auckland	36–12			Centre
240	26/6/04	New Zealand	Argentina	Hamilton	41–7	1		Centre
241	10/7/04	New Zealand	Pacific Islands	Albany	41–26	1		Centre
242	17/7/04	New Zealand	Australia	Wellington	16–7			Centre
243	24/7/04	New Zealand	South Africa	Christchurch	23–21			Centre
244	7/8/04	New Zealand	Australia	Sydney	18–23			Centre
245	14/8/04	New Zealand	South Africa	Johannesburg	26–40			Centre
246	18/9/04	Wellington	Bay of Plenty	Mt Maunganui	13–17	1		Second-five
247	25/9/04	Wellington	Taranaki	Wellington	73–28	1		Second-five
248	2/10/04	Wellington	Northland	Wellington	65–12			Second-five
249	9/10/04	Wellington	Southland	Invercargill	30–0			Second-five
250	15/10/04	Wellington	Waikato	Wellington	28–16		NPC semi-final	Second-five
251	23/10/04	Wellington	Canterbury	Wellington	27–40	1	NPC final	Second-five
252	13/11/04	New Zealand	Italy	Rome	59–10	2		Second-five
253	27/11/04	New Zealand	France	Paris	47–19			Second-five
2005								
254	26/2/05	Hurricanes	Reds	Brisbane	24–10			Second-five
255	5/3/05	South	North	London	54–19	1	Tsunami Relief	Second-five
256	11/3/05	Hurricanes	Sharks	Durban	29–23			Substitute
257	19/3/05	Hurricanes	Bulls	Wellington	12–21			Second-five
258	25/3/05	Hurricanes	Stormers	Palmerston North	12–9			Second-five

#	Date	Team	Opponent	Venue	Score	Tries	Points of Interest	Position
259	1/4/05	Hurricanes	Chiefs	Wellington	28–16	1		Second-five
260	10/4/05	Hurricanes	Waratahs	Wellington	26–24			Second-five
261	22/4/05	Hurricanes	Highlanders	Wellington	16–26			Second-five
262	30/4/05	Hurricanes	Brumbies	Wellington	49–37	1		Second-five
263	6/5/05	Hurricanes	Blues	Auckland	22–10			Second-five
264	20/5/05	Hurricanes	Crusaders	Christchurch	7–47		Super 12 semi-final	Centre
265	10/6/05	New Zealand	Fiji	Albany	91–0	2		Centre
266	25/6/05	New Zealand	Lions	Christchurch	21–3			Centre
267	2/7/05	New Zealand	Lions	Wellington	48–18	1		Centre
268	9/7/05	New Zealand	Lions	Auckland	38–19	2		Second-five
269	6/8/05	New Zealand	South Africa	Cape Town	16–22			Centre
270	13/8/05	New Zealand	Australia	Sydney	30–13			Centre
271	27/8/05	New Zealand	South Africa	Dunedin	31–27			Centre
272	3/9/05	New Zealand	Australia	Auckland	34–24			Centre
273	30/9/05	Wellington	Auckland	Auckland	22–29			Second-five
274	7/10/05	Wellington	Taranaki	New Plymouth	31–17	1		Second-five
275	5/11/05	New Zealand	Wales	Cardiff	41–3			Second-five
276	19/11/05	New Zealand	England	London	23–19	1		Centre
277	26/11/05	New Zealand	Scotland	Edinburgh	29–10			Second-five
2006								
278	10/2/06	Hurricanes	Blues	Auckland	37–19	1		Second-five
279	24/2/06	Hurricanes	Cats	Wellington	29–16			Centre
280	4/3/06	Hurricanes	Cheetahs	Bloemfontein	25–27			Second-five
281	16/4/06	Hurricanes	Highlanders	Dunedin	29–13	1		Second-five
282	22/4/06	Hurricanes	Brumbies	Canberra	16–21			Second-five
283	29/4/06	Hurricanes	Chiefs	Wellington	35–10			Second-five
284	5/5/06	Hurricanes	Reds	Wellington	26–22	1		Second-five
285	13/5/06	Hurricanes	Waratahs	Sydney	19–14			Second-five
286	19/5/06	Hurricanes	Waratahs	Wellington	16–14		Super 14 semi-final	Second-five
287	27/5/06	Hurricanes	Crusaders	Christchurch	12–19		Super 14 final	Second-five
288	22/7/06	Wellington	Waikato	Hamilton	45–24	1		Centre
289	29/7/06	Wellington	Taranaki	New Plymouth	30–14			Centre

#	Date	Team	Opponent	Venue	Score	Tries	Points of Interest	Position
290	4/8/06	Wellington	Bay of Plenty	Wellington	11–6			Centre
291	10/9/06	Wellington	Tasman	Wellington	39–25	1		Substitute
292	17/9/06	Wellington	Canterbury	Wellington	26–24			Centre
293	23/9/06	Wellington	Waikato	Hamilton	21–37			Substitute
294	29/9/06	Wellington	Otago	Dunedin	21–14	1		Second-five
295	6/10/06	Wellington	Canterbury	Wellington	36–23		Air NZ Cup quarter-final	Second-five
296	13/10/06	Wellington	Auckland	Auckland	30–15	1	Air NZ Cup semi-final	Second-five
297	21/10/06	Wellington	Waikato	Hamilton	31–37	1	Air NZ Cup final	Second-five
2007								
298	3/2/07	Hurricanes	Reds	Brisbane	16–25			Substitute
299	9/2/07	Hurricanes	Chiefs	Hamilton	39–32	1		Centre
300	17/2/07	Hurricanes	Blues	Wellington	23–22			Centre
301	23/2/07	Hurricanes	Brumbies	Wellington	11–10			Centre
302	9/3/07	Hurricanes	Force	Perth	17–18	1		Second-five
303	17/3/07	Hurricanes	Sharks	Durban	14–27			Second-five
304	24/3/07	Hurricanes	Lions	Johannesburg	7–30			Second-five
305	13/4/07	Hurricanes	Cheetahs	Wellington	37–15			Second-five
306	20/4/07	Hurricanes	Crusaders	Christchurch	13–23			Substitute
307	27/4/07	Hurricanes	Highlanders	Wellington	22–21			Centre
308	5/5/07	Hurricanes	Waratahs	Wellington	14–38			Second-five
309	20/7/07	Wellington	Auckland	Wellington	44–21	1		Substitute
310	27/7/07	Wellington	Otago	Wellington	68–7			Substitute
311	4/8/07	Wellington	Hawke's Bay	Napier	6–8			Substitute
312	11/8/07	Wellington	Manawatu	Wellington	37–7			Centre